"TRASHED SHOES ARE LIKE A WAR WOUND.
EVIDENCE OF HOW HARD YOU SKATE,
NOT SOMETHING TO BE EMBARRASSED ABOUT!"

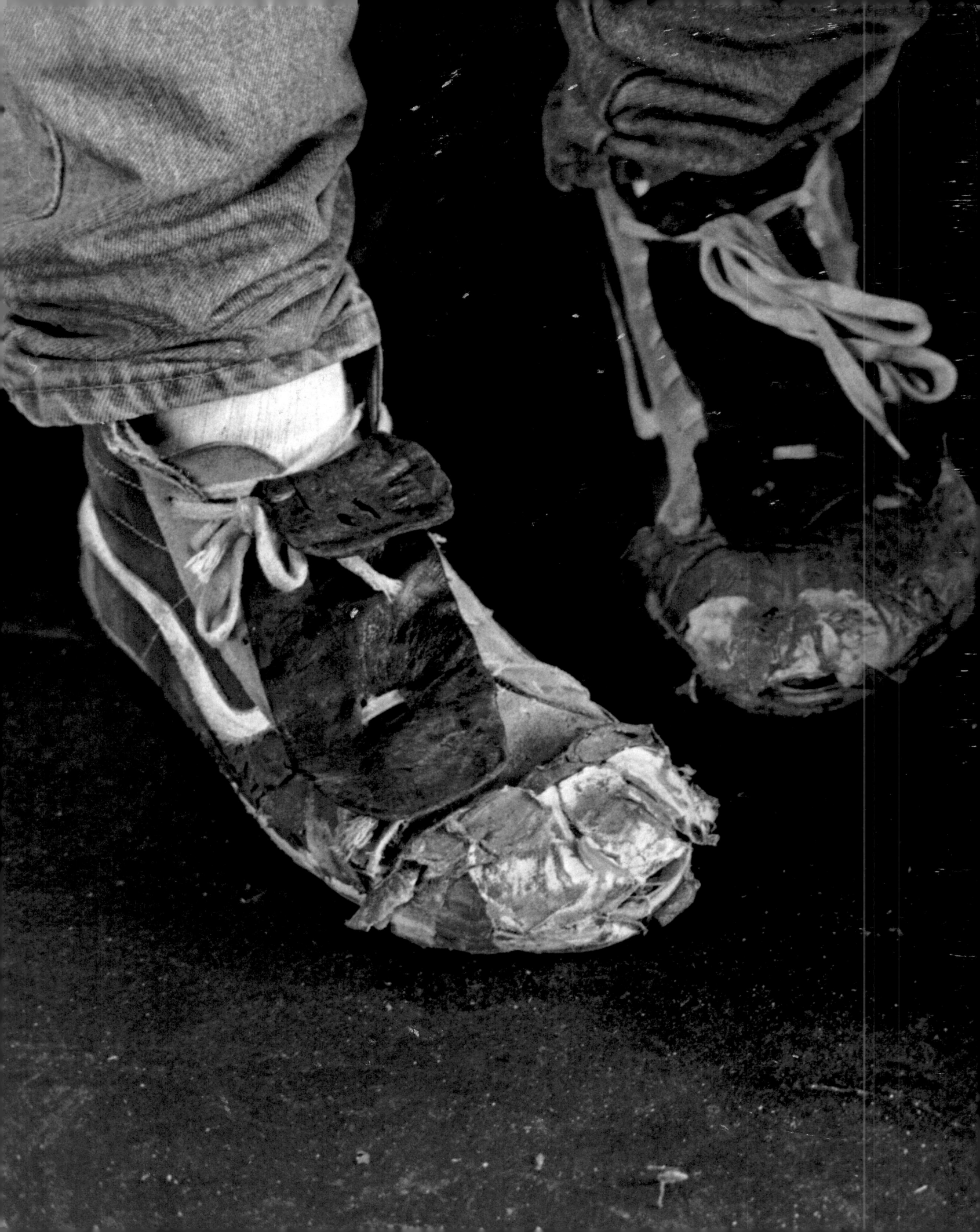

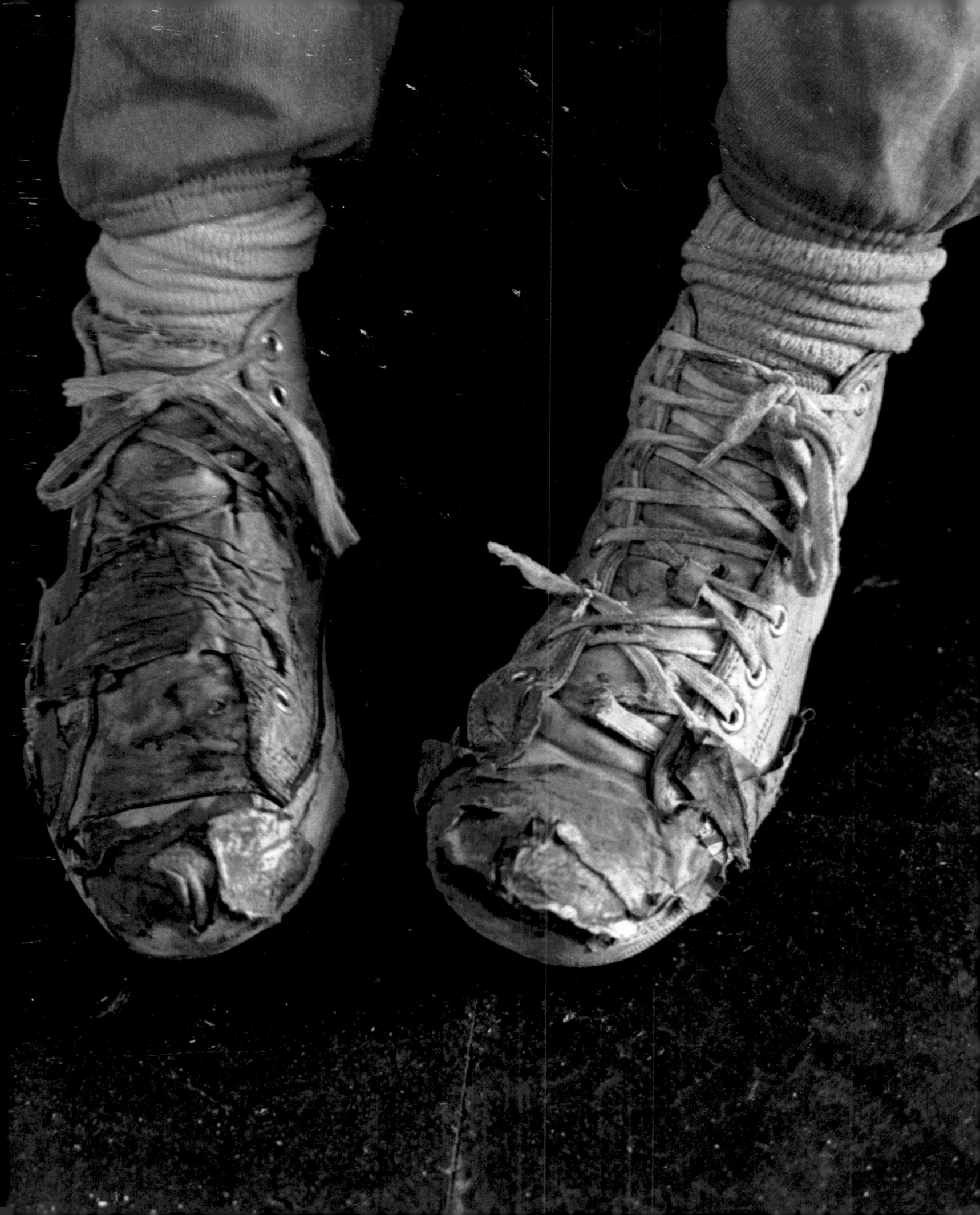

MADE FOR SKATE

Published by

FauxAmi Exhibitions
-
SKATEBOARD MUSEUM STUTTGART

in association with Gingko Press

MADE FOR SKATE
THE ILLUSTRATED HISTORY OF SKATEBOARD FOOTWEAR

FIRST EDITION

Conceived and created by
Jürgen Blümlein & Daniel Schmid

Written by Dirk Vogel

Additional text by Holger von Krosigk

Shoe pictures by

Cap10

Additional photos by Bernd Deuber, Sven Daubenfeld and Axel Görger

FauxAmi Exhibition Blümlein and Schmid GbR Postfach 205 Rungestraße 22-24 10179 Berlin Germany www.FauxAmi.com	Gingko Press, Inc 5768 Paradise Drive, Suite J Corte Madera, CA 94925 USA (415) 924-9615 www.gingkopress.com	Gingko Press Verlag Hamburger Strasse 180 22083 Hamburg Germany (040) 291425

ISBN 978-158423348-0

Copyrights 2008 by FauxAmi

All rights reserved. No part of this publication may be reproduced or transmitted in any form or by any means, electronic or mechanical, including photocopy, recording or any information storage and retrieval system, without prior permission in writing from the publisher.

Printed in Hong Kong

CONTENTS

10-13 .... **THE INTRO**

14-23 .... **THE 1 ROOTS**

24-83 .... **THE 2 SHOES**

84-177 .... **THE 3 EIGHTIES**

178-309 .... THE **4** NINETIES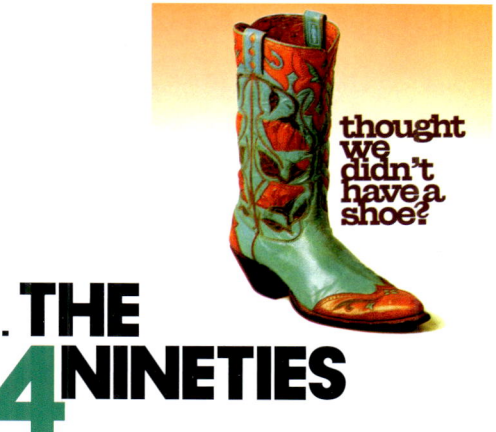

310-379 .... THE **5** NEW CENTURY

380-395 .... THE **6** FUTURE-EPILOGUE

396-399 .... THE **7** INDEX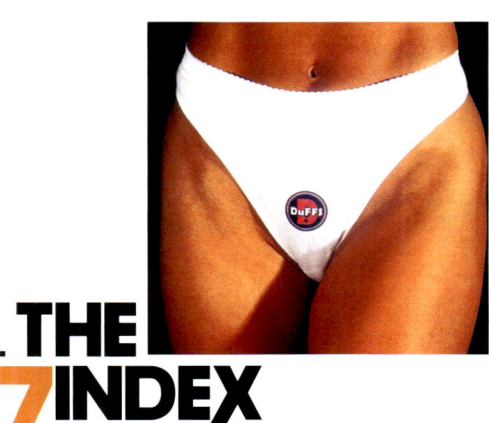

"... and as I said on the phone already, the [Airwalk] Prototypes are totally ! like HOLY RELICS to me (!!!), don't lose them whatever happens!!! the grey ones even have a special feature; the lace savers have been autographed by Tony Hawk and Jimi Scott."

– Extract from an e-mail by a friend submitting his 20 year-old skateboard shoes for the MADE FOR SKATE exhibition.

THE INTRO

INTRODUCTION - WE KNOW SHOES

"There's a lot you can tell about a skater by looking at his shoes. Where he skated, how many times he's ollied..."
- Tim Brauch (impersonating Forrest Gump), *411 Video Magazine*

There used to be a time when you could spot fellow skaters by looking at their shoes. You knew it right away – the telltale ollie holes on the sides, some patched-up with Shoe Goo™. The worn down soles, the frazzled laces. You made eye contact and exchanged a knowing nod or a quick what's up. A little *Fight Club* moment at the corner store. You knew right away that you were both into the same thing, sharing the same daydreams of spots and tricks, the same victories and agonizing defeats. You knew all that, just by looking at someone else's feet.

Skateboarders have always paid a lot of attention to shoes. After all, they're what connects us to our boards – and to the world at large. Skaters know what difference a pair of shoes can make. We not only wear shoes – we UTILIZE them. We test them to the limits, wear them down, skid them across griptape and hot pavement. And when they're all beat up, we go to lengths to make them last a little bit longer, stand some more abuse, even when there's hardly any more sole left to walk on. We're an authority on which shoes have good grip and which shoes don't. We know which features make sense and which ones are just bells and whistles thrown on top for extra flair. We KNOW shoes, because we live in them.

Nowadays it's harder to pinpoint those who actually skate in their kicks, with millions of skate shoes walking around out there, some of which have never seen a board. And even if you could identify another skater, chances are it wouldn't be cool to talk to him, him being too hesh, too hip-hop, too punk, too whatever. Skateboarding has grown into such a broad church that we're split into a number of sects – some kind of schism in the 90's when the Rock'n Rollers and Hip-Hoppers parted ways – and ever since then, never the twain shall meet. What we ALL share as skateboarders, though, is a long history, and shoes are a big part of it.

FOOTPRINTS OF HISTORY

It was this rich history of skateboarding, which we at FauxAmi set out to document with our very first "Skateboardfieber" exhibit in 2003. This planted the seed for what is now a permanent Skateboarding Museum at the Stuttgart Filmhaus with over 1,000 exhibits on display. Honestly, we never believed this would happen.

At the time we just asked around for old skate equipment among friends, collectors and captains of the European skateboard industry for what was meant to be a two-week show. Things just kind of skyrocketed from there and branched out way past running the museum (check www.skateboardfieber.de for details). We were invited to stage follow-up exhibits in Barcelona, Berlin and Zurich, which opened up ever so many doors for us. These days, a large number of collectors and skate history nuts from around the world are supporting us with pieces from their private collections.

The whole skate history story ran its own course, but it took a while until skateboard shoes came into play. They kind of snuck up on us, actually. At first, the exhibit focused almost solely on the evolution of skateboard hardware: mostly decks, wheels and early predecessors of the modern skateboard, like the skate-scooter. Shoes were marginal at best, although they play such a big part in everyday skating.

Then one day, we realized that some people actually keep their 20-year-old, run-down-to-the-toes skate shoes. When the museum received the first pair of 1988 Airwalk Prototypes – it was all over. "We HAVE to do something with shoes!" we said. It is just too powerful."

MEMORY LANE

There are so many memories that come back when you see a pair of old sneakers. "I used to have those," you'll say, and all of a sudden the floodgates break open and the images pour in like a tidal wave. That launch ramp at your grandpa's house, the first video you watched. Your first kickflip. Or when you went skating that concrete ditch by the lakeside.

Skateboard shoes not only connect us to our boards, but to our personal history. There's a powerful sense of getting back into synch with your past that sets in when you remember wearing a certain type of shoe. You remember what your world was like back then in vivid colors. You come to realize that all these images are burned into your memory somewhere – you just never had a trigger to access those memories. The shoes do just that. No wonder you remember them so well. After all, those were the shoes you saw every single time you looked down at your board when you did a trick. For as long as they lasted, at least...

The first *MADE FOR SKATE* exhibit was a runaway success. And we knew it whenever we saw people causally stroll around the rooms, and finally stopping dead in their tracks in front of the display with those old Airwalk Protoypes. That look on their faces! You could tell that their memories transported them somewhere else in their mind at that moment – far away from the hectic tradeshow routine with sales reps preaching the gospel of vulcanized soles just two rooms down the hall. Far away in their minds to a place in time when they had a pair of these on their feet, and skateboarding was different, and skaters were just skaters.

ALIVE AND KICKIN'

As *MADE FOR SKATE: The Illustrated History of Skateboard Footwear* will document, skateboard footwear has come a long way. Look at all the choices you have today when you buy a pair of kicks at the local skate shop: Retro or ultra-fresh? Heel-shock-system or not? Mid-top or low-cut? Synthetic or suede? Vulcanized sole or stitched rubber? Run-of-the-mill or limited edition? Skatin' shoes or chillin'? Have your pick!

Even though skateboard shoes have spilled out into the mainstream in a big way – skateboard footwear at the time of this writing is an $800 million Industry – even the most modern shoes are part of an ongoing tradition, laid down in terms of elementary design patterns and choices of materials in the mid-1960s. Just how closely shoes today still adhere to this blueprint, is just one of the aspects we are trying to show in this volume. At the same time, we're fully aware that any attempt at documenting the evolution of skateboard footwear can be fragmentary at best.

It's been a good run so far and still, more and more shoes for the exhibit keep pouring in all the time. Thank you to all our contributors for making this book and the exhibit possible (although their shoes kind of stink, but hey – what did we expect?!).

What it all boils down to is this: Shoes are still what connects us to our boards, and we'll keep looking at them with a keen eye – both on and off our boards. We hope that the exhibits and this book will help connect people with the rich history of skateboarding, as well as their own individual histories as skateboarders.

Skateboarding might be diversified and sometimes even split into cliques today, but as skateboarders, we all share the same roots. And we all know a whole lot about shoes – that much we can surely all agree on.

FauxAmi

The first *MADE FOR SKATE* exhibition at the BRIGHT Skateboarding Tradeshow
January 2007 - Frankfurt

Nike SB celebration 10 Years of BLUEPRINT Skateboards with *MADE FOR SKATE* and MOVING UNITS exhibition at the Old Trumann Brewery - June 2007 London

MADE FOR SKATE exhibition at the URBAN LAB Gallery / Stil
August 2007 Vienna

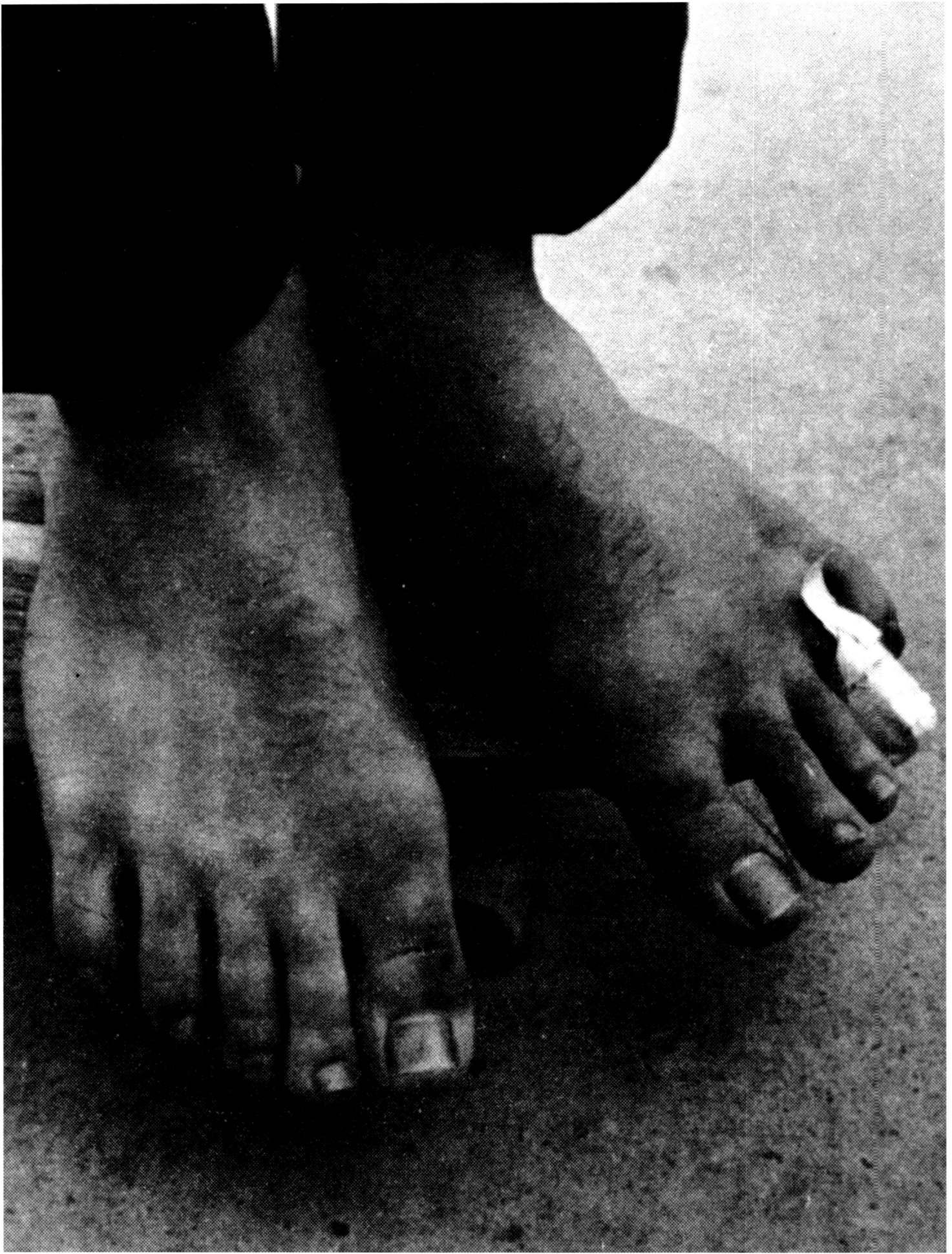

THE ROOTS

BLOODY TOES - JUST KID STUFF OR A REAL SPORT?

SKATE BOARDS
KID STUFF OR REAL SPORT

No one, except possibly the skateboard manufacturers, took them seriously until recently. Tabbed by many as one step above rollerskating and strictly "kid stuff," the young skateboarders went about their business perfecting their style and stunts. Recently, LIFE Magazine, among others, sat up and took notice of the "sidewalk surfers" and gave them a two-page spread under the heading of Sports. Recognition like this will probably catapult skateboarding into a national sport and will provide the landlocked surfer with still another outlet for his frustrations.

The movements and maneuvers are much the same as surfing and many a skateboarder has become completely wrapped up in his ride, only to be startled back to reality with a wipe-out. At that time asphalt just doesn't seem like a fair exchange for water. Among maneuvers the skillful skateboarders can manage are hanging five and ten, drop-knee turns, arches, 360's, tandem riding, and even the "Paul Strauch crouch."

Some of the skateboarders have set up slalom courses, timing each other from stand-still starts. Teams have been formed and exhibitions put on.

One thing in favor of the skateboarders is that there seems to be a lot more sidewalk than surf. The younger participants don't have to own a car to get to their favorite spot (they can skate there) and, as a matter of fact, they don't need wetsuits for cold days, wax for their boards (maybe a little oil now and then), and trunks are optional.

What kind of future can the skateboarder look forward to? Perhaps inter-club contests, city championships, or maybe someday the Grand Slalom Skateboard Finals at the Olympic Games. One thing they can all look forward to for sure are a few bloody elbows and knees.

To find out what the public and the surfers and skateboarders themselves felt about all this skateboarding activity, we posed the following question to a random selection of innocent bystanders: "What do you think of skateboards — are they kid stuff or real sport?"

Well, the boys are careless on them. Before they learn how to handle them they endanger other people. I had to do the same thing with my electric car. I learned to operate it before I endangered anyone. But getting back to skateboards, I think they're a real sport and here to stay.
Charles Frost, Huntington Beach, California

I think they're real sport — I love them. I think they help you with surfing. I practice almost every night.
Jan Gaffney, Long Beach, California

Well, I don't know. A lot of kids own them, but it's probably becoming a sport. I know of a surfboard manufacturer who is going to sponsor one of the kids in our club (Long Beach Surfing Club), Bobby Hill, who is very good on a skateboard. It seems that when they can't go out in the water and surf, they can do it on land with a skateboard. There's a lot of similarity between the sports.
Chris Hertel, Huntington Beach, California

I think it's really good, actually. It requires a lot of balance and it's a lot of fun. I've done it many times myself recently.
Tim Kelly, Hermosa Beach, California

I think they're boss. I get a real kick out of them, especially if it's flat (the surf). You know, when there's nothing to do, there's always a lot of hills.
Mike Compton, San Marino, California

I think that skateboarding is going to be a real sport. It's becoming more popular every day. It's not just kid stuff; it takes a lot of skill to ride a skateboard. It's very challenging. There's more to it than you think. There's downhill racing and many maneuvers on flat areas. I think someday we'll see giant contests with skateboards.
John Boozer, Huntington Beach, California

Skateboarding has changed my style of surfing quite a bit. I changed my backside turns after several days of skateboarding. It's definitely a sport that helps surfing.
Mike Doyle, Inglewood

Skateboards are the link trainers for the yo-yo set and wonderful therapy for the surfer without a wave. Depending on where you roll your portable surf machine, it can be either a kiddie game or a sport to test the reactions of the best surfer.
Carl T. Herrman, East Northport, New York

STEP ON IT...

When skateboarding first made a big splash in the 1960s, it was hardly more than an adaptation of surfing on pavement. Landlocked surfers would hit up schoolyard embankments when the waves were flat, acting out all kinds of turns and surfing moves such as Hang Tens and Laybacks on the hot concrete. Little known fact: In those early days, skating pioneers were divided on the issue of wearing shoes or not. After all, you weren't wearing shoes in the water, right?

So getting your toes bloody was just part of the game for many!

Despite the bloody toes, skateboarding soon attracted a huge following. What started with homemade skateboards called "popouts," had turned into a $30 million-a-year market by 1965, dominated by a handful of early manufacturers. Nevertheless, the media remained skeptical about the life expectancy of this new phenomenon, which according to pundits was mainly "just kid stuff." Many observers predicted "sidewalk surfing" would go the way of 90-day wonders such as Frisbees, Puka Shells, Hula Hoops and Beethoven sweatshirts. In other words, the media saw skating headed for a total burnout into oblivion quickly.

The skaters couldn't have cared less. A couple of decades later, "Give Blood, Go Skateboarding" would become a punk rock motto for going big and paying the price. But for the early pioneers, giving blood was just a natural part of skating. And with this kind of dedication, it soon became apparent that skateboarding would not just burn out like some kind of fad. It was here to stay. And it's been bloody from the ground up.

HOW TO BUILD YOUR OWN SKATEBOARD

MATERIALS:
One 18-inch length of 1 x 4 finished hardwood.
One #4 MacGregor, Red Head Roller Skate. This is a clamp-on skate made by Union Hardware.
Six #10-¾ sheet metal screws.
One #14-¾ sheet metal screw.
Paint, lacquer or varnish.

TOOLS:
Pliers, hacksaw, file, hammer and centerpunch or nail, medium fine sandpaper, ruler, pencil, hand drill with 5/32 and 13/64 drills, a screwdriver and vise or C clamp.

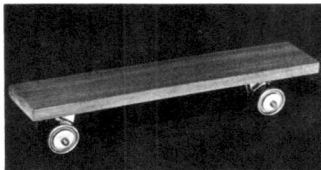

The skateboard pictured above can be constructed in one afternoon for less than $2.50, and using all new materials.

Here are the basic materials required to build a skateboard. Shown with materials is board finished with paint, imagination.

First step is to use ordinary pliers to loosen the nut that holds the toe section to the heel section of the skate.

Making sure that the board is level, draw a guideline along the exact center of the board from the nose to the tail.

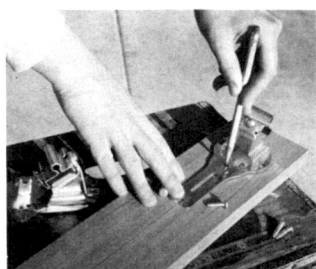

Align the skate sections on the guideline of the board and mark the locations of the mounting screws with a pencil.

Illustration clearly shows the placement of the skates and the location of the mounting screws in the finished product.

1964 - Article in a surf magazine

BARE FOOTED SIDEWALK SURFERS

Joey Cabell - Winner of the 1964 Makaha Surfing Championship...

As far as riding technique went, early skateboarders followed the blueprint set up by Californian and Hawaiian surfers. And to say that skateboarding in the 1950s was surfing's little brother would be an understatement. Skateboarding WAS surfing in those early days - surfing on concrete.

Try to separate the two - you were on shaky ground.

The letter pages of surfing magazines at the time were full of heated diatribes bashing folks who wanted to call themselves "surfers," when all they did really was roll down the streets on four wheels. They should learn "real" surfing first, was the clear verdict. This was a heated issue. After all, the whole lifestyle that surrounded skating on concrete had been built on beach culture - the clothing, the moves and of course, the bare feet.

A "NATURAL" EXTENSION OF SURFING

Pro surfers like Joey Cabell (pictured top right) could often be seen messing around with skateboards in their pastime. They used the little boards as a welcome opportunity to fine-tune their balance and control for taking on bigger challenges in the water, much the same way golfers take to putt-putt. The whole thing was also catching on quickly outside the pro ranks.

Due to growing demand for skateboards among surfers, Carl Jensen in Hermosa Beach, California, produced the first mass marketed skateboards in 1958 under his Humco label. Around the same time, the publisher of *Surf Guide Magazine*, Larry Stevenson, began promoting skateboarding as a natural extension of surfing culture.

...speeds trough a slalom course

1964 the quarterly SKATEBOARDER cover Vol.1 No.1

1964 the SKATEBOARDER cover Vol.1 No.3

The two went hand-in-hand and surfers switched back and forth between beach and sidewalk on a daily basis. Skateboard hardware continued to progress while major surf companies like Hobie and Gordon & Smith added skateboards to their line-ups. More and more skilled shapers stepped in, experimenting with redwood, walnut or oak laminated together for a fine, smooth finish reminiscent of surfboards. This also meant a smoothed top with no griptape. But hey, no one gave a second thought about wearing shoes anyhow, as sidewalk surfers collectively swore by the feel and control achieved through barefooted skating.

In 1963, Stevenson's surf company Makaha took it to the next level by producing the first-ever pro skateboard. Not for a pro skateboarder, mind you, but for a pro surfer – world famous surf icon Phil Edwards. At 6" by 22" in size, the rounded edges and "mini surfboard shape with beveled rails" left no doubt about where the inspiration for the shape had come from. As technical novelties, the Phil Edwards pro model introduced double-action trucks with adjustable truck tension for the first time, while clay wheels back then presented the state-of-the-art in wheel design.

SURFING THE SIDEWALKS

Out in the field, skaters were riding skateboards – but thinking surfing. In terms of rideable terrain, they sought out either smooth flat ground or embankments on schoolyards reminiscent of ocean waves. Downhill riding also soared in popularity, and a few "concrete waves" such as driveways and curb cuts thrown in along the way were always welcome treats. One notorious downhill area of San Francisco was even known among locals as "Waimea Bay," named after a famous Hawaiian surfing spot.

The only problem with downhill skating remained getting the board to stop! Hopping off at last second offered the main escape route, because power sliding – today the most popular way for controlling your speed on the street – at the time proved impossible with clay or metal wheels. Dragging your bare toes across the pavement for stopping was definitely not an option, either.

There remained major room for improvements. But despite the technical shortcomings in board construction, skateboarding touched a nerve and drew large crowds with its promise of speed, thrills and a highly marketable aura of carefree beach living.

The first major skate competition was held in 1965 in Anaheim, California. Sold out at 5$ a ticket (equivalent of $30 today), the International Skateboarding Championships saw competitors facing off in freestyle and slalom racing. These were also the prime days of high jump (pictured top left on the cover of a 1964 issue of The Quarterly Skateboarder), as well as barrel jump and slalom – all elements taken from "real" sports.

Steve Hilton at the Anaheim National Championships 1965 - Slalom Downhill

1975 *SkateBoarder* cover Vol. 2 No. 1

But among hardcore skaters, freestyle remained the creative outlet, the flow-and feel part of skateboarding that was closest to the spirit of surfing. The repertoire of tricks remained quite limited at first, because after all, trucks wouldn't turn that well and the whole no-shoes part was inherently risky. A 360° gone bad could mean serious damage to your toes!

BUST A MOVE - BUT WATCH YOUR TOES!

Style was everything in distinguishing yourself from others, especially since most of the moves that skaters are taking for granted today would not be invented for the next 20 years. Most riders preferred a crouched down, low-to-the ground style adapted from surfing, gliding and turning along as well as the hardware allowed for.

They compensated for the lack of flexibility in skateboard trucks by adding acrobatics to the mix, like handstands or the infamous Coffin, where the skater lies down on the board. Anything went, as long as you kept rolling – and kept your toes off the street.

Even swimming pool walls were getting hit already in the early 1960s. But at exactly this point, clay wheels had surely reached their limitations – as documented in the "Lords of Dogtown" movie – by being too slippery and unwieldy for this kind of demanding terrain.

Soon enough, skateboarding itself seemed to have reached its limits and the masses started walking away from it. Many surfers started getting their kicks back in the water again with a surge in big wave surfing at a new level of danger and risk-taking. For them, big boards equaled big cojones. Little boards, not so much.

Back on the mainland, only the dedicated skateboarders remained. The ones who skated the hell out of clay wheels and tore through pair after pair of rickety trucks. And the ones who didn't mind that there was nowhere legal to skate anymore.

Giving blood to skateboarding, they stayed around, and would continue to lead skateboarding into becoming its own culture and medium of expression. Skateboarding would live on through many peaks and valleys.

But first, sidewalk surfing had to die.

GET BLOODY

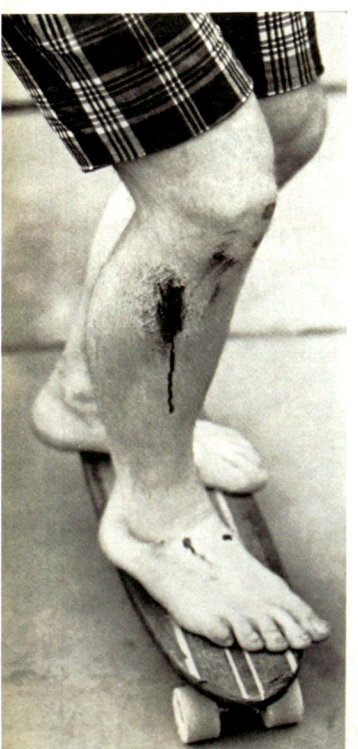

Soon enough, sidewalk surfing had not only picked up millions of followers, but also a questionable reputation as a very dangerous past time. This is hardly a surprise – harsh wipeouts have always been a major part of surfing and many risks abound when you're stepping to big ocean waves. But ultimately, surfers land in the water when they wipe out. And with skateboarding, well, eating it is a whole different story on concrete.

THINGS WERE GETTING BLOODY

It's hard to imagine today how anyone would think it a good idea to step to the hot concrete without any shoes on. Did the constant abrasion help develop some kind of extra-thick skin, some protective membrane? Probably not, as many a pair of feet on old photos appears downright mangled. Just look at Chris Yandell's banged up feet up there. Hurts just to look, doesn't it?

TOO MUCH ATTITUDE?

With all the gory pictures and horror stories, the public at large began casting a doubtful eye on what skaters were doing pretty early on. Health concerns across the U.S. were picking up quicker than board sales. In 1965, the California Medical Association reported that skateboards had surpassed bicycles as the major source of childhood injuries. Around the same time, orthopedists coined the term "skateboard fracture" for shattered elbows. Not to mention reports of skateboarders colliding with pedestrians or skaters getting hit by cars.

It was only a matter of time until The Man stepped in. By August 1965, skateboarding was banned from the streets and sidewalks of twenty U.S. cities from Rhode Island to California. Medical associations issued warnings about the new "dangerous fad," while police officers would even urge stores to stop selling skateboards to their customers.

But the growing public dislike of skateboarding was hardly due to safety concerns only. Yes, the bloody feet and accidents were an eyesore to the public. But what hurt the establishment even more was the fact that skateboarders would just go out and skate on whatever they saw fit. Anywhere they wanted. At any given time. This remains the biggest reason for anti-skate legislature to this day. In the eyes of skateboarders, even the most useless architecture can hold an enormous potential for getting your kicks. No memberships, regular hours or entrance fees needed to have X-amounts of fun.

And that kind of thinking – it just needs to be stopped, right? Cracking down on skaters has never been easy. Out in the street, skaters not only knew what was good for skating, but soon figured out how security was enforced and how it could be bypassed.

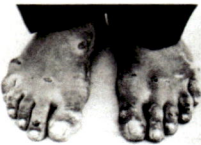

1975 *Skateboarder* "Who´s Hot" Chris Yandell

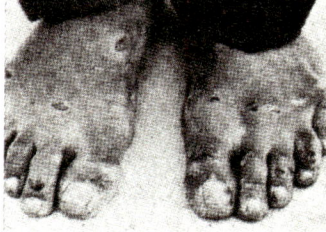

1977 article in German *Skateboard* magazine urging skaters to use "proper" skate footwear.

One 1960's hot spot awaited skaters right at LA International Airport; a banked area called "the Trestle" after a famous surfing spot outside camp Pendleton Marine Corps Base on Oahu. Riding the concrete tube at LAX usually implied being chased by police officers, but the morning and late night hours provided hope of some undisturbed sessions.

It was exactly this free-wheeling appropriation of the public domain into skateable terrain that worried the average man. A cover article from LIFE magazine in May 1965 portrayed skateboarding as "Mania – and menace." Next to accident statistics and gruesome tales of rebellious misconduct, the article featured a picture of a mangled foot. "It's easier to get bloody than fancy," the article concluded, and upright citizens should leave it alone. Skateboarding, after all, was for punks.

Following the *LIFE* article, an editorial in the *Quarterly Skateboarder* urged skaters to clean up their act: "[Skateboarding is] not a sport of destruction – of others or yourself. It's a sport of control. It's up to you to see that skateboarding does not become a sport of rebels and radicals. It's a sport for young sportsmen. We look forward to a great future in skateboarding and we ask you, the pioneers, to make it great."

But it was too late. The damage was done and the masses walked away from skateboarding. The die-hard skaters stayed on, but they were tired of getting their toes banged up.

Z-BOYS TAKE A STAND

The new breed of hardcore skaters – personified by original Z-Boys Stacy Peralta and Tony Alva – took a different stance on the issue of shoes. After all, their new and more aggressive way of skating was getting more and more demanding and physical.

"I never skated barefoot," Stacy Peralta remembers. "I couldn't stand skating barefoot as I felt it held me back and gave me no control."

Looking back on the skate scene at the time, Peralta adds: "Jay Adams is the only person I remember ever skating barefoot and he only did it once in a while. No one I skated with back then preferred skating without shoes – it was too hard on the feet when you came off the board, which was all the time."

"And remember, we were riding clay wheels, which were the equivalent of skating on round pieces of ice!"

Enter the first skate shoe.

1965 - The first skateboard shoe ad in skateboard history!

THE 2 SHOES

1965 RANDY´S - THE FIRST SKATEBOARD SHOE

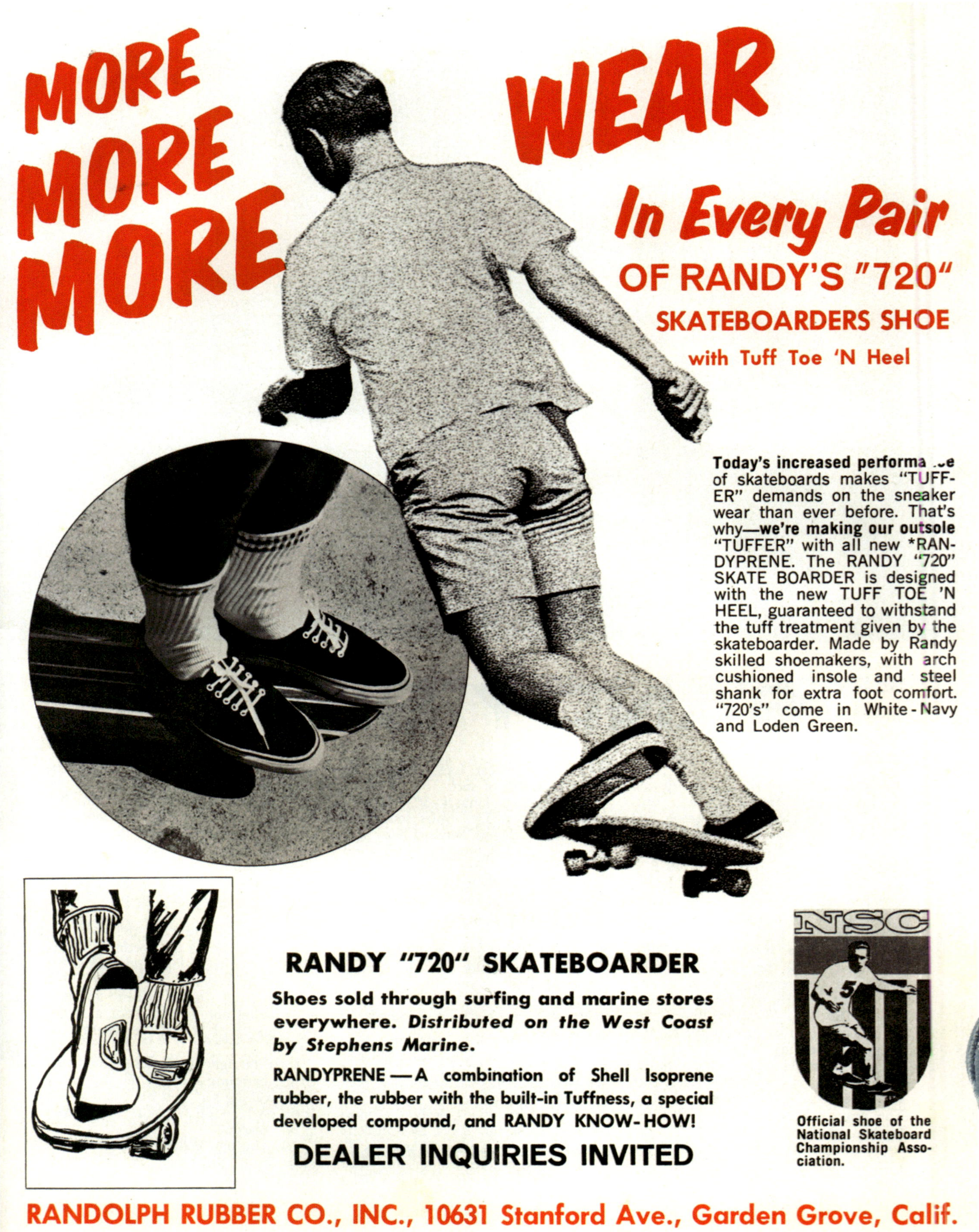

MORE MORE MORE WEAR In Every Pair OF RANDY'S "720" SKATEBOARDERS SHOE

with Tuff Toe 'N Heel

Today's increased performance of skateboards makes "TUFFER" demands on the sneaker wear than ever before. That's why—**we're making our outsole "TUFFER"** with all new *RANDYPRENE. The RANDY "720" SKATE BOARDER is designed with the new TUFF TOE 'N HEEL, guaranteed to withstand the tuff treatment given by the skateboarder. Made by Randy skilled shoemakers, with arch cushioned insole and steel shank for extra foot comfort. "720's" come in White - Navy and Loden Green.

RANDY "720" SKATEBOARDER

Shoes sold through surfing and marine stores everywhere. *Distributed on the West Coast by Stephens Marine.*

RANDYPRENE — A combination of Shell Isoprene rubber, the rubber with the built-in Tuffness, a special developed compound, and RANDY KNOW-HOW!

DEALER INQUIRIES INVITED

Official shoe of the National Skateboard Championship Association.

RANDOLPH RUBBER CO., INC., 10631 Stanford Ave., Garden Grove, Calif.

The Randy 720°, made by the Randolph Rubber Co, was the first-ever skateboard-specific shoe. Arriving on the scene in 1965, the shoe was based on two main design objectives: offering protection during sharp turns and spins, while providing the intense feel and control of barefooted skating. The shoe sold for about $14.95 (equivalent of $90 today) at surf and marine shops, as well as the first-ever skate shop, legendary Val Surf in North Hollywood.

Featured in the Randy's ad is Mark Richards, skateboard pioneer and co-owner of Val Surf. "They approached me to skate in this ad as they knew of our history and because I had been doing some commercials and TV spots at the time," Richards remembers. The ad was shot by surf and skate photographer Leroy Grannis. With their bold colorways, Randy's made quite a fashion statement. "Being the first to wear a blue shoe like that was pretty brave. I remember taking quite a bit of flak for it."

How did the promise of TUFF TOE'N HEEL come through in the streets? "The shoes were of good quality for the time but did not really hold up well under skating conditions," Richards says. "We would constantly drag our back foot doing kick turns, spins and landings which would wear through quite quickly."

But nevertheless, the Randy 720° marked an important beginning. And with its signature combination of soft sole and the use of suede in a casual low-top cut, it laid down the blueprint followed by skateboard footwear design to this day.

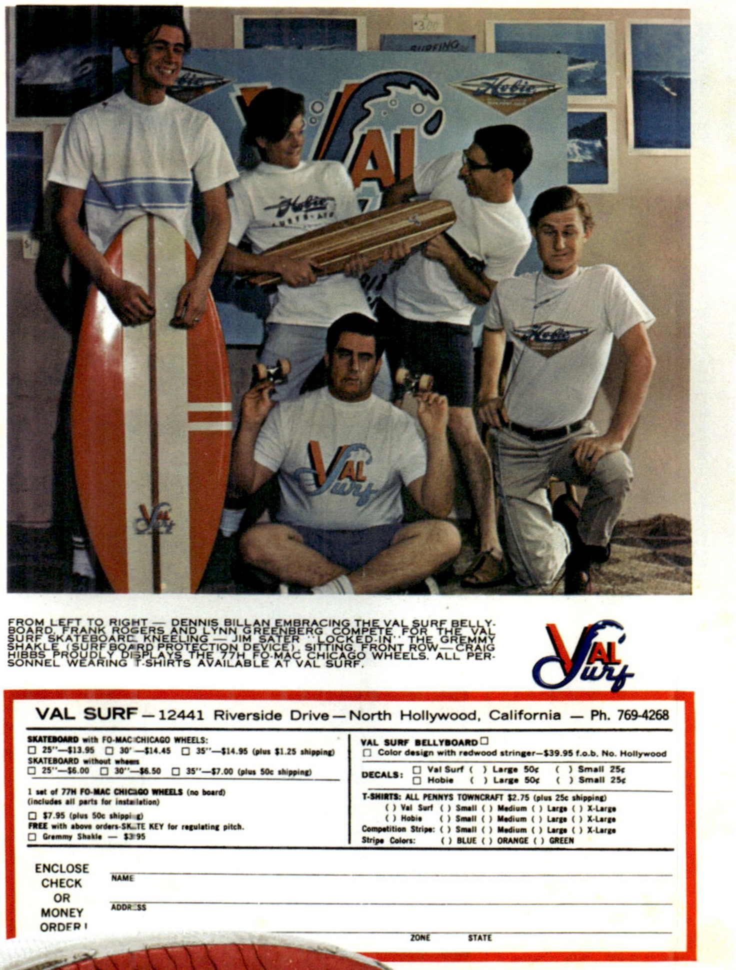

1965 June *Surfing Magazine* Val Surf ad

OFF THE WALL - THE VAN DOREN RUBBER COMPANY

Nowadays, made-to-order shoes are all the hype, but in the early days of the Van Doren Rubber Co., they were the standard mode of operations. When seasoned shoemakers Paul and Jim Van Doren came out West and set up a shoe factory in Southern California with their partners Gordon Lee and Serge D'Elia, they offered shoes made to order – delivered on the same day. An idea that would have sneaker heads today drooling from the side of their mouths.

The first Vans store opened on March 15, 1966, on 704 East Broadway in Anaheim, California. They were offering three different shoe styles, priced $2.49, $4.49, and $4.99 (equivalent of $14.99, $27.00 and $29.99 today). Customers could pick the style of their choosing by looking at a range of sample shoes on display – the only actual shoes in the 400-square-foot store. The rest of the store space had been decorated with empty boxes for lack of actual stock.

After deciding on their style, customers could spend a day on the beach and return in the afternoon to pick up their custom-made sneakers. Pretty cool.

A DESIGN CLASSIC

As far as shoe design went, early Vans were much in the tradition of casual beach shoes inspired by sailing sneakers and the like, with a soft sole and canvas top construction. Sticking to this basic formula, Vans shoes would continue to evolve through constant experiments over the years. Soon enough, the small shoe brand from California had grown into a successful business with over 70 outlet stores open all across California by 1974. Their eye for hands-on learning also led to improvements in the company's trademark soles.

The first models came in a diamond pattern with two choices of sole colors – blue and gray, with the gray ones made from harder rubber. Skaters would mostly opt for the blue soles for more control – they were still warming up to the idea of wearing shoes in the first place. But under the pressures of riding in the streets, the soles soon turned out to break along the ball of the outsole. This problem was fixed by adding horizontal lines in the pattern together with the trademark waffle pattern that helps distribute shock evenly.

Even though skaters started wearing Vans early on – mostly because of their functionality, durability and affordable price – it took the company until 1976 to fully realize their standing in the skate community. Starting that year, Vans not only started running ads in skateboard magazines and sponsoring riders, but also began making their shoes more skate-specific with models like the #36 "Jazz" model, as well as the "Off the Wall" and high top models. New features included a padded collar below the ankle – where earlier models only had single stitching – as well as reinforced heel and toe sections.

The new generation of Vans also featured the signature stripe on the side. "I think my dad basically came up with that stripe doodling in his office," Paul Van Doren's son Steve says remembering the genesis of the emblematic ornament. Over the next few years, Vans became THE iconic skate shoes worn by pioneers like Tony Alva, Stacy Peralta and Jerry Valdez.

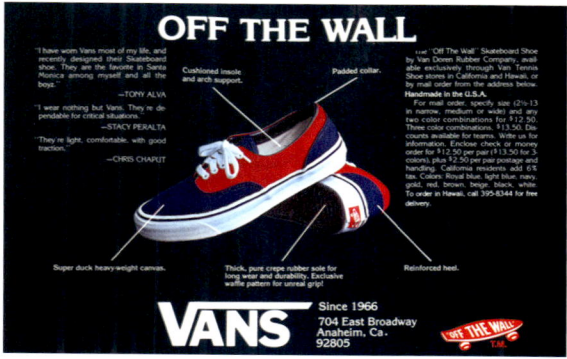

VANS Style #95 - custom-made leather

RIGHT ON THE SPOT

Reflecting on what exactly made Vans hit the right spot in terms of shoe design, skate pioneer Stacy Peralta said: "I don't like bulky shoes – I like easy-fitting, lightweight shoes that breathe and that have a flexible sole that grips well."

So what is to Stacy Peralta the iconic skate shoe? "Basically, the original Vans deck shoe is the blueprint for the perfect skate shoe. It's as simple a design as the thumb tack and still hasn't been improved upon."

What also made Vans a number one choice for skateboarders was their commitment to the scene. "Vans was the first company to recognize us as skateboarders and treat us seriously," Peralta said. "They started providing us with shoes many years before any other companies would even look at us. When all the other companies looked at us as vandals and losers. When no one wanted anything to do with us because they felt it would tarnish their image. Vans was so ahead of their curve they were almost behind."

And since the Van Dorens had always believed in taking out the middleman, Vans continued to be available only at Vans stores – skyrocketing in growth – while skate and surf shops continued to sell other (less successful) brands of shoes.

CUSTOMADE FOR YOU

VANS Style #34 - custom-made at any possible colorway to choose

IN THE EARLY DAYS,

Vans stuck with the custom-made idea of the Anaheim factory days, visualized in the 1979 advertisement featuring a shoemaker sewing together shoes for skaters waiting to go pacing out the door. After all, the Van Dorens had over 20 years experience in the shoe business under their belts. So a customer, to them, meant someone who would receive custom-made shoes.

Did we mention that you could bring your own materials, meaning ANY KIND OF FABRIC into the store to be made into Vans? Yep, snake leather, tiger fur, corduroy - if the shoe makers could stitch it together, it could be turned into a shoe, ready to be picked up at the Anaheim factory after a week. Hard to believe in today's age of mass-manufactured kicks - but even two separate colorways for each foot were an option.

While sneaker enthusiasts today spend their time musing over off-the-wall shoe design ideas - "Dude, leopard hide front section, wouldn't that be dope?!" - skaters back then could head to the Vans store and just get it done. Even beats customization on the Internet, doesn't it?

WHEELS, GRIPTAPE AND KICKTAILS

After taking a big dive in popularity, skateboarding underwent a decisive period of technical improvements throughout the early 1970s. The introduction of the urethane wheel remains THE most important achievement of that era, marking „the beginning of modern skateboarding" according to an article by Don Redondo on the history of skateboarding in *Thrasher* magazine.

As legend has it, professional surfer Frank Nasworthy came across urethane wheels in a backyard shop named "Creative Urethane" in Virginia in 1970. Replacing the clay wheels on his skateboard with the new radials, Nasworthy stepped into a whole new level of riding experience. Applying his technical design knowledge from college, Nasworthy then proceeded to create his own blend of skate-specific urethane wheels, which he mass-produced under the "Cadillac Wheels" label in 1972.

The new wheels were off to a rough start, mainly because of their high price at $8.00 a set (equivalent to $35 today). But once skaters would experience the difference – they'd never go back to clay or steel wheels. And consequently, sales took off while other manufacturers followed suit.

With the grip and control afforded by urethane wheels, skaters were ready to step to new terrain and finally move out of the shadow of surfing. The heyday of skate parks began in 1976 with the opening of the first facility in Port Orange, Florida, offering pools, snake runs and vertical ramps. The same year, hundreds of parks shot up all across North America.

Given the demands of this more challenging terrain, skateboard decks also evolved into an entirely different beast, thanks to the kicktail, invented by Larry Stevenson in 1970, and commercially sold griptape that replaced make-shift sandpaper top layers for better grip in 1975.

Over time, skateboards grew wider for more stability, as manufacturers changed board shapes from 6 inches to almost 9 inches, while aerial moves and inverts started their rapid progress. Not to mention knee slides, the new method of bailing to safety that took a heavy toll on the top section of skate shoes. A sure grip became the prime focus of skate equipment in these days, and skaters would even hammer small nails into the board's surface to achieve a non-slip stand. This called for footwear that could take the abuse without falling apart under the constant friction in contact with griptape. With boards and wheels taking the next step, it was time for footwear to evolve.

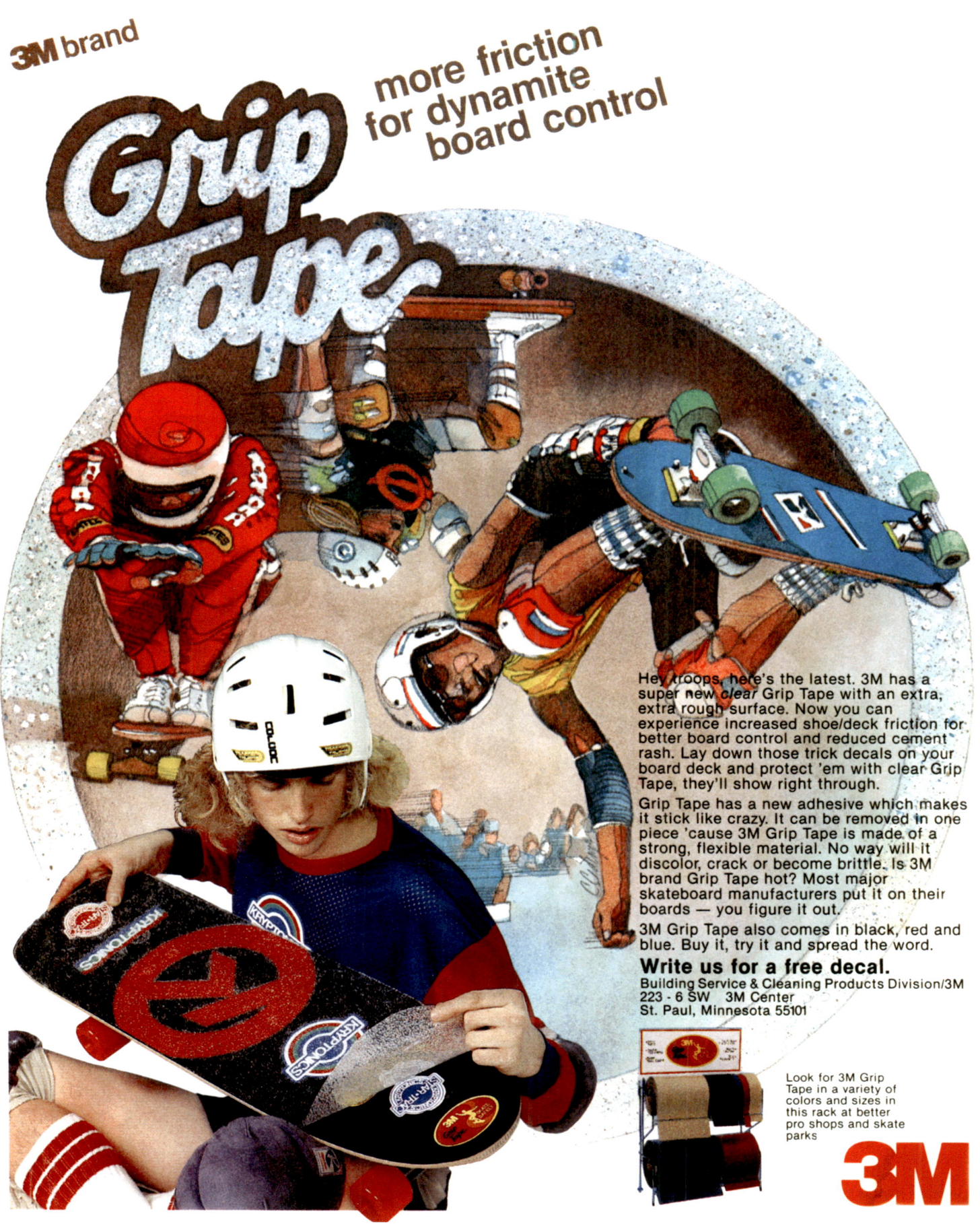

MAKAHA RADIALS - FOR THE SOLE

How many skateboard companies today are making their own shoes? Well, back in the day it was almost expected of brands to carry the entire range of equipment for whatever sport they were specializing in. So in 1976, Makaha Sportswear introduced their first skate-specific shoes – the Makaha Radials.

The shoe's main promise was to "break the deck / shoe barrier". Or in other words, allow for a barefooted skate experience while keeping your shoes on (Makaha was a surf company, after all). To achieve this, the grippy rubber sole featured a radial pattern, reminiscent of the suction cups on an Octopus's tentacles. According to a 1978 ad for the Radials, this sole design was adapted directly from shell ski boots, allowing a direct transfer of motion energy from sole to board.

The shoe was available in three colorways: red/white, blue/white and green/yellow. Next to the trademark radial edges of the sole, Makaha Radials featured reinforcement in critical areas exposed to excessive wear and tear during skating, like a double-layered toe section to withstand knee slides on pools and ramps.

And with nylon as the main material for the top section, the Radials may have felt a bit stiff and unwieldy – but man, did these shoes last! The pair we received for the exhibition has aged timelessly, withstanding the onslaught of griptape and concrete with hardly a scratch. Nevertheless, nylon and radial sole patterns have long since disappeared into obscurity. But who knows, maybe they could be the next big thing.

Jay Adams, barefoot pool skating. Tony Alva pulls back. Nice shot of the very special sole of Makaha shoes, 1976 "Who´s Hot" in *Skateboarder Magazine*.

MAKAHA MAKO - A GRAY SUEDE SHARK

In search of new shoe design ideas, most skateboard footwear companies either turn towards their riders or emulate what the rest of the industry is doing at the moment. Thinking outside the box, early skateboard company Makaha found inspiration in oceanic marine life.

For the Mako model, Makaha drew on their surfing roots and built the shoe's dark blue and white colorways on the Shortfin Mako shark, a warm-water shark native to the Atlantic Ocean from the Caribbean to as far north as the Gulf of Maine.

The Mako shoe was a direct follow-up to Makaha's almost identical Radial model, but with a key difference: While the Radial's upper section had been constructed from nylon - which was nearly unbreakable but cumbersome - the Mako was one of the first shoes to introduce an entirely suede 'upper' to satisfy the demand for more board control among the new generation of skaters in the late 1970s.

With their metallic blue-gray backs and white-colored bellies, Mako sharks are known for putting up an acrobatic battle when hooked, which makes them the perfect model for a skate shoe.

SKATE SHOES ON SKATES

Disco balls and roller skates – the spinning 1970s were all about things revolving, twisted and flashy. Those were the glory days of roller derbies and Roller Disco. The first Super Skating Center opened its doors in 1977 in the town of Kendall, California. As roller skate mania spread, millions of roller skaters around the world were soon going, going and going like Energizer bunnies around strobe-lighted skating rinks in most major cities. The movement gained great momentum thanks to the flow of effortless gliding afforded by ball-bearings and urethane wheels.z

Almost every "cool" shoe company in the 1970's was going along with the whole hype and put a shoe on skates. Vans shoes in cooperation with ACS released an Off the Wall roller skate that proved a huge seller. And numerous other skate companies like Santa Cruz jumped on the 8-wheel market.

THE CONNECTION?

Well, rollerskating was far from limited to a bunch of bubblegum popping disco freaks going in circles at the local roller rink. Eight-wheel culture also packed a growing hardcore element, with roller skaters stepping to vert on halfpipes and pools. The publishers of *Skateboarder* even started a roller skate magazine to give enthusiasts a forum (Who wouldn't wanna give it a try with a cover like this?). And as with many trends, the mainstream craze eventually faded, while hardcore rollerskating remains a fixture to this day.

THE DYNAMIC DUO!

HANG TEN'S NEW 'WILD, WIDE RIDE' SKATEBOARD AND 'SKATEBOARDER' SHOE.

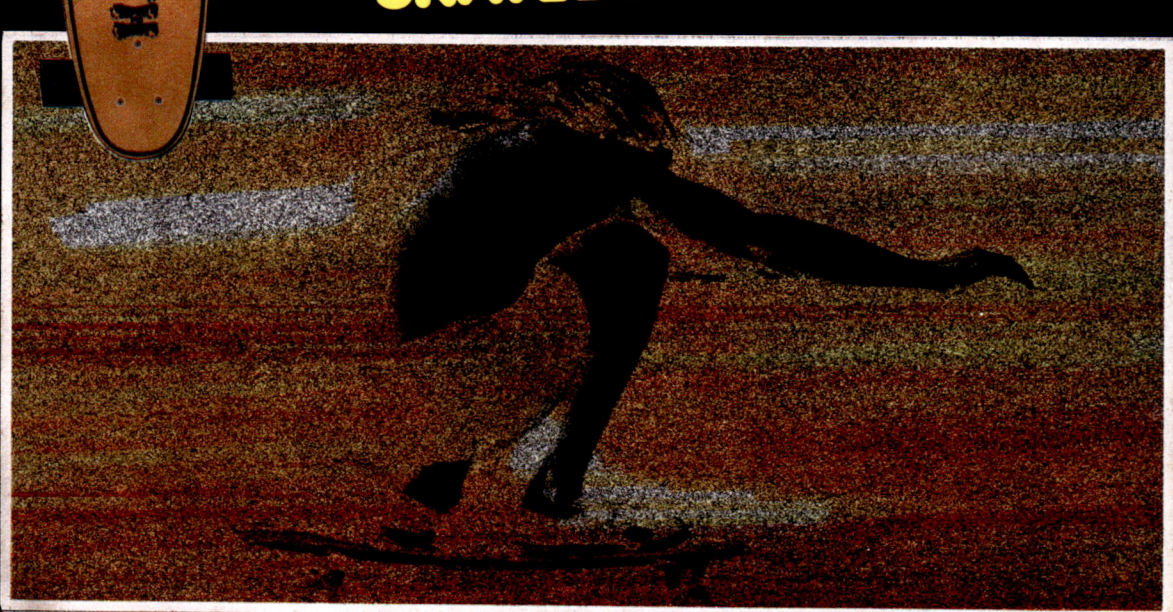

Hang Ten's new 450 SL "Wild Wide Ride" seems to create its own speed... with perfect control

Features extra wide 7" fiberglass deck with measured flexibility... new generation 7" wide trucks with smooth, hardened independent suspension axles... designed to put you into faster turns, bring you out with more stability.

New Mercury Blue Hang Ten "Big Dog" 2 inch wide precision-molded urethane wheels have a rigid core and soft tracking edge for top speed and sure grip. Double-sealed precision bearings keep out dirt and dust, last longer and ride smoother.

Unique ¼" rubber cushion between truck and board gives smoother, quieter ride, more road clearance.

Get Hang Ten's "Wild Wide Ride"... the new standard of excellence... for competing pros or weekend wonders.

Hang Ten's tough new "Skateboarder", the first shoe designed exclusively for the sport.

The famous Hang Ten feet... the mark of excellence in this new shoe designed by skateboarders for skateboarders!

Only the tough, long-wearing "Skateboarder" gives you:

Extra Control and Stability — Especially designed wedge-bottomed sole... Taslan laces... reinforced cowhide... high collar.

Extra Wear and Protection — Double-thick toe... riveted at stress points for superior strength... gumbo crepe sole with reinforced steel shank outlasts all other shoes.

Extra Comfort and Durability — Padded collar... cushioned insole super-soft Velura cowhide.

For the surest way to protect your feet, look for ours.

"The label that became a lifestyle"

Hang Ten Skateboards and Footgear • 751 Seventh Avenue • San Diego, CA. 92101

HANG TEN - DESIGNED "EXCLUSIVELY"

Following in Hobie's footsteps, surf manufacturers Hang Ten offered a complete skateboard with urethane wheels and their own version of a skate shoe. Marketed as "the first shoe designed exclusively for the sport," the Hang Ten looked like an unorthodox blend of a bowling shoe and a Clarke's Wallabee.

One of the shoes' biggest sales points was their sturdiness. A classified ad for a skateboard mail order store at the time even listed the shoes under "Skateboard Safety Equipment": HANG TEN SHOES - TOUGH SOLE W/ HARD TOE: $23.95

For added resilience, the gumbo crepe natural rubber sole came reinforced with a steel shank insert – not exactly offering the flex and feel of skating barefooted. The wedgeshaped sole rose in thickness toward the heel for added heel padding – a design principle that has not seen many follow-ups. Most skate shoes to this day rely on evenly thick sole layers, while gel inserts and the like have become the top choice for heel protection.

SKATE-SPECIFIC SHOES

One major contribution to shoe design lay in Hang Ten's extra sturdy Taslan laces, which may be worth re-visiting, with most laces these days still breaking easily. However, the shoe didn't hit home among skaters. Hang Tens were too bulky, plus, the polished leather finish proved too slippery for manoeuvring across griptape, so a major re-design was in order.

As a follow-up, Hang Ten introduced an all-suede skate shoe in late 1979 that righted all the wrongs of the premiere model. This low-cut model was closer to the shoes created by Makaha and Hobie, and also abandoned the wedge-shaped sole in favour of an evenly shaped soft gum rubber sole.

While Hang-Ten's shoe offering ended with skateboarding's second big death a few years later, one feature has endured the test of time: If you look closely, you will see that the logo stripes on the side of the shoes are almost identical to those found on contemporary Globe Shoes models. Oops, can we say that here? Guess we just did...

KID POWER – FOR FUTURE SUPER SKATERS

Back in the days before kids were a much sought-after demographic targeted by heavy marketing and research, offering kid-specific shoes was a big step. But it did fill a big gap in the lower size ranges, and with many kids taking up skating, Kid Power Shoes became a smash hit with youngsters. Or should we say, their parents, since these were the days before five-year-olds had their own credit cards and mobile phones.

Aside from cutesy stripes and a sturdy toe cap, the upper shoe section pretty much followed in the low cut tradition established by Vans and Hobie, while the extra-wide sole stuck out significantly on the sides to give youngsters solid balance and control. In terms of sole texture, the two-colored profile of Kid Power Shoes broke new ground with a differently patterned section around the balls of the foot – a principle that grown skaters would come to appreciate in later years.

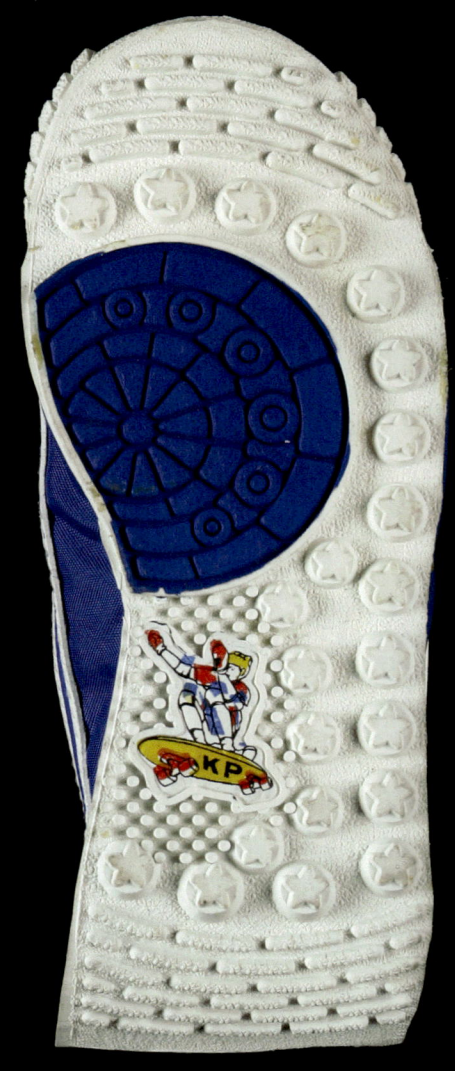

Your KID POWER® Skateboard Sneakers have been designed to help you be a super-skater—and a safer one! Wipe-outs are no fun— that's why the soles are especially made to grip your board. But before you tie up your new KID POWER® shoes and skate off, check out these tips from our skateboarding pros. They'll help you skate the best way there is . . . safely!

Ride safely . . . and enjoy your KID POWER®

FOR SKATEBOARDING ONLY - STEP INTO A HOBIE

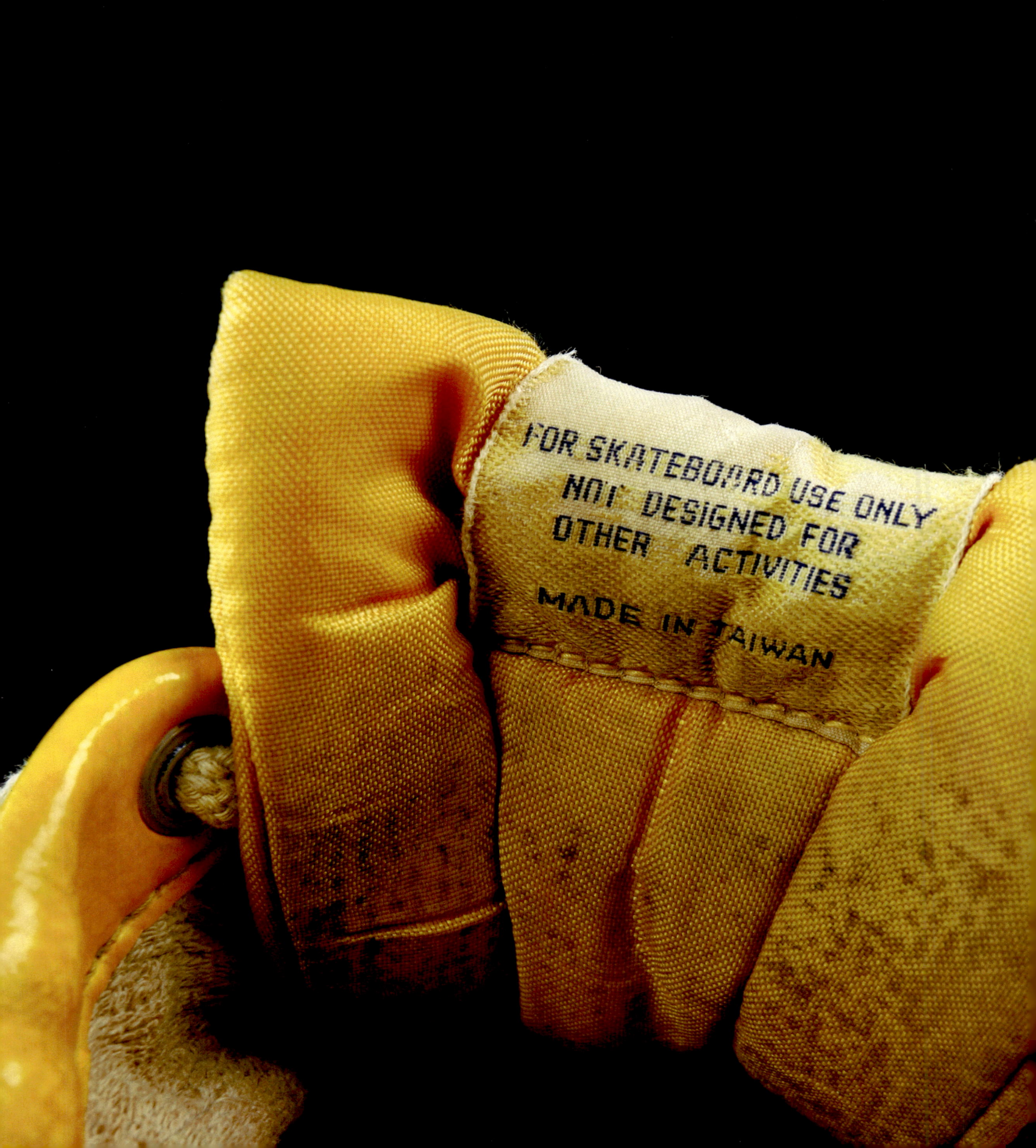

Paving the way for countless others to follow, Hobie was one of the first surf companies to get involved in the skateboard market. This is even more remarkable considering Hobie's early beginnings in the garage of company founder Hobart "Hobie" Alter in 1950.

With the success of Hobie's skateboard line, the next logical step was to branch out into the shoe business. The launch of Hobie Athletic Footwear coincided with the rise of pool skating, to which the design and functionality of the shoes paid attention.

The Hobie shoe came in blue suede with yellow and red ornaments, replete with a plastic-protected toecap. Other features included a reinforced padded ankle section with the company's signature "H"-logo on the back and a flexible, grippy sole.

Due to growing popular demand, the Hobie was also available as a high-top model, which more and more skaters realized was the way to go for skating large pools.

"I always fall good..." Shogo wipes clean

SKATE SAFE

SKATE SHOES
by Doug Schneider

One of the major dilemmas in the life of any skateboarder comes each time he buys a new pair of tennis shoes. It always seems that just when you break your shoes in to the point where you like them, they begin to wear out. There isn't much you can do to make a pair of shoes last longer, but there are a few points that you should consider before your next purchase so that you don't get stuck with something you don't want.

Most of the more well known shoe companies, such as Adidas, Converse, Nike, and Puma, have several styles of shoes which are ideal for skateboarding. Vans and Hobie sell shoes that are made especially for skateboarders. All of these companies sell both high tops as well as low tops. Low tops offer added mobility to the ankle while high tops provide more support and protection. Many people who use low tops wear ankle guards to protect their ankles. Most ankle guards restrict ankle movement to some degree, though less than wearing high top tennis shoes.

Price is a big difference between low and high tops. (Example: a Nike Bruin low top retails for about $18.00, while the same model in a high top costs between $38.00 and $40.00.)

Next thing to consider is the material you want the tops to be made of. For instance, suede stretches a lot more than canvas. If you buy a suede shoe which fits perfect when you first buy it, it will tend to stretch out and you may end up having to wear two pairs of socks after awhile. In other words, suede and leather shoes should fit really snug at first, not necessarily in length, though definitely in fit.

Another important point is the relative advantages and disadvantages of soft (rubbery) soles as opposed to stiff soles. Vans and Nike shoes are fairly soft soled, which enables more 'feel'' of the board. Hobies and Pumas, on the other hand, are stiffer, which makes it harder to sense where your feet are at all times, but offer more support when jumping off of your board and, naturally, last a bit longer.

Tread patterns vary greatly and *do* tend to affect grip. The more tread that touches the board, the better the grip. Nike treads resemble ripples and work best with regular grip tape because only the tip of the ripple is touching the board (especially when the shoe is new). The dotted and square treads are usually a little stiffer and grip better with pizza deck (again, particularly when the shoe is new). Once the soles are broken in, the grip tape used doesn't matter as much.

Finally, when buying your shoes, check soles for loose glue joints, loose threads and imperfections on the bottom of the soles. In the final analysis, don't buy a shoe because it works for someone else — buy it because it fits your own style and needs. They're *your* feet — treat them right!

Skate shoes affect performance . . . Doug, showing a good "feel" for equipment and terrain.

Nike Blazer ca. 1979

OLLIES, AIRS AND HIGH TOPS

As the 1980s approached at breakneck speed, pool skating at skate parks all over the world was progressing to unseen heights. Quite literally, with pioneers going well above the lip with new and increasingly higher variations of airs, aided by the traction and speed afforded by urethane wheels. On behalf of the shoes, the extensive shock of landing on concrete from aerials demanded extra support.

"It made quality and durability the most important factors," said Tony Hawk, who was turning heads as a gifted rookie at the time. "Low-tops didn't cut it anymore, and some thinner footwear was more dangerous than functional."

In search for the ultimate ankle support and protection, skaters branched out into wearing non-skate shoes like Nike basketball shoes for added resilience and padding. At the same time, all skate shoe manufacturers began adding high tops to their line-ups while experimenting with new padding. The most groundbreaking maneuver of that era was the Ollie air, named after its inventor, 15-year-old Alan "Ollie" Gelfand from Florida, who in 1978 learned how to "pop" no handed airs above the lip by hitting his tail on the way up. The Ollie not only dazzled outsiders – "Look, dad – no hands!" – but emerged as the new benchmark for separating the men from the boys. The only way was up.

Air at the "Mad Dog" Bowl - England
1979 Tony Alva Europe tour

Nike Blazer - movie-props *Lords of Dogtown*
Tony Alva's shoes at the Dog Bowl scene

Everywhere around the world, skaters were pushing the limits of how high and fast you could go on a skateboard, while shoe manufacturers struggled to develop just the right kind of shoe for this new demanding way of skating. Pool skating also added an extra element of physical danger to the game. Injury levels were up again and once more, the media jumped on the "dangerous fad" angle, portraying skateboarding as a reckless and dangerous craze. Eventually, the whole skatepark era would go down in flames fanned by feisty insurance lawyers across the USA.

Meanwhile, skate park owners were doing all they could to make skating as safe as possible at their facilities. Park hours were divided by sessions according to skill level. Helmets and full pads were the standard protective gear required at parks – but they didn't protect the ankles of skaters who still mostly relied on low-top shoes.

Protection was highly needed, though, as skaters would knock their relatively heavy boards into their ankles quite regularly on grinds and airs gone awry.

SHIELD YOUR ANKLES

Despite rising demand among hardcore pool skaters, high top shoes took a while to catch on among the skateboard community as a whole. Some riders still preferred the control and flexibility offered by low cuts. At the same time, extra ankle protection couldn't hurt during the occasional pool session.

Offering an optional safety upgrade for low top shoes, Vans introduced a custom-built ankle guard sold at skate shops around the world. The advertisement at the time read: "The VANS Ankle GUARD - A Breakthrough in the Industry! A safety product designed specifically for ankle protection."

 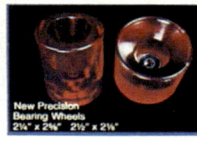 

STYLE #37 - TAKE IT "HIGH TOP"

The add-on Ankle Guards struck a nerve among skaters and remained in the company's line-up even when Vans introduced the Style #37 Hi-Top in 1977. In late 1978, Vans replaced the Style #37 with the even higher cut Style #38, which established high top shoes as a solid fixture in skateboarding. Soon thereafter, Vans Ankle Guards were discontinued.

Despite these safety measures, The Man was ready to strike again, as park after park succumbed to the onslaught of insurance lawsuits. The bulldozers were rolling in, and skateboarding was getting ready to die for the second time.

STYLE #38 - TAKING IT HIGHER

Meeting the demand for high-top shoes, in late 1977 Vans introduced their Style 38, a design classic also known as the "Skate Hi." To endorse their new model, Vans went all out and signed man-of-the-hour Stacy Peralta as their sponsored athlete of choice.

At the stroke of a pen, Stacy Peralta became the first skater ever to receive endorsement checks from a skateboarding shoe company. And not a bad sum, either. Vans was paying young Stacey $300 a month, which equals nearly $1000 today, making the trailblazing pioneer one of the best-paid men in skateboarding at the time.

Did Stacy Peralta have any idea at the time that skateboarding shoes would continue to grow into the biggest gravy train in any pro skater's salary? "My current bank account would reflect it had I known," he said.

Next to a reinforced ankle with sewn-in padding and the signature waffle-grip sole, the Skate Hi also featured an early version of an ollie pad on the side. Staying up-to-date with the demands posed by riding technique, Vans would continue to involve their sponsored riders into the design process of their shoes, with models like the first "Era", designed by Tony Alva and Stacy Peralta. This formula for implementing hands-on experience into the design process later found its extension in pro skaters starting their own shoe companies, such as DC, Lakai and Etnies.

SKATEBOARD SHOES - NOW ON SALE

To some skaters of that era, the death of the second wave of skateboarding is immortalized in images of demolished skate parks and shut down swimming pools. But the price tags on this shoebox also tell the story.

These skate-specific Wilson shoes had sold for a regular $17.99 during the height of the 1970s skateboard boom. But when skateboarding died without any warning due to spiraling insurance costs and lack of attendance, they practically turned from hot selling items to slow sellers overnight.

The dwindling popularity of skateboarding is reflected in the price for this pair, which had slumped from a harsh early drop to $10.79 all the way to $3.00. If anyone still doubted that skateboarding had hit rock bottom, here was solid proof.

Imagine how long these must have hugged the shelf before someone finally placed them in their garage where they collected dust for 20 years, before they sold for $30 to a collector on eBay. Which is why a trip to the local flea market or garage sale can still reveal mint-condition treasures in the most unlikely places.

SKATE SHOES FROM A TENNIS BRAND

YOU KNOW WHAT THEY SAY ABOUT TEACHING AN OLD DOG A NEW TRICK?

Behind the Wilson brand name is one of the oldest shoe companies in the US. Started in 1913 in Chicago under the name Ashland, the company was renamed Wilson in 1916 after its president Thomas Wilson.

The company rose to fame during its 35 years as the main distributor for Converse up to 1977 and was initially synonymous with tennis shoes.

HOW DID THE CONNECTION TO SKATEBOARDING COME ABOUT?

As legend has it, the company's signature shoe for legendary NCAA basketball coach John Wooden became a big success with skaters in 1977. According to pro basketball player Brother Ray, the shoes "were indestructible. They were the first sneakers I saw with a polyurethane bottom. I loved them. I had them in natural nubuck which was between leather and suede."

The John Wooden shoe was discontinued after a year, and instead of abandoning skaters, Wilson followed up by serving their own version of skate-specific shoes. The verdict? Not bad, especially for a tennis company. The nubuck upper material, reinforced lower ankle section in the back and ankle padding under the top sleeve would hold up quite well according to current standards.

SKATEBOARD SHOES UK AND EUROPE

Getting your kicks wasn't easy for skaters in the UK and Europe in the late 70s and early 80s. You really had to scramble to get your hands on a pair of skateable shoes.

Simply walking into a skate shop was only an option in a handful of metropolitan cities, and high street stores or shopping centers were still decades away from carrying skate brands.

"No one really carried skate shoes back then, you had to mail order them from the US," said Don Brown about growing up skating in England. "And even Converse were hard to come by. You basically had to catch a train to London for a few hours from where I lived." How did European skaters get by?

Like they always did. By using that quintessential Do-It-Yourself-spirit on which European skateboarding is built. Already undeterred by the scarcity of rideable terrain and hardware, early European skaters would press on and appropriate anything they could into skate shoes.

"A lot of people would get some kind of generic shoes out of department stores, anything that was cheap and disposable," Don Brown said.

BOTTOM FEEDING FOR CHEAP KICKS.

All over Europe, any shoe was game to be tried out for skating. "Way back in the early days, we had any kind of no-name, cheap-o-sneakers," said former professional skateboarder Claus Grabke from Germany. Another option consisted of fishing at the bottom of the sales bin for the cheapest models by your country's native shoe brands, such as adidas and Puma in Germany or Clarke's in the UK.

Over years of trial-and-error testing, a number of classic shoe choices emerged as mainstays of the continental skate scene. "I remember skating these adidas shoes called 'Nizza' a lot," Claus Grabke said. "There were also those low-cut Puma shoes and of course the first high-top Nikes."

Over in England, Don Brown would rely on Dunlop's "Green Flash" sneakers that were a staple among skaters at the time thanks to their flexible sole and good grip. The roots of the Dunlop company go all the way back to the mid-19th Century, when the Liverpool Rubber Company owned by John Boyd Dunlop patented a way of sticking rubber to canvas. The Green Flashes were "green" in more than one way, relying on entirely vegan materials – which is among the biggest selling points of a recent re-issue aimed at fashion-conscious club kids.

DOING THINGS DIFFERENTLY

Soon enough, traditional English shoemakers Clarke's filled the gap with their Stunter model, a canvas high-top much in the image of a Chuck Taylor with a number of additional skate-specific features. These included ribbed ankle padding, as well as wrap-around toe rubber support and a padded heel section.

Although the company declared in full page ads that "Sports Science Professors" had helped create this skate-specific shoe, the Stunter scored poorly in reviews in British *Skateboard* magazine, mostly due to the rubber crepe sole being "not very grippy" with an overall "knobby feel." The review concluded: "It's hard to believe that a major manufacturer could get it so wrong."

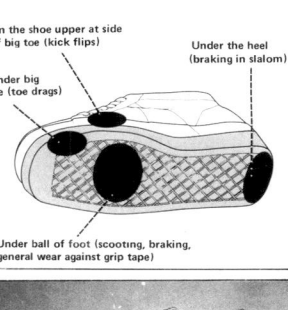

However, the legacy of the Stunter may lay in its ads, which pioneered the high-tech, scientific angle for marketing skate shoes that would become popular again in the mid-1990s - you know, "scientifically advanced footwear" and "skate-specific technology" and all that.

Another phenomenon mostly limited to England was the popularity of Pro-Keds "Park Plus" skate shoes by automobile tire corporation Uniroyal. Pro Keds basically followed the formula of a plain canvas sneaker in the mode of the Vans deck shoes, although the grip and longevity of the Pro Keds' soles fell short of the original. Nevertheless, Pro Keds were heavily marketed through magazines at the time under the slogan "The Skater's Edge."

Dunlop also stepped in, maybe driven by skateboarders embracing their Green Flash shoes, who knows?

In the late 1970s, Dunlop introduced their "Skateboard Superstars" - essentially Chuck Taylor's with added ankle padding and rubber soles with a "suction cup" pattern reminiscent of Makaha Radials. Their launch coincided with another Chuck Taylor clone entering the British market, so-called "Speed Rites" by shoemakers Marbot from Essex.

Over in France, Freestyle skateboarder Pierre André Senizergues was also experimenting with shoes in the lower price range: "I didn't have a lot of money, so I would get shoes from a supermarket called 'Monoprix', which means one price. Then I would duct tape them and put super glue on to make them last longer."

IF YOUR SHOES WON'T GRIP, BRING OUT THE MONSTER GRIPTAPE!

Although these generic shoes posed an affordable option, they had serious performance issues: "Most of the shoes we used wouldn't grip that well, so we used extra coarse griptape on our boards to make up for it. That kind of griptape was definitely deadly for your fingers, but it would make any shoe grip," he laughs.

"I also remember [US shoe company] Pony sponsoring a lot of skaters, so I always wanted a pair of Ponys, although they also fell apart quickly. I knew that if I ever made shoes one day, I'd find ways to make them last," said Senizergues, who now owns Sole Technology, makers of Etnies, és and Emerica.

ausse le skate.

America :
...ris : blanc/bleu/rouge
...bleu/rouge/blanc
...intures : du 28 au 46.

chaussures de sports
PHOENIX
PALLADIUM

These Boots are made for Skateboarding

When we decided to make a skateboarding boot we gave ourselves some headaches.

Because we didn't just take an ordinary boot and say it's for skateboarding.

Instead, we consulted two Sports Science Professors who analysed what was needed in a skateboarding boot.

Then we designed and made one to their specifications.

Around the vulnerable ankle bone we put shock-absorbing ribbed padding. For real protection and flexibility.

Inside the boots we built an arch support and padded tongue. After all, who needs bruised, flat feet?

Our natural rubber soles were given special forward ridging. For highly flexible gripping-power and positive contact with your board.

We also developed a specially strengthened wrap-around toe and heel. And extended the rubber to protect the sides and front of the foot.

Finally, we put together some really sharp styling in rugged natural canvas. To make you look as good as you feel.

See the result at your Clarksport Stockist.

Wrap Around Toe

Wrap Around Heel

Forward Ridging

Ribbed Ankle Padding

Colours: White/Navy, Black/Red, Navy/Orange. Sizes 2–5 recommended retail £7.99. Sizes 6–12 recommended retail £8.99
Send for free brochure and list of stockists to: Clarks Ltd. 21 Seymour Road, East Molesey, Surrey. KT8 0PE

Skate shoes became more readily available in the 1980s, but the exchange rate for US-dollars remained rather steep in those days. "I would always see people wear Vans in magazines", Pierre André Senizergues said. "But they were $100 a pair for us, which was a lot of money, so we really had to make them last with a lot of trial and error, super glue and duct tape."

To support the scene, French shoe makers Phoenix Palladium provided a low budget skate shoe with their "Trial America" model that looked like – guess what?! – a red-white-and-blue colored Chuck Taylor with fancy laces.

Things changed when the big skate boom of the 1980s hit Europe and stores and distributors made skate shoes available to the masses. But all the early skaters still remember a time in Europe when getting your kicks meant searching high and low for shoes you could skate.

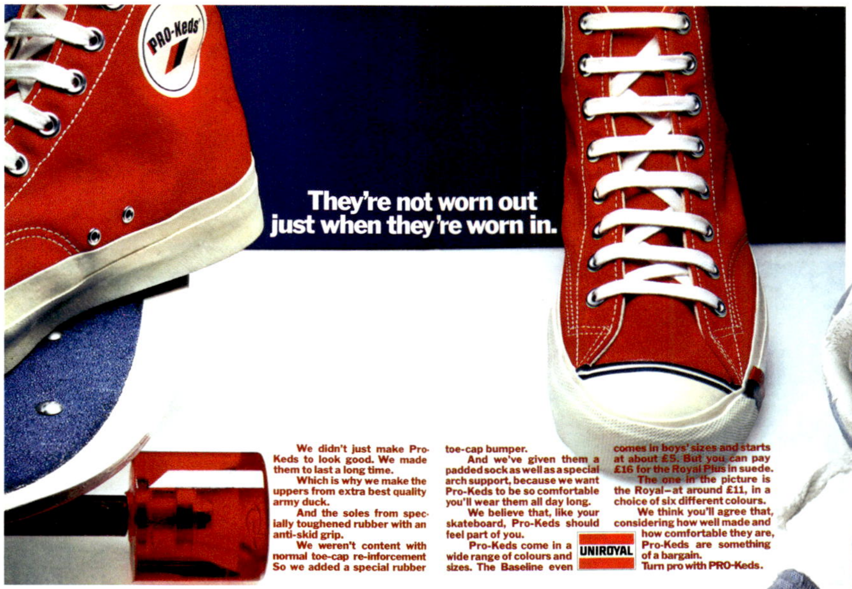

THREE STRIPES FOR THE SECOND WAVE

With many technical innovations and new, spectacular maneuvers, skateboarding's second wave was creating a new demand for resistant, grippy and comfortable footwear. Since the skateboard industry wasn't able to provide shoes on a large scale yet, most riders were sporting those from the established athletic shoe brands. A famous three-striped company from Germany called adidas was on board too – and soon launched some of the first skate-specific shoe models in Europe.

At this point adidas was strongly associated with mainstream team sports such as football. When skateboarding first made its way into California schoolyards in the early 50s, adidas had just helped Germany's football team win the 1954 World Cup. adidas had equipped the team with cutting-edge football shoe having removable studs. When Nasworthy's "Cadillac Wheels" were beginning to fly off the shelves, Germany had just beaten the Netherlands 2 to 1 in the 1974 World Cup final in Munich. There was no way around the three stripes, especially in the 1970s. At the 1976 Montreal Olympics, 83% of the athletes wore adidas. Apparently, that wasn't enough to scare off skateboarders.

Halfpipe legend Claus Grabke of Germany, one of the most popular riders in the 80s, still remembers the red adidas "Handball" shoe worn by many riders in the early days. As skateboarding turned into a countercultural movement, Grabke and others turned away from mainstream shoe models "because my father was also wearing "Handball" shoes. He was actually a handball player. Skateboarding was an escape from the world of the parents, so there was no way I could have worn those."

Thanks its sense of freedom and individuality skateboarding was now getting the glory that had been reserved for mainstream sports like football. In another reversal, football was now stigmatized as being strict and team-oriented. Despite this fact, adidas quickly gained a foothold in skateboarding.

Among the most popular models in Europe was the "Nizza", a canvas basketball shoe first introduced in 1976. t was fashionable and had all the features a 1970's skateboarder wanted: The transparent suction cup sole was grippy. A good ankle and heel cushioning provided proper support, and a rubber toe cap offered further protection.

Quickly after the successful launch of the "Nizza", adidas realized the potential of skateboarding and produced some of the first shoes designed specifically for the sport – the "Skate" and "Superskate". They were released in 1978, in the same year that Adi Dassler, the founder of the company died. The shoes were designed at Landersheim, France, and launched in France first. Both low- and high-top were vulcanized in their original version and made of wear-resistant kangaroo leather. The three stripes were more than just a brand logo. Actually, the middle stripe provided some well-needed stability for radical skate action.

A 1970s British skateboard team, replete with manager, coach and skateboarder.

THE 3 EIGHTIES

FUNCTION - FASHION - SIGNATURE SHOES

The 1980s were an age of youthful experimentation in riding technique and fashion. The sky was the limit for what was possible on a skateboard. Skateboarding grew and matured as an underground culture in its own right. These were the good old days. Skateboarding came up big everywhere. On bill-boards, in movies, on television and in the streets. This new breed had come a long way. After the demise of concrete skate parks and the end of the second huge wave of skateboard mania, skateboarding had gone underground.

Or some bugged-out geek speak along these lines, sing e-handedly "inventing" skateboarding during a chase scene with his arch nemesis and small-town bully supreme, Biff. The airs and stunts portrayed on the big screen had a captivating effect on audiences. Most viewers had never even imagined you could do all this stuff on a skateboard. Consequently, skateboarding was no longer seen as a toy – but something entirely different. Something really cool! And millions around the world wanted a piece of it.

Backyard vert ramps and schoolyards had become the places where the remaining hardcore skaters survived and honed their skills. Having picked up momentum throughout the first half of the new decade, skating was ready to come back toward the mid 80s – bigger and badder than ever. All over the United States, the number of skaters shot back up into the millions. And this time around, the wave spread all over the world, as young people discovered skateboarding from Moscow to Rio de Janeiro.

BACK IN THE SPOTLIGHT

It was back on and popping in every sense, considering the adaptation of the ollie pop to street skating and the tremendous impact on mainstream culture. Skateboarding appeared in blockbuster movies like *Police Academy 4* and most crucial of all, *Back to the Future* starring Michael J. Fox. Millions of viewers watched average kid Marty McFly travel back in time to the 1950s in order to avert a fatal shift in the time-space continuum.

SKATE CHIC

With their newfound attention in the public eye, skaters had come out of the backyards and into the spotlight. The "skater dude," epitomized by Sean Penn's character Jeff Spicoli in the 1981 smash hit *Fast Times at Ridgemont High*, became a sought-after fashion icon. After all, Spicoli's checkered Vans slip-ons had already moved on to be the company's best selling shoe ever after *Fast Times* hit cinemas, and the slacker cool of skating struck a nerve as a "look" that people liked to emulate – whether they skated or not.

Hot fashion items of the day included berets, painter's caps – worn shield up with bobbing bangs out front – and full-print sweat pants, preferably with skull patterns. The iconic skate fashion brand of the hour, Vision Street Wear, offered an extensive collection sold not only at hardcore skate shops – which proved to be the brand's downfall in the eyes of the hardcore scene.

"Function before fashion" emerged as a counter-movement to the polished street chic sold to the masses and die-hard skaters started abandoning Vision in favor of more hardcore companies. Vans shoes still enjoyed a reputation as the prototypical skateboard footwear company, but a new competitor on the core market had arrived with Airwalk shoes, created in 1986 by George Yohn.

Practically overnight, Airwalk rose to dominate the market with a powerful combination of promotion strategies and technical innovation. In an unprecedented team-building power move, Airwalk swept up key pro riders including Tony Hawk, Chris Miller and Tony Magnusson to endorse their brand, while introducing key design features such as the lace saver for added protection and functionality.

At the same time, skaters kept appropriating footwear from other sports for their purposes. The 1986 edition of Nike's Air Jordan turned out an inexpensive and resilient alternative to skate shoes. From a design standpoint, it would also inform skate footwear for generations (see story on Air Jordans and Animal Chin).

TRANNY DAYS

Throughout the 1980s, skateboarding still primarily revolved around ramps and all kinds of transitions. Vertical skating reigned supreme, with pro skaters such as Christian Hosoi, Tony Hawk and Steve Caballero receiving pay checks of over $10,000 a month. Competitions on the scale of the North American Skateboard Association's (NSA) cup series or the Munster World Cup drew thousands of spectators and were always the place to see newly invented moves like the McTwist (by Mike McGill, 1984) or the 720° (by Tony Hawk, 1985).

On the streets, the glory days of launch ramps were in full swing, with airs and grabs that had been invented on vert transferred to the street setting. Freestyle skating on flat ground had its heyday as a competitive sport, with freestyle skaters performing choreographed routines –cued to music (preferably dramatic and bouncy, we've seen people skate to Meat Loaf, seriously!) – including handstands, finger flips and all kinds of footwork such as shove-its and varials. There's an amazing clip of Rodney Mullen in Japan in 1984 on YouTube to give you an idea of how diverse and finely-tuned freestyle riding had already become at this early stage.

The invention of the flatland ollie by freestyle skater Rodney Mullen in 1984 opened a new chapter of street skating. This would prove to be THE most important street maneuver in skateboarding as it literally opened the floodgates for the invention of all kinds of new street tricks. At the same time, the ollie made a number of urban objects accessible that had been considered unskateable before, allowing for a continuous and undisturbed ride up and down stairs, curbs and ledges.

Two new skate-specific magazines proliferated the latest developments in riding technique to readers around the world. The attitude and style-driven *Thrasher* magazine started publication based in San Francisco in 1981. It would grow to become a defining force in hardcore skate culture, commenting on and shaping skateboarding with a watchful eye on keeping things legit until this very day. The second title was *Transworld Skateboarding Magazine*, started in Southern California in 1983 with an emphasis on high-quality photography and a spotlight on leading athletes of the sport.

LIVING ON VIDEO

In hindsight, home video may have provided the medium that defined the 1980s. The technology also proved the perfect way for skaters to see new moves and stay up to date on riding technique. Stacy Peralta soon realized the potential of video and started the iconic line of Powell-Peralta videos in 1984 The Bones Brigade Video Show. The video turned out to be a smashing success among skaters who now had a way to view tricks performed in moving images, instead of being limited to photographic proof in magazines.

As far as filming styles and editing techniques went, Bones Brigade laid down the look and feel for how skateboarding would be presented for decades to come. Fisheye lenses emphasized the scale and difficulty of tricks, while Peralta employed fast-paced editing together with a carefully chosen soundtrack for an engaging overall viewing experience. Almost every company in the business followed suit and produced their own videos, and skate videos have remained a crucial factor in the progress of skateboarding to this day.

In terms of cultural interconnectedness, video footage of new and outstanding tricks would show skaters around the world, what could actually be done on a skateboard. When Natas Kaupas and Mark Gonzales started board sliding the first handrails in 1986, the footage sent shockwaves around the globe and forever changed the way skaters looked at the built environment.

Thanks to the growing number of tricks, the city no longer appeared as just a space for passing through on the way to the skate park – the city WAS the skate park. Which didn't go down all that well with the public at large, fearing for the safety of street architecture, paid by tax money. The new breed of skaters would cause notable damage to benches, planters and walls. And they wouldn't leave! Instead, skaters would linger around and session a set of stairs or rails for hours, scraping up the edges and waking up the neighbors with their noise.

Something had to be done. Before long, "No Skateboarding" signs popped up around the world, while skaters were claiming the streets and everything in it. This was just the beginning and skaters didn't mind being branded as outcasts at all. Actually, they kind of liked it.

SKATE AND DESTROY

Skateboarding once again became labeled as a menace, which hardcore skaters welcomed as part of a punk rock attitude that had grown into a big movement since the early 1980s. The soundtrack for rebellion came from bands like Suicidal Tendencies, led by Mike Muir, brother of Jim Muir of Dog Town fame and produced by photographer Glen E. Friedman. Their 1987 single "Possessed to Skate" provided an anthem for an entire generation of skaters, together with songs by Black Flag, the Dead Kennedies, The Red Hot Chili Peppers, and the Descendents, to name but a few.

In all its intensity, skate punk was worlds apart from the neatly styled skate chic that the masses could buy in pre-packaged doses. This was something raw and gnarly. Driven by the skate and destroy attitude... street skating proved more and more dangerous with skaters stepping to bigger stairs and rails – all the while facing increased

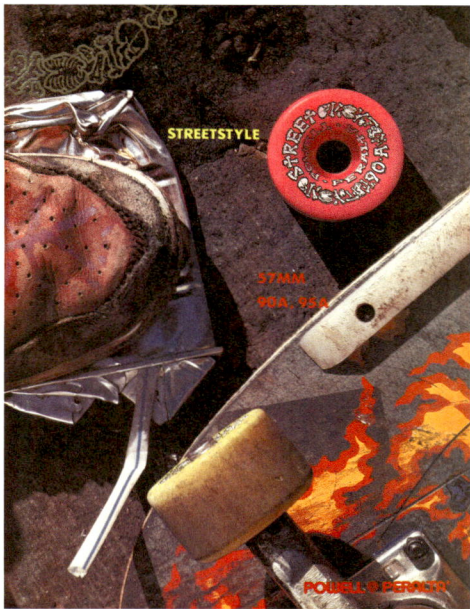

risks of arrests and citations. "Give blood, go skateboard," became the motto for a new generation of street skaters who were ready to pay the price for taking skating to the next level.

On the other side of the spectrum, "Skate and Create" was a new catch phrase for musicians, photographers and artists, who took their drive and motivation directly from skateboarding. These individuals are far too numerous to be specifically named in this book, but let's suffice it to say that their contributions helped skateboarding evolve into a full-fledged culture known for its non-conformist originality and spontaneity.

THE SHAPE OF THINGS TO COME

As the 1990s drew near, a number of key developments in riding technique presented the shape of things to come. The late 1980s saw the beginnings of technical street skating, for which the early videos by Tony Magnusson's company H-Street proved a driving force. And skaters no longer had to skate vert to make a living in skateboarding, as more and more skaters received paychecks as street pros.

Before the turn of the decade, a number of technical elements from freestyle skating – such as impossibles, 360° kickflips and shove-its – had been added to the street repertoire and performed in an urban setting. At the same time, pioneers like Frankie Hill, whose mind-boggling gap ollies were the curtains in many a Powell video at the time, raised the bar in terms of how big a gap could be cleared on a skateboard.

The lines between skating goofy and regular were already blurring, with Mark Gonzales throwing down the first switch stanced tricks on street, while Tony Hawk proceeded to baffle skaters by doing the same on vert. In line with this development, skateboard decks started featuring double-tail designs – like the groundbreaking Mike Vallely Barnyard model released by World Industries in 1989 – so they could be ridden either way.

Skateboard footwear emerged as an important factor in sponsored skateboarding with the arrival of the first signature shoes, most noteworthy the Natas and Steve Caballero models, backed up by substantial endorsement checks. Although frowned upon at first, pro shoes would grow into an integral part of sponsored skateboarding – and the biggest gravy train for pro riders.

THE ALL STAR CHUCKS

SHADES OF ANOTHER TIME

Reintroducing the Chuck Taylor Classic All Star® *from Converse.*®

Old movies, comic books, songs from the sixties.

Seems like whatever was big in the past, is huge now. And the comeback everybody has their eye on is being staged by one of the most vintage classics of all—Chuck Taylor All Stars, from Converse.

They give you the timeless look of original *'Chucks.'* The black leather eyelets. The ankle patch. The black rubber outsole. It's a look that's been away just long enough to be 'discovered.' You'll be seeing them on the street, in khaki, black, red, navy, and olive canvas. Which is why you'll want to see them at your local Converse dealer.

Chuck Taylor Classic All Stars. They're a fashion idea whose time has come. Again.

It was 1917. Before there was an NBA. Before anybody was playing basketball for a living.

Chuck Taylor, like most semi-pros, needed a second job so he could continue playing the game he loved. He went to Converse, a small company in Malden, Massachusetts. They had just started making basketball shoes, and hired Chuck as a salesman. But before he started selling the shoes that would soon be called "Chucks," he suggested Converse make a few improvements. The young company took the advice of their new salesman, and "The Ambassador of Basketball" went on to single-handedly make "Chucks" the most famous shoe in the game.

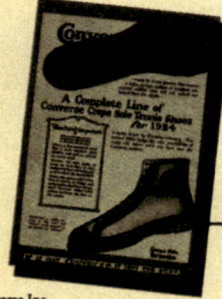

The first ad for our new shoe ran 63 years ago.

© 1988 Converse Inc.

THE *Chuck Taylor* CLASSIC ALLSTAR®

Chuck Taylor All-Stars go a long way back. They're still around today, same-as-ever after over 1 billion pair sold around the world – quite a feat in itself.

In the sidewalk surfing days, skaters had already "discovered" Chucks as an inexpensive footwear option that offered good grip and board control. Appropriating the shoe for their purposes, skaters made All-Stars a classic part of skate fashion.

Chucks also feature prominently in the skateboard chase scene in *Back to the Future* – after all, they were the only piece of Marty McFly's attire that he didn't need to change after traveling back in time.

EARLY PRO SHOES

Converse first started producing the iconic rubber and canvas shoes in 1917. They were simply called "All Stars" at first and did fairly well among basketball players – until All-State player Chuck Taylor of the Buffalo Germans started making them "his" shoes. Taylor would even become one of the main salesmen for the shoe later on.

Since then, regular variations in colorways would generate a lot of appeal for the shoes – and make them a classic fashion item in popular culture as THE All-American sneaker – especially since Converse made sure to fit the club colors of all the basketball teams and colleges on the national championship circuit. Available materials ranged from leather to suede, vinyl, denim, and hemp. Throughout the years, Chuck Taylor himself would stay involved in the design of his pro shoe until passing away in 1969.

The one pro skateboarder who almost single-handedly brought Chucks into the skate spotlight in the 1980s is Christian Hosoi. At the height of his career as one of the world's top vert skaters, Hosoi's look was characterized by cut-off t-shirts, spandex shorts and Chuck Taylors, preferably red. Young Rodney Mullen could frequently be spotted skating in Chucks, and Mike Vallely wore them throughout his entire part in the legendary "Speed Freaks" video.

Was this a reflection of Vallely's vegan / vegetarian attitude back then? "Perhaps that had something to do with it or a lot to do with it but really I also have always loved and preferred Chucks," Mike Vallely said.

"Those are the shoes I grew up skating in and going to punk shows. I wore Chucks during the most crucial of times." As it turns out, the iconic street skater had his start on the All Star shoes: "I skated in Chuck Taylors or Vans for pretty much my first two years of skating from '84 to '86 before I started wearing basketball shoes," Vallely said.

When we asked skateboard icon Tony Hawk about what for him is the ultimate shoe design of all time, he had this to say: "Chuck Taylor's. Not the best for ankle support, but I skated in them before ever having a sponsor. A basic design that is timeless."

A TIMELESS CLASSIC

Around 1988, Converse started running their iconic "Every Artist Needs His Canvas" ads in skate magazines like *Thrasher* and *Transworld*. For a few years, Converse even supported their own skate team with Chucks, while leaving the shoe itself unchanged in terms of design and material. Why would they? Skaters liked their Chucks just the way they were!

All around the world, All Stars were flying off the shelves of skate shops –and into the trash soon after, as their durability for street skating was highly limited. Some skaters found ways to make Chucks last by adding handmade Shoe Goo ollie pads, while others kept them strictly for ramp skating, where they lasted okay.

LICK MY BOOTS

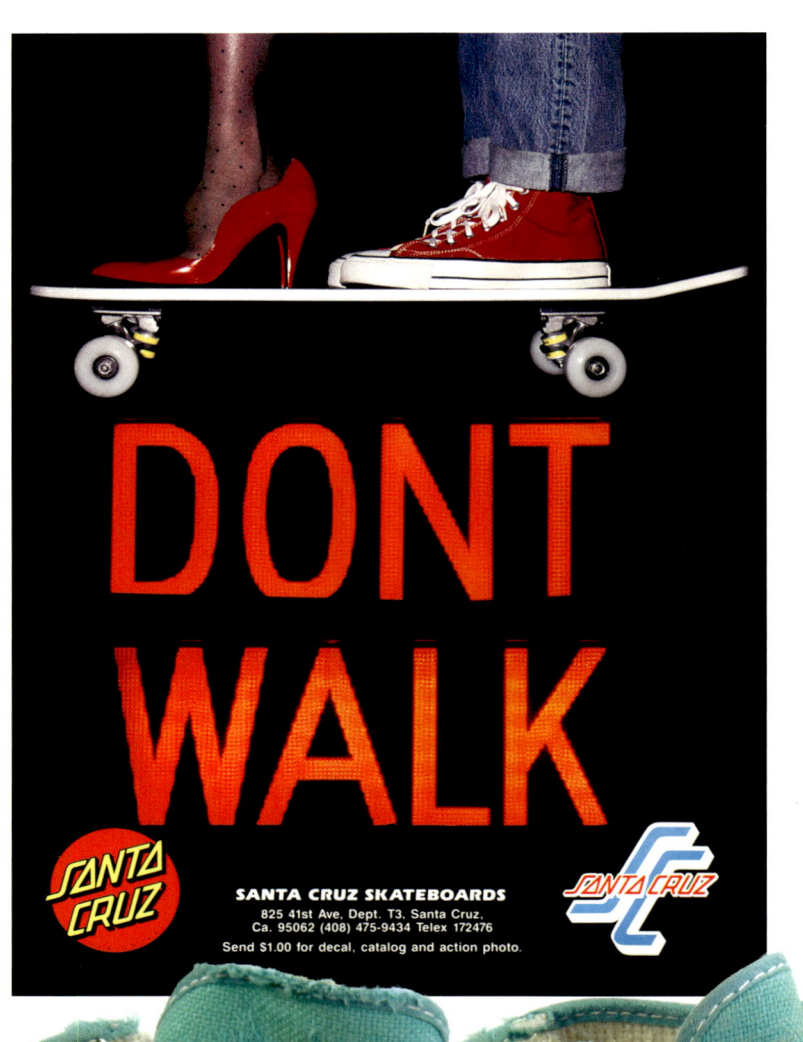

Talk about striking a nerve! The late 1980's saw a big wave of imitation Chuck Taylor boots from all kinds of skate shoe manufacturers. They all stayed with the classic design formula laid down by Converse as early as 1917; a simple high top canvas shoe with a soft sole, a rubber toe cap and glued rubber lining on the side.

The only noteworthy changes that skate companies were really offering on the original were more garish color variations and "zany" print patterns. Meanwhile they copied the shoe itself almost down to the T (short for Taylor, in this case). Airwalk's flashy zig-zag patterned "Havoc" model pretty much led the pack as far as screaming colors went, while the black and neon colored Airwalk pictured here looks like something straight out of a Prince video.

In recent years, the faux Chucks have seen a renaissance across the board, as more and more shoe companies take the old formula and spice it up with attitude and new prints. Someone really needs to bring back the "peace and love" doodles, though, that would be tight.

lick my boots

A bonus to skint *Skateboard!* writers are the free samples sent by manufacturers; this month our poor old postie has been staggering up the stairs with sacks of the hardest footwear on the market; Vans, Pacers, Converse, Airwalk — we got 'em all! There's nowt wrong with a cheap pair from Woolies, but these cuties do the business for the full-on skater. Lick these boots, punk!

Vans low top 'Dinosaurs'

Jeez, I wish these Cobweb and Newsprint Vans were Hi-Tops, you wouldn't see my board for dust! Styling à la *Sunday Sport*.

Above and right: Converse — not the Chuck Taylor baseball classics but the lighter Allstars for board sensitivity. Canvas and rubber, available in Navy, Green, White (impractical), Denim and the truly hideous Raspberry!

Above: for Hardcore purists, Hogs by Pacer are designed with Skate moves in mind; check the ollie patches and new, improved padded sole. Hogs also come with a packet of silica gel to maintain them in top condition, Bostik days are over!

Below: Acidic Airwalk; Blue Suede "Peace" shoes for your mum's CND march, Velcro lace flaps and well sound ankle padding; tuff!

Above: Airwalk Hi-Top "Havoc". Health Warning; do not wear on sunny afternoons without eye protection!

Airwalk "Shockwaves", still some of the best toe caps around.

Airwalk Hi-Top "Jagged Edge", Black suede and Velcro trimmings. Vans low top "Dinosaurs" (Vans sold TOO well this year, they had no Hi-Tops left to send us!) "Lost Weekend" boardshorts by Mambo.

Many thanks to M-Zone, Croydon for providing the last available Vans in the country. Nice one, boys.

un-nakedness

GLUE YOUR SHOES

TRANSAXLE

SHOES (What to do about them)

Take steps to prevent your shoes from turning out to look like Bob Smeltzer's (above). Patch them when they are new!

If you have bought a new pair of shoes in which to skateboard, don't even think about knee sliding in them and don't even walk in them until you have prepared them in the following way. Here, first, buy a tube of Shoe-Goo. Drive to K-Mart to do this. Find a roll of duct tape as well. You just don't want to be found without a spool of such a powerful adhesive such as this. I tell you, duct tape can repair about anything it needs to. It just tears.

Gather together a few sheets of newspaper or any other sort of mat (like gift wrap) which will prevent a mess. Place this sote down onto the work area. Take and cut scrap sections of leather clean off your old Van's, or whatever kind of (leather) shoes you had. For an example, cut off the tongue and sides, then you will have leather. Cut shapes from these scraps to fit the frontal sides and toe of each of your new shoes. (See Fig. A-26).

Put Shoe-Goo on each scrap patch, as well as the area where it is to be applied. Do not, repeat, don't use Shoe-Goo sparingly. It just tears if you know how to use it.

After you have pressured all of the scrap patch guards into place, release the shoes into the sunlight and allow the glue to fester for at least 24 hours. Then you'll be ready. You'll find that your shoes will last at least 30 to 50 percent longer. You will be stoked.

Send in some of your own ideas to the people here. Ideas on how to patch up new shoes to keep them from getting holes. Maybe your ideas will be printed in the letters column. Clean off your hands before you write the letter. I just now Shoe-Gooed my new Van's, but didn't have any patches to put on them. So I put the glue on very thick. My fingertips are sticky. I will wear my old low tops until my new shoes are dry. Then I'm going to enjoy vertical.

—Garry Davis

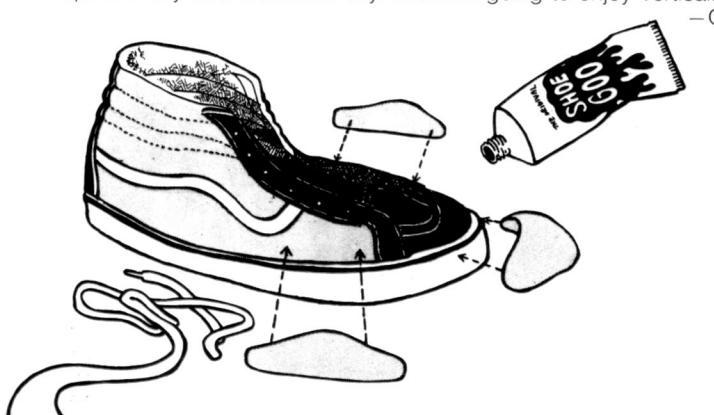

Finger Tips

This tip is written to give you some insight on how to prolong the life of your fingers.

Have you ever just put together a new board, rode for an hour, did about 20 finger flips and on your twenty-fifth one, you couldn't do any more because your finger tips were hurting? As you examined them more closely, you saw they were red, raw, almost bleeding, and totally delaminated?

This happened far too often to us, until we found the answer. No, it is not covering your fingers all up with tape. Tape wears out, tears, then falls off. Let's go right to the problem. It is your grip tape itself. If you take a close look, you can see little shiny rocks almost like glass.

The solution is to knock off the rough sharp, jagged tops. You can do this by simply scraping the top with an object such as a rock. Rocks work very well, plus they are in abundance.

Now if you want your shoes to last longer, do it to the middle of the board also. Skate safe and have fun.

—Primo and Diane

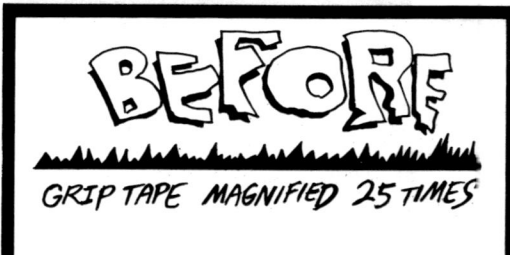

GRIP TAPE MAGNIFIED 25 TIMES

GRIP TAPE WITH TOPS SCRAPED

Skate-specific shoes offered professional riding comfort and performance, no doubt. But at pretty steep retail prices, they could also burn quite a professional hole in your pocket. In 1988, a pair of Airwalks easily set you back $69 (equivalent of $119 today), and you had to wash a lot of cars in the summer to score a pair.

Next to leaving considerable holes in your wallet, soon the shoes themselves would resemble Swiss cheeses from damage incurred by ollieing and dragging your foot on downhills. And no use trying to convince your mom that the flashy shoes you just blew your entire allowance on were gone – Finito! – after just three weeks. Could you get another pair?! Might as well forget about it!

A much more popuar answer to millions of skaters around the world came in a white and red tube labeled Shoe Goo. The gooey liquid was available in only two colors (black and clear), but that was more than enough. As it turned out, Shoe Good worked miracles in patching up all parts of the shoe: The blown-out side stitching, the ollie holes with the socks poking through, even the soles themselves. Originally created to repair tennis shoes and the like, Shoe Goo was a blessing that the skate community avidly embraced.

Soon enough, skaters would get quite prolific at crafting professional-looking repair jobs with Shoe Goo. The verdict on technique was split: Most skate rats applied their 'Goo straight out the tube, while others swore by using a special glue gun. Some skaters even found ways to mold their own sole patterns out of Shoe Goo.

At one moment in time, a whole generation of skaters was gluing and patching together what was left of their fading kicks to make them last that extra stretch until the inescapable moment when the whole shoe finally succumbed to the laws of physics – and fell apart.

At the same time, the industry was aware of the short lifespan of skate shoes. Protective gear specialists Smith introduced their attachable Lace Protectors for all scrounging skaters who couldn't afford kicks with built-in lace guards. Stick-On ollie pads, marketed as Ollie Armor, presented another approach in commercially sold shoe upgrades. But none of them ever came close to the success of good old trusty Shoe Goo.

this is the Stuff

I can remember messing around with Shoo Goo in the hope that it would resurrect my beloved Vans that would cost more than a week's socialising to replace. It never worked — the stuff just peels off. But this stuff is different!

As is so often the case with these cheesey substances, it was Royce who turned me on to it. He'd used it to stick together the upholstery of his latest prototype spacerocket (registered with MOT as a "motor bicycle"). He even built handgrips and shock absorbing washers with it.

It's called Sikaflex and is not based on rubber like Shoo Goo but is instead a urethane in liquid form. It sets in a day to comprise a soft, grippy thane of about 50-60A durometer. (Vans soles are about 60-70A rubber). It should wear quite quick but who cares if you can just squidge some more on?

If you're a third lung merchant and used to enjoy a whiff of Evostick just completely forget it with Sikaflex. Its vapour contains isocyanates which are viciously cancer causing. And if you're dumb enough to smoke while inhaling some of these nasty urethane setting agents the heat of your fag is exactly right to synthesise some of the most powerful cancer creators on the planet. You have been warned!

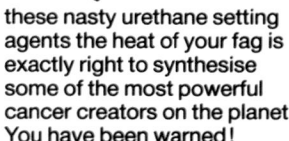

The gun you have to buy to session the industrial sized tubes this comes in are very controllable, cost £3 or so and should last for dozens of tubes. I found that that you can use thick upholsterer's canvas tape to act as patches. I put a layer on the outside surface of the shoe around the hole and stuck the tape on and just covered it in Sikaflex. You can then put a second layer of tape and just seal the edges with the mastic.

Stick delammed bits of rubber with contact adhesive like Evostick first if you like, as Sikflex doesn't grab and hold until its setting, you can then Sikaflex over the top. Where you need it very thick put it in on in layers letting it go off for a few hours between them. One major priority is not to create nasty lumps on the inside of the shoe. This is why it's best to put all patches on the outside. It's so sticky that they will not peel off so long as this super goo is all around and over the edges.

Always use it outside in a breeze, or in a very well ventilated place, and don't expect to wash or clean it off anything unless you're very lucky and get if off straight away. You can buy rubber surgical gloves quite cheap to protect your hands. If you are worried about getting it absorbed into your skin, or use the polythene disposable type. Royce reckons you could use it to stick a one piece steel surface on a ramp as it will flex and allow for shrinkage etc. (See his metal ramp feature next month). You can stick recaps on pads and even make grabgrip on decks if you key the surface by scratching the varnish, just pipe a nose or edge grab onto the surface and let it set.

The joy of it is that it sticks like nothing on earth. You can hardly scrape it off a stainless knife when it's set, let alone get if off clothes, carpet etc. I still have a bit on my hand and no way can I peel it off. This is bad news for mums of Sikaflexers but red hot news for skate shoe rejuvenators.

Get the shoes good and clean, if they're canvas and plastic or rubber you can give them a session in the washing machine. Then they must be fully dry (don't put them in the drier – they'll melt!). Put the stuff on with the nozzle on the tube cut so it delivers a thin worm.

It's always a real drag getting enough life out of shoes and who can afford forty quid every three weeks or so? Anyway aren't they always just nice and comfy just before they fall apart. So expect to see the test teamers skating around with blobs of this stuff all over them this summer.

Sikaflex cost me about £6 from my local branch of Strand Glass, the fibreglass people, and they had it in black, grey or white. It's distributed by:

Sika Inertol, Welwyn Garden City, GB-Herts AL7 1BQ

or: Sika Chemie Gmbh D 700.
Stuttgart 40 Deutschland

or: Sika BV, NL 3606 EA, Maarssen, Nederland. And other Sika agents around Europe.

I don't know if it's sold in the States but its official description is all-purpose polyurethane sealant. Don't be fooled by silicone bathroom type sealants that come in a similar form; they don't cut the mustard.

N.B. I/we accept absolutely no responsibility for any mess or disease you or yours may get yourselves into as a result of mis-using this stuff: You have been adequately warned!

Words and photos Steve Kane.

TAPE YOUR TOES

For a quick solution to pretty much anything that needs fixing –ANYTHING– look no further than duct tape. The sturdy adhesive tape is a staple in every North American household, thanks to its military-grade resilience and unmatched ease of use.

Just tape up whatever needs holding together, and simply tear the tape with your fingers. No scissors needed, yet the holding power is ultra-tight. And duct tape even rescued the astronauts on Apollo 13.

Duct tape enjoys a cult following across the United States, with the annual Duct Tape Festival in the town of Avon, Ohio as an epicenter of duct tape mania. Compared to the almost infinite amount of uses these hardcore enthusiasts come up with every year, simply duct taping your battered skate shoes may seem rather pedestrian. But it works.

Chad Muska looks back at his first skate shoes that had their lifespan expanded by the power of duct tape. "I think they were a pair of Converse Chuck Taylor's," Muska remembers. "I must have used them for like four or five months. Lots of duct tape!"

The technique is very effective, especially for feisty toe section damage from knee slides on vert. Or for ollie holes on the side. Or for an improvised lace saver. You can go completely MacGyver with it, as long as you don't try sealing the ducts in your home, for which studies have proven duct tape to be totally ineffective. Bummer.

SLASH Duct Tape & Skateboarding

Duct-tape: a strong, sticky, and fiberous stuff that is usually grey, and costs about five bucks a roll. Sure we all know what duct-tape is. Many of us use it to patch up all kinds of different stuff that is involved with our skateboarding. But for those out there who perhaps don't know about duct-tape, here are a few pointers. Hightops are probably the most common of all things that skaters plaster with duct-tape. Wear and tear on skate shoes is usually caused by kneebailers who drag their toes, or from just all out skating in general. The method of fixing shoes with duct-tape is fairly simple. Just tear off strips of tape from your handy roll and stick them down over any holes or worn spots on your shoes. Make sure that the first layer of tape you put down onto the canvas or leather of your shoe sticks well, otherwise it will eventually peel up, and with it will come all of the other layers of duct-tape that are on top of it. As you do more kneebails or ollies and the tape on your shoes begins to wear down, you can build it up again by adding more tape onto your existing duct-tape foundation. Kneepads are also good receptacles for duct-tape. Stock recaps can be held on more securely, or you can make your own custom recaps out of plastic containers and worn out recaps, and tape them onto your pads with heavy-duty duct-tape. You can even tape over spots on the fabric of your pads where it might be wearing out. If the velcro straps that hold your pads on tightly are starting to come loose on their own, you can stop that from happening by fastening them down with a few pieces of good ole duct-tape. Another spot where a role of duct-tape comes in handy is at the ramp. If your ramp's pool or pvc coping is starting to crack up or break, you can temporarily fix it with some duct-tape and make it skateable for a bit longer. Worn or loose spots on your ramp's surface can be patched up with duct-tape. Any holes in the tarp you might be using to cover your ramp during winter storms can be patched with duct-tape. Also, a role of duct-tape is a good thing to have around at the pool. You can use it to help cover holes that might be there because of a missing drain, light fixture, or plaster ornament. And, of course, you could always use it to hold together cracked pool coping. When it comes to improving your board, duct-tape can be used in many ways. If your board is too flat, you can add more concave to it by piling up layers of duct-tape on top of your un-griptaped board. That's right, build up the top of your board with duct-tape, then put on the griptape, and end up with a custom concave that is the exact shape you want. This method actually works pretty well. The duct-tape concave is kind of soft, which allows your shoe to sink into it a little, making for good contact between shoe and board. You can also use duct-tape to make the tail of your board steeper, or more concave. If you need help with your street ollies you can use duct-tape to make a little bump beneath the griptape of your board near the front truck to increase front foot grippage there. On the bottom of your board, you can use duct-tape to make bumps for grabbing. When making such bumps, you need not use solid layers of tape, you can roll up some paper and use it in between a few of the layers. Put a small piece of griptape over your gripbump, so that it won't be too slippery for grabbing. If you have ever gouged your fingers on the threads of your front truck's mounting bolts, you can stop that from happening by wrapping a small piece of tape around them. You can also wrap duct-tape around your thumbs and fingers to help stop abrasion there. I think you get the gist of what I am saying here: duct-tape can be used in many ways. And when you think about it, that five bucks you might have to spend on a roll of the grey sticky stuff will be quickly paid back by the benefits you'll gain from the tape's usage. So get some if you want. Skate happy and be prepared to have a lot of skaters asking you if they can have some.

Alec Schroeder

No

Yes

THE CHIN JORDAN STORY

One of the era-defining photographs of the 80s shows four members of the Bones Brigade team hoisting simultaneous inverts on the Animal Chin Ramp. Taken in 1987 by photographer J. Grant Brittain, the image solidified the legendary status of the best-known team in professional skateboarding at the time. The photograph originally appeared in *Transworld Skateboard Magazine* coinciding with the launch of the *Search for Animal Chin* video directed by Stacy Peralta and was available for a limited time as a special poster print.

The odd thing about the photo is that Steve Caballero, Mike McGill, and Lance Mountain are skating Nike Air Jordan 1s, when all of them had their own respective shoe sponsors. What happened?

"This time in skating was bleak for everyone," said original Bones Brigade member Lance Mountain, "and Vans were the only ones who had sponsored skaters up to this point. The market was just too slow maybe to give skateboarders shoes anymore."

Left without the support of their sponsors - and suffering from seriously battered shoes – the team received help from Craig R. Stecyk, art director at Powell-Peralta skateboards, who had a go-to guy at Nike. A few days later a shipment of Air Jordans arrived on the set of Animal Chin. And the rest is history.

"I just wore shoes that someone would give me", Lance Mountain remembers. "Vans gave me shoes, then Nike. Then Airwalk started giving me shoes." Out of all team members, only Tony Hawk had a new pair of Vans left, which he's wearing in the picture.

OPEN THE DOOR

The impact of the *Animal Chin* video, which also featured a full-blown plot detailing an epic quest for the legacy of a mysterious skateboarding monk, was unlike any other video before it. The Bones Brigade skaters were super stars, and skaters all around the world emulated their tricks and memorized the oft-hilarious plot lines of the video.

At the same time, the Air Jordan 1 became the shoe of choice for what would go down ass the Launch Ramp Era of skateboarding, thanks to its air-padded sole for extra cushioning around the heels.

"I was getting heel bruises for months during the jump ramp days – heel bruises and back pain!" said Lance Mountain. "So at that time, shoes with a little more support around the heel were good. Then I found out that if I didn't skate jump ramps anymore, it was better…"

In magazines and videos, all the big name riders were skating the Jordan 1. Mark Gonzales, Natas Kaupas, Mike Vallely and Tommy Guerrero took it to the streets, while Chris Miller, Neil Blender and others rode the shoe on ramp.

As a matter of fact, vert legend Chris Miller liked his Jordans so much that he wore them despite his sponsorship contract with Airwalk – the biggest skate shoe company on the market at the time. Only for contests and other public outings would he slip into his sponsor's shoes to meet his contract obligations. Otherwise, the Jordan just felt right to him.

Finally, Airwalk's senior designer Lenny Holden took Miller's input seriously. After a number of brainstorming sessions and a thorough dissection of the shoe's every feature, the Jordan's design served as the basic blueprint for the Airwalk Prototype series, to which Holden added a number of skate-specific twists like ollie padding and extra reinforcement where it was needed. But as opposed to the Jordans, Airwalk prototypes sold at full retail prices around $50 a pair. Which still made the basketball shoe a budget solution for broke skaters.

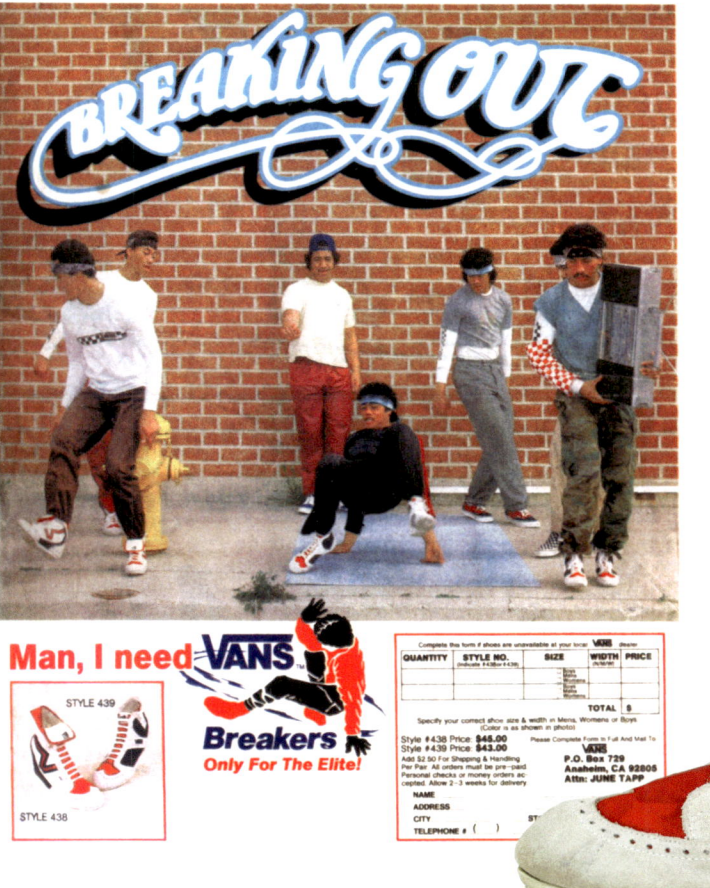

A LOW BUDGET SOLUTION

After all, what had really sent the shoe's mass popularity skyrocketing was the price. Since development of the Jordan 2 was in the finishing stages in the late 1980s, Nike was keen on clearing out their old stock. So for a few magic months, the shoe was on sale for $19.99 ($35 today) – instead of $64.95. Quite a deal! Many skaters went ahead and bought three pairs at once. With supplies lasting well into the sale, the shoe stayed on the streets – and pictured in skate magazines – until the end of the 80s.

To Nike SB's designer James Arizumi, the Jordan 1 is THE quintessential skate shoe: "Yes, yes, I know Jordan is very cliché and it was never really designed for Skateboarding but if you look at the way that it was constructed, panelled, and colored it pretty much defined what skate shoes looked like for decades to come."

The designer continued to pinpoint the exact makings of the Jordan 1's classic status: "If you break down the shoe to its core components the design lends itself very well for skateboarding. The toe cap is perfect for abrasion resistance and shape structure for the toe box, the perforations on the vamp for breathability, the way the shoe color blocks is classic and iconic skate shoe design."

"The Jordan 1 has intentionally or unintentionally influenced footwear designers both in Skate and in fashion for years," Arizumi concluded.

End of the story? As the 90s were approaching, the skate shoe industry as a whole was picking up in terms of sales again, and companies could finally afford sending their team riders proper packages – first of all the big name members of the Bones Brigade. But to this day, the Quadruple *Animal Chin* Inverts photo remains an emblematic product of its time, reminiscent of an era when even the best skaters in the world had to scrounge for shoes.

WALKING ON AIR

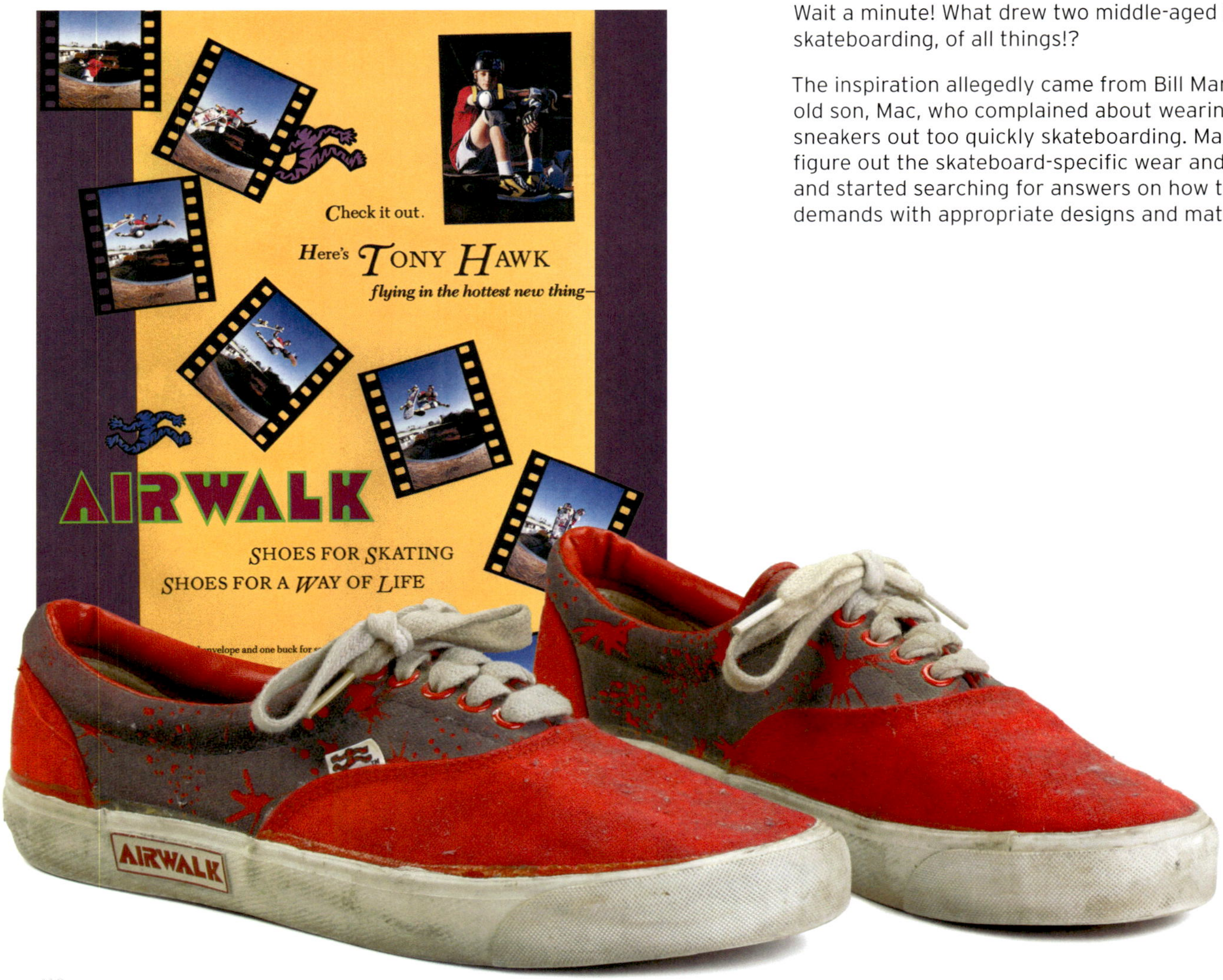

If you weren't around at the time, it's hard to explain in retrospect how HUGE a company Airwalk was in the late 1980s. Having appeared on the scene practically over night in 1986, Airwalk became a major player in the industry and a defining force in the evolution of skateboard footwear.

Despite Airwalk's popularity in the skateboard scene during their peak years, the company fell from grace in the mid-1990s. When Airwalk was at the top of its game, their shoes were a style statement almost synonymous with skate culture. Today, you can find them battling it out for pole position in the low price point range at Payless ShoeSource. But that's a long way down, so let's start at the beginning.

BARGING ON THE SCENE

Airwalk was the brainchild of footwear entrepreneur George Yohn and businessman Bill Mann from California. George Yohn had been a pioneer in outsourcing shoe production to Asia in the 1970s, for lower cost of labor and higher profit margins. This earned him a track record of building multi-million dollar footwear companies, mostly for unbranded men's dress shoes. Bill Mann had been a buyer for athletic retail chains in the US and knew the sales side of things inside out. When the two started Airwalk in 1986, they combined Mann's marketing insight with Yohn's 30 years of experience in the shoe biz. A powerful combination, it would turn out.

Wait a minute! What drew two middle-aged businessmen to skateboarding, of all things!?

The inspiration allegedly came from Bill Mann's then 11-year-old son, Mac, who complained about wearing his Reebok sneakers out too quickly skateboarding. Mann proceeded to figure out the skateboard-specific wear and tear on shoes and started searching for answers on how to meet these demands with appropriate designs and materials.

The duo's inside man in terms of the skate scene was Australian-born skateboarder Sinisa "Sin" Egelja, who worked at the Carlsbad skate park at the time when Bill Mann was shopping for ideas for shoe designs. As it turned out, Sinisa would spend 16 years with Airwalk managing the skate team and running the design department. But his most crucial contribution to the company may have been steering the two owners towards functional skate shoes.

Nevertheless, both Mann and Yohn understood skateboarding well enough to know that a merely good product would only get them so far in causing a splash on the scene. It would take style and image – as well as a large dosage of legitimacy – to become a "real" skate company.

Consequently, the two built their company around the name Airwalk – allegedly suggested by *TWS* Art Director Garry Davis – taken from a popular launch ramp move at the time. Their image-driven marketing campaign targeted the skate community with double-page color ads featuring the rapidly growing Airwalk team. Soon enough, some of the best skaters rode for Airwalk, and the yellow logo and dinosaur graphics became ubiquitous at skate parks and spots all over the world.

TECHNICAL IMPROVEMENTS - SAVE THE LACE

The proliferation of the street ollie made "ollie holes" along the side toe sections a common occurrence, and Airwalk addressed the problem by introducing double-stitching and reinforcement around the toe areas, as well as composite rubber "ollie pads" on the sides. On vert, frequent knee slides were taking their toll on the laces. Airwalk provided the solution with so-called "lace savers," suede flaps held in place by Velcro.

The new guys were now giving long-time industry leader Vans a run for the top spot with all guns blazing. By the end of 1987, Airwalk shoes were available in over 100 styles.

PROTO-TYPICAL

One of the most iconic Airwalk shoe lines is the Airwalk Prototype series. Allegedly, the shoes were designed by Lenny Holden at Airwalk for their team rider Chris Miller, who had taken to wearing Nike Air Jordans during practice sessions.

Although he remained loyal to his shoe sponsor, Miller continued vert skating in Jordans because of their ankle protection and sturdiness. Their design served as the basic blueprint for Airwalk Prototypes, to which Lenny Holden added a number of skate-specific twists.

The Prototype "Bruiser" and "Jolly Mambo" models were immortalized by Mike Vallely wearing one of both models on each foot in Powell Peralta's *Public Domain* video, in which he runs across a graveyard and opens the gates for modern street skating with his performance. Mike Vallely remembers: "I mixed the shoes on purpose, for no particular reason other than I thought it looked cool and I vibed on it."

How does Vallely feel about the video in hindsight? " I enjoy watching the footage and seeing the photos from that time period when I wore the Prototypes, those shoes really stand out."

But soon after shooting the *Public Domain* video, Mike V left Airwalk: "I did a lot of business for Airwalk back then but wasn't really interested in maintaining the relationship," he explained. "At that time I was actually moving away from wearing leather and animal products and when I told the people at Airwalk that I didn't want to wear their shoes anymore."

"They actually made synthetic versions of Prototypes for me to wear but I wasn't into it. I felt like I was being used to sell leather shoes and I didn't want anything to do with it."

Mike V. joined the team of short-lived vegan shoe brand Zero-Two, while Airwalk continued updating the Prototype models up until 1992, before focusing on their unofficial successor, the highly technical NTS model.

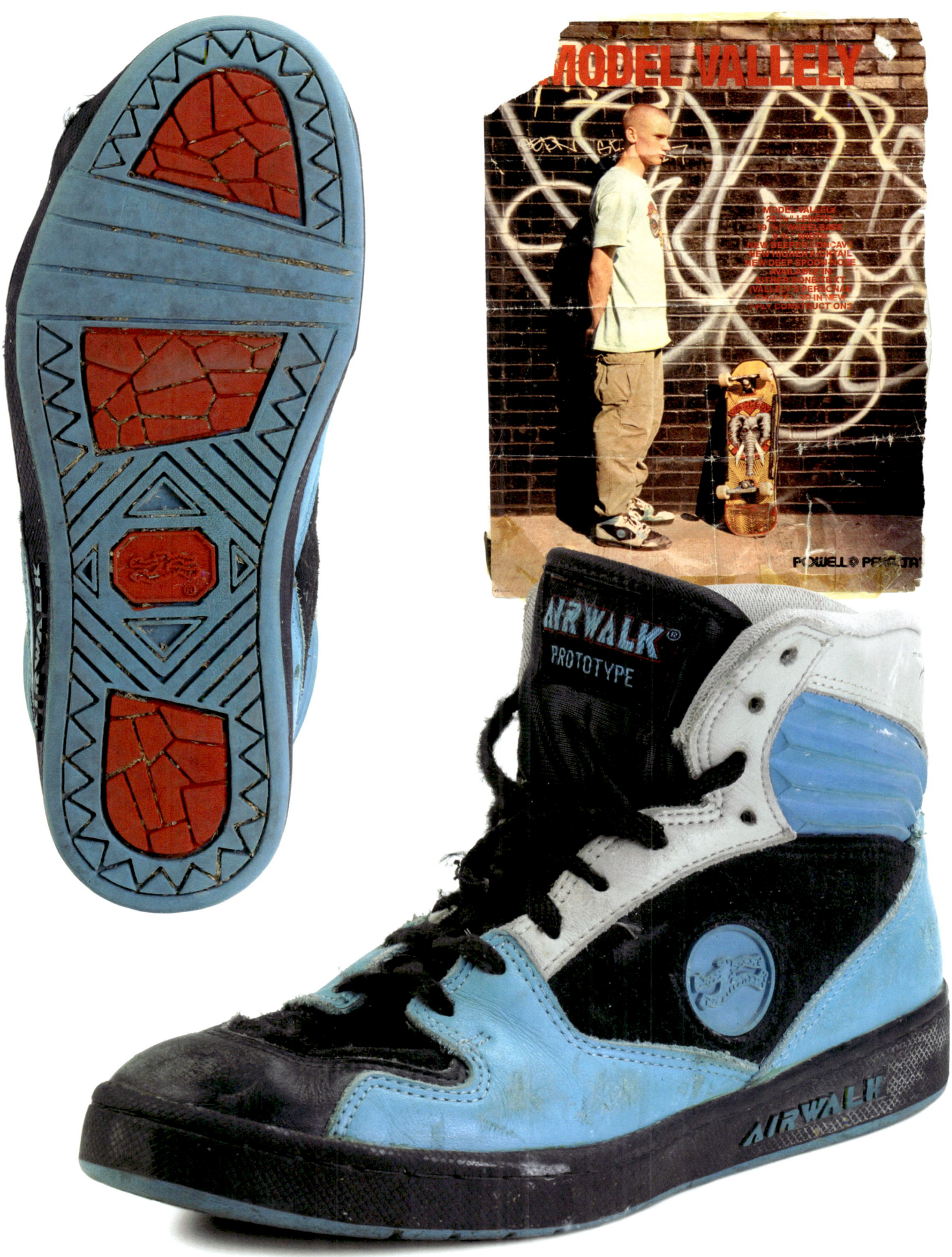

FLYING LIKE AN ARCHOPTERIX

The original concept art of the Airwalk Prototype "JOLLY MAMBO"

Airwalk Prototype "VORTEX"

A sample of the Prototype in multi colors "13 Colors"

JOIN THE CLUB - MEET VICTOR NOVETTIPOLAE

Another classic is the Airwalk VIC – still available, by the way – with ads centered on a fictitious character named Victor Novettipolae (which means "new shoes" in Yugoslavian).

In reality, Vic was the alter ego of designer Sinisa "Sin" Egelja, shown in ads performing the most awkward, humorous stunts ever seen on a skateboard – our favorite is a Hang-Ten smith grind on a ramp, which just defies the laws of physics. The VIC shoes were high tops combining a soft natural rubber sole reminiscent of Vans shoes. It has a sturdy suede upper section replete with extra padding around the toe section, and a Velcro lace saver.

FADE OUT

At the turn of the decade, Airwalk was doing better than ever, with sales topping $20 million in 1990. Team riders included new talents Danny Way, Pat Duffy and Kris Markovich. The future seemed wide open for the company. But the tide was about to turn, while skateboarding as a whole lost its mass appeal and went back to becoming a hardcore sport shunned by the mainstream media and general population. Skating once again saw itself headed away from the big contest arenas and skate parks to the "real" streets, which also meant a more rugged, low-fi aesthetic. At the same time, skaters were growing distrustful of companies that had become too large for "keeping it real" in their eyes – which had already sealed the downfall for Vision Street Wear – and Airwalk came under scrutiny for selling their shoes at Footlocker and other retail chains.

As a compromise, they decided to sell their skate-specific shoes exclusively at skate shops, while leaving the more fashion-oriented models to the shoe chains. And voila, this seemed to work at the time.

Meanwhile, backyard operations including World Industries and Foundation skateboards took the spotlight. But the whole industry felt a major dip in sales within just a matter of months. Airwalk saw their sales slump to $8 million in 1991, down an entire $12 million in just one year.

Instead of a complete slump, a period of refinement and evolution set in. Skateboarding – especially street skating – continued to mature away from the spotlight. Airwalk coasted along quite well into the early 90s and kept introducing functional footwear that stayed in line with the progress of street skating.

The Enigma shoe championed by Jason Lee became an instant classic and showed the shape of things to come in terms of skate shoe design: Lower cut, lightweight suede shoes with soft soles and thicker tongues for padding against flip tricks gone awry. Skaters continued to like Airwalk – but being well liked by practitioners of a fading sport won't pay the bills, so the upper echelons at Airwalk started looking for a way out.

HIGH FASHION, LOW STREET CRED

For founder Bill Mann, this way out consisted of leaving the company in order to join the marketing department at Vans in 1992. See ya! Mann was replaced by Lee Smith (as in: Businessman Lee Smith, not American Expatriate Pro Skater Lee Smith from San Francisco). Smith's rescue plan for Airwalk consisted of branching out into other markets, including high fashion.

The skaters got the message, and collectively walked out on Airwalk. Despite all this, Airwalk successfully branched out into other sports and kept on trucking. But after moving to Pennsylvania the company was finally sold to a new management team in 2001.

These days, Airwalk shoes are still around in skateboarding - although low key, with snowboarding being the main area of activity - and even support a team headed by Andy Mac-Donald. Maybe the whole retro/nostalgia thing would work in their favor if they decided to re-release their Prototype line due to popular demand (that would be our rescue plan).

MAD FLY

No matter what the name might suggest, Madrid Pro Designs are not a European skateboard company, but named after North California surf icon Jerry Madrid. Madrid started making his own skateboards out of fiberglass in the late 1960s. With the help of his brother Jeff, Jerry Madrid turned Madrid Pro Designs into a full-fledged company in 1976.

Their legacy lives on today, as the Madrid brothers not only introduced concave pressing techniques to skateboard manufacturing, but also invented the less harsh, yet grippy "Fly Paper" griptape that is the established norm for gripping your board today.

The best possible grip also formed the main design objective for Mad Fly Shoes, produced in the mid-1980s in cooperation with Vans. This was basically an enhanced version of the Vans #38 model, with added suede leather ollie pads for extra durability, and reinforced toecaps for protection on knee slides.

Most notably, the Mad Fly shoe featured the Madrid brand's iconic "Fly" pattern printed on the shoe's upper, as well as a stenciled Fly pattern on the rubber sole – a more "fly" take on the Vans waffle sole, if you will.

Variations included slip-on versions of the Fly shoes, as well as different colorways on the high tops. At the beginning of the 1990s, Madrid Shoes were discontinued, but the company is still successfully manufacturing boards, trucks and wheels – and of course their legendary Fly Paper griptape today.

TITUS SHOES - GERMAN NEW WAVE

Titus Dittmann is widely credited as the man who brought skateboard enthusiasm to Germany in a big way. The former schoolteacher made a steep climb from selling imported skateboard product out of his living room in the 1970s, to building his own empire of distribution assets and Titus branded goods. Along the way, Titus also found time to launch his own line of footwear.

Titus Shoes started at the height of the 1980s skateboard boom. In 1987, the first shoe hit stores all over Germany and became an instant success with customers. "Skaters and punk rockers at the time were digging Titus Shoes, since they were the only real alternative to Vans and Chucks," remembers Markus Koenig, designer at Titus headquarters. "You have to remember that even Airwalk was hardly available in Germany at the time."

In terms of design, Titus Shoes combined elements like the Lace Savers used in Airwalk VICs and the overall cut of Chuck Taylors. Produced in Asia, they could be offered at stores at a much lower price point than imported shoes from the US - another plus among customers.

The team was composed mostly of the Titus hardware pro team including Florian Boehm, Anders Pulpanek, Hans "Puttis" Jackobson, Martin van Doren and Ralf Middendorf with the addition of Santa Cruz pro Claus Grabke, who had a short stint on the team. "Claus was pro on Titus Shoes for a brief time, but we never did a pro shoe," said Titus Dittmann. "This was highly unusual back then and no shoe brand was really doing pro shoes."

"But nevertheless, it was a pretty exalting feeling to add shoes to our product line," Titus added, "especially since it's a difficult and risky endeavor with all the minimum quantities and production molds that are involved in this sector."

ETNICS - JOIN THE FRENCH REBELS

To modern-day observers, the shoes on the bottom of this page may look like shameless Etnies knock-offs with the name spelled wrong all over them. But when the company was launched in 1986 by French company Rautureau Apple in collaboration with skateboarder Alain "Platoon" Montagnet, it was actually called "Etnics" – derived from the word "ethnic." Then what happened? "The name needed to be changed because an American shoe company named "Ethonic" was threatening to file a lawsuit," says Ruedi Matter.

A EUROPEAN REBELLION

True to their tag line "Rebel Sports," Etnics broke a few rules upon entering the scene. For once, they bridged the gap between the US and Europe by taking pro skaters from both continents on their pro team. And since the company was based in France, they could offer shoes at a much lower price point in Europe than competitors from overseas.

Visually, Etnics added some spice to the shoe market, standing out from the rest of the pack with their distinct colorways and – for lack of a better word – "ethnic"-looking print patterns. A great amount of thinking had gone into the designs: The very first batch of Etnics already featured reinforced suede ollie pads with double stitching, as well as an extra layer of grippy rubber around the lower toe area as inventive features.

However, when it came to finding a new name because of Ethonic in 1987, the French Rebels flipped a single letter and called their company "Etnies."

WELCOME TO THE CONCRETE JUNGLE

Many years before the rise of Hip-Hop and camouflage patterns, Etnics produced a camouflage shoe. And not only did the Fighter model released by the French company in 1988 beat the whole Camo-craze to the punch by a solid seven to eight years, it also broke new ground in many other ways.

First of all, the Fighters powerfully juxtaposed a "regular" military camouflage on the shoe's inside(!) lining with a neon remix of the theme on the outside. The Camo inside lining would later be picked up by many other brands, including Nike SB and DC. And neon, of course, was huge in the 80s – the garish pinks and yellows would also make a big return at the turn of the Millennium.

Even Tony Hawk and Rodney Mullen could be spotted skating in pink Powell skull shirts and shorts. In terms of skate-specific features, the shoes boasted Michelin 500 rubber coating on the outsoles, as well as double ankle lining and padding around the upper heel section.

And finally, the packaging raised the bar for skateboard footwear companies with a transparent plastic "Pure, Fortified and Proven Concrete Jungle Box," in which the shoes themselves came wrapped in delicate paper imprinted with a treasure map of sorts. So all in all, the Fighters blended style and functionality into a full package.

A NAME STITCHED INTO A SHOE

Almost 25 years went by between the introduction of the first skateboard-specific shoe – The Randy 720° in 1965 – until someone put the name of a professional skateboarder on a signature shoe. Twenty-five years!!! What had taken the skateboard industry so long?

Traditionally, skateboarders had frowned upon pro shoes, seeing them as the domain of "established" sports – bear in mind that professional basketball shoes have been around since the 20s – and thereby a staple of ball sport (or "jock") culture. And while it was okay to appropriate B-ball shoes for skating, you became a skateboard pro with the release of your own pro board, not shoe.

NATAS - THE FIRST SIGNATURE SHOE

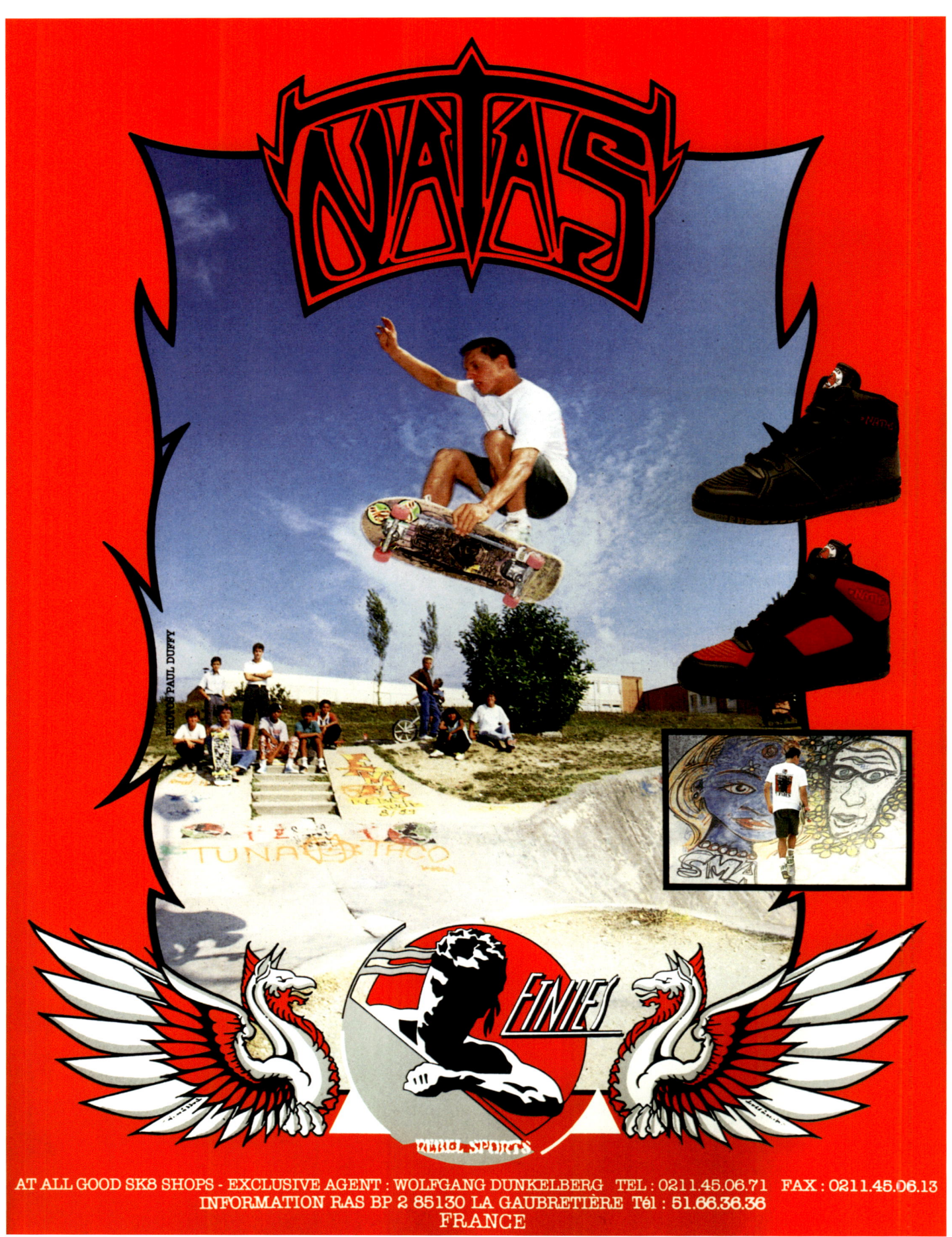

This was how things had been done for decades. Ultimately, it took an outsider's perspective to break the spell. A French perspective. Young shoe company Etnies thought nothing wrong with the idea of a pro skate shoe. In 1988, Etnies introduced the first ever signature skateboard shoe for legendary street skater Natas Kaupas from Santa Monica.

"Yvon from freelance shoes in France started the whole thing and contacted me after my interview in *Thrasher*," Natas Kaupas remembers.

They could not have picked a better rider for the deal. Widely credited with opening the doors to modern street skating, the name Natas was synonymous with progression and style all around the world. Single-handedly, Natas Kaupas opened the doors for pro shoes to become an accepted part of skateboarding.

"The whole pro shoes thing goes back to Natas," says Don Brown at Etnies. "All the way to how shoes are created by talking to the riders to see where they get their inspiration from, then taking that input to create the best possible products that they can endorse with their name."

PART OF A MASTER PLAN

To Natas himself, the whole thing seemed rather unspectacular at the time: "It never seemed that groundbreaking to me," he said. "Chuck Taylor had a shoe out for how long before? 100 years? Stan Smith, Jack Purcell – this was not a new idea!"

Initially, the Natas pro shoe had been part of a bigger idea at Etnies. The company had planned to introduce a series of three pro model shoes, with additional signature models for German vert rider Claus Grabke and French freestyle skater Pierre André Senizergues, who now owns Etnies.

"The idea behind the signature shoe was to feature and represent a champion vert ramp rider with Claus, a champion freestyle rider with my own signature shoe, and a champion street skater with Natas," Pierre André explained.

What had been the motivation to contact Claus and Natas for a signature shoe? "Claus and Natas have always been very creative and innovative," Pierre André said. "Claus's other interests outside of skating have been his art and music, combine that with Natas and his talent as an artist – it was a natural decision."

THE FIFTH BEATLE

In hindsight, Claus Grabke is almost like the fifth member of the Beatles, namely bassist Stu Sutcliffe, who left the band on the verge of their breakthrough. The German pro actually was first offered the deal – and thereby could have made skate history as the first pro to have his own shoe. If he hadn't declined.

As Grabke remembers: "One day I received an offer by my friend Pierre André, asking whether I could imagine designing and riding my very own pro model shoe. I found the idea pretty strange and uncool – a pro model shoe." Etnies backed up the offer with a few shoes from their current line. "But they all had leather," Grabke said – a clear deal breaker for the strict vegetarian who insisted on cruelty-free footwear.

Consequently, Etnies incorporated Grabke's input into a leather-free prototype sample: "It was a shoe with a skull pattern, looking similar to Chucks," Pierre André revealed. However, when Grabke received the shoe, he was not into them one bit: "The shoes made a really unstable impression. The sole was thin as paper and the design was so uncool that only a freestyle skater could have come up with it," Grabke remembers. "Everything was in pink and day-glo, little skulls and gimmicky stuff. I really didn't see it going anywhere."

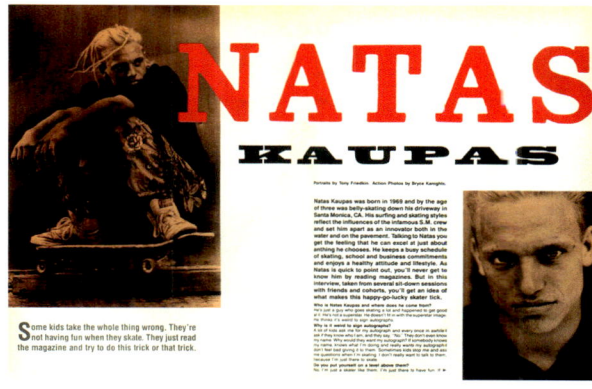

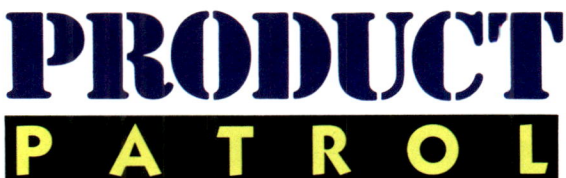

How does Grabke feel about the decision today? "Well, my son by now is 18 years old and also skates. Of course he's well familiar with pro shoes and can't really understand why I turned down the offer back then. He says 'Dad, you would have been the first pro with his own shoe!' But I just didn't think the idea was that good back then. And I still don't think, despite a few exceptions, that it's too great now."

So Etnies ended up canning Grabke's shoe. As Pierre André puts it: "It was ultimately decided that we would focus more on Natas and shoes for street skaters."

A SHORT-LIVED DEBUT

A little bit of basketball influence can hardly be denied when it comes to the shoe's design. The Natas was a high top boot much in the mode of a Nike Air Jordan or the adidas Hi-top basketball or Converse Hightop models that Natas sported during his pre-shoe-sponsor days. "I had a big part in the design, probably too big," Natas said. "I was too new to designing. I never liked Jordans, though. They were too narrow for my feet and I thought the soles were too hard. So I used an Ellesse high top as inspiration."

Despite its popularity, the Natas pro model was discontinued after the second edition. "The second edition of my shoe came out without my approval," Natas said. "They didn't fit my feet, I couldn't wear them and that ended my relationship with Etnies." Soon afterwards, Natas sustained what seemed like a career-ending injury in 1991. And although the evolution of shoes continued, there was never a low-top Natas shoe.

BACK AGAIN…

But in 1998, Natas came out of retirement with a pro board on Element skateboards and also formed Vita Shoes along with longtime friend Mark Oblow, known as the man behind Color and Prime skateboards and a professional skate/surf photographer. One year later, Vita released the Natas Pro Model shoe. In 2002, Natas also designed a Nike SB Dunk low with colors by Reese Forbes and one year later Etnies re-released the original Natas shoe in a limited 15th Birthday edition.

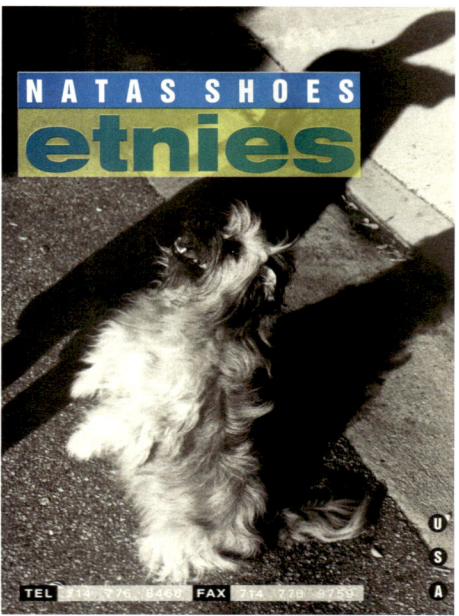

Although short-lived, the original Natas model had succeeded in convincing the skateboard scene that pro shoes weren't only for jocks – especially judging by the number of pros that have had their name stitched onto a shoe ever since. As Claus Grabke puts it: "Etnies should really build a monument to Natas! Without his shoe the whole idea [of pro skate shoes] probably would have died quickly!"

"It really started a trend with a lot of other people," said Don Brown. "And it's great to put pro skaters up on a pedestal and turn them into these role models by giving them a shoe. They deserve all the credit they can get. After all, they are the ones that are out there every day, always killing themselves on their skateboards."

For riders like Chad Muska, the board on wheels has opened many doors: "I owe everything in my life to skateboarding. The pro model shoe is just one part of it. I have made really good money at doing what I love and that is a blessing," Muska said.

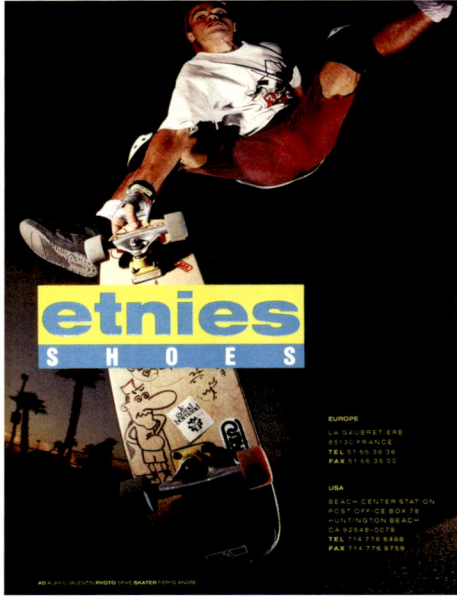

ETNIES GOES U.S.A.

Fueled by the soaring success of Etnies in Europe, the French company soon needed someone to open up the US market. That man was professional freestyle skateboarder Pierre André Senizergues, who had joined Etnies as a pro in 1988. A year later, he set up Etnies U.S.A. in Huntington Beach, California, and started distributing the shoes through a licensing agreement with owners Rautureau Apple.

But Pierre André Senizergues had more in mind than just selling the shoes. Having been involved with footwear design since the inception of his first pro shoe, the Senix in 1988, the former computer programmer would play an increasing role in creating the look and style of Etnies shoes.

"For the first shoes I used lots of 500 Michelin rubber for protection around the outside and also a mouldable arch support that fitted itself to the foot," Pierre André recalled. "We also added impact support very early on, because people were skating launch ramps in those days."

DESIGNED IN THE US

In 1991, Pierre André hired his friend and fellow professional freestyler, Don Brown from England to help operate Etnies U.S.A. And since Brown had gathered extensive design experience from testing shoes for Vision Street Wear, it was soon clear that the two wanted to expand their creative influence on the entire brand. To this end, Etnies U.S.A. struck a licensing deal with Rautureau Apple in 1992 to start designing the shoes in the US with the rights to worldwide distribution.

The timing proved ideal for getting the original owners to surrender creative control. Skateboarding was undergoing a major slump and times were especially tough in Europe.

To keep an ear to the street for new ideas, they had to look no further than their own warehouse: "I was hooking a lot of people up with shoes and they would give me feedback," Pierre André said. "There is a crazy list of people that used ride Etnies that no one knows about. Even the Gonz used to wear Etnies! So did Christian Hosoi and Chris Miller. Everybody would switch around back then. The only ones officially in ads were Rodney Mullen, Eric Dressen, Rudy Johnson, Natas and later Sal [Barbier], of course."

"I think that the evolution of skateboard footwear has had the biggest impact on skateboarding," Pierre André said. "When skateboarding crashed suddenly after the high in the Eighties, I thought about how to prevent that in the future. Making shoes can actually make skateboarding survive, with the revenue from people outside of skateboarding redistributed to support it."

Etnies literally blew up during the mid-90s shoe boom, spawning a number of spin-off companies including éS, Emerica, and ThirtyTwo, operated under the umbrella of Sole Technology Inc.

"The importance of shoes has always been around in skateboarding, even though our industry was not focussed on footwear at first," said Don Brown.

SPRAY AND PAINT YOUR SHOES

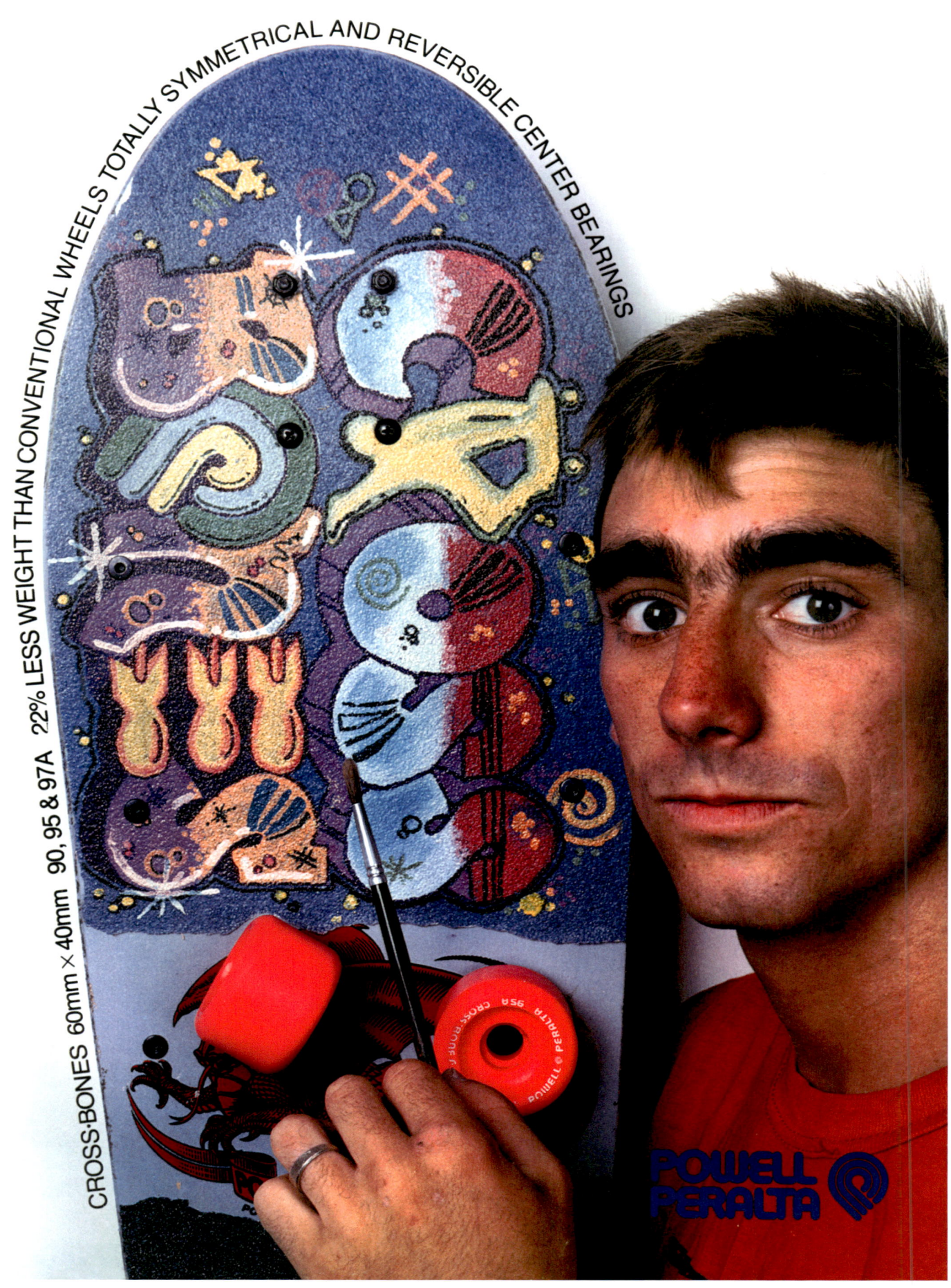

In the mid 80s, an overly infectious virus spread throughout the skateboard pro ranks. Its name: Art! Armed with paint markers and spray paint cans, victims would wander about in a perpetual state of euphoric bliss, doodling and slathering paint on whatever crossed their paths.

As the unforgettable Jason Jesse so eloquently summed it up in a video part at the time: "My mind is a garden. I skateboard, but I'm an ARTIST! I love art and I love you. Come to me and kiss me!!!"

Suddenly, art would be popping up wherever people popped ollies, and everything was fair game to receive the treatment. Neil Blender ornamented his backyard mini ramp with a paintjob combining elements of Cubism and Claus Grabke's name written all over the place for some reason only known to the artist himself. Art works in mysterious ways like that...

PAINT MARKERS - SO 80S!

Blender would also pen his own board graphics on his G&S Skateboards pro models, and skaters such as Mark Gonzales and Lance Mountains also personalized their pro decks by creating their own artwork. Soon enough, skaters turned their attention to the top of their skateboards as well, where 32 inches of black griptape provided the perfect canvas for manifesting their art in physical form.

Painting on griptape with paint markers became a creative outlet for many pros. Some of the more elaborate pieces even made the pages of skate magazines, like Lance Mountain's griptape art in a Cross Bones wheels advertisement. Mark "The Gonz" Gonzales would also turn heads on the regular, not only with his revolutionary skateboarding, but also with his griptape artwork. One of the Gonz's pro models on Vision even featured a printed top layer graphic that invited skaters to rock it with clear griptape.

A special technique among griptape artists at the time consisted of using hair spray to fixate the artwork on the griptape, proofing it against the wear and tear from soles skidding up and down the deck. And speaking of soles, skateboard shoes also provided ample space to get artsy.

PAINT YOUR TOES - NO WAIT! - YOUR SHOES

Painting your shoes actually goes back a while longer than the 1980s. Claus Grabke remembers tie-dying his white adidas "Nizza" high tops in his mothers sink as early as 1979. "The painted shoes by Gonz came around 1988, so that was about 11 years later," Grabke pointed out.

Over in the US, painted shoes also started popping up at concrete skate parks. "The first time I saw home-modified shoes was in this Steve Olson ad in '79, when punk came into skateboarding," says Lance Mountain. "He'd spray painted stripes on his shoes."

The time marks the start of the "SK8&CRE8," DIY spirit among skateboarders who tried to give a personalized, more individual note to their gear. "Towards the end of '79 and the beginning of 1980 we had to modify EVERYTHING," Lance Mountain said. "We were dying stuff pink or purple. White Converse were the choice of canvas, you could do anything on them. Around 1987/88 I got shoes from Nike", Mountain continues, "and I liked to mix and match the colorways."

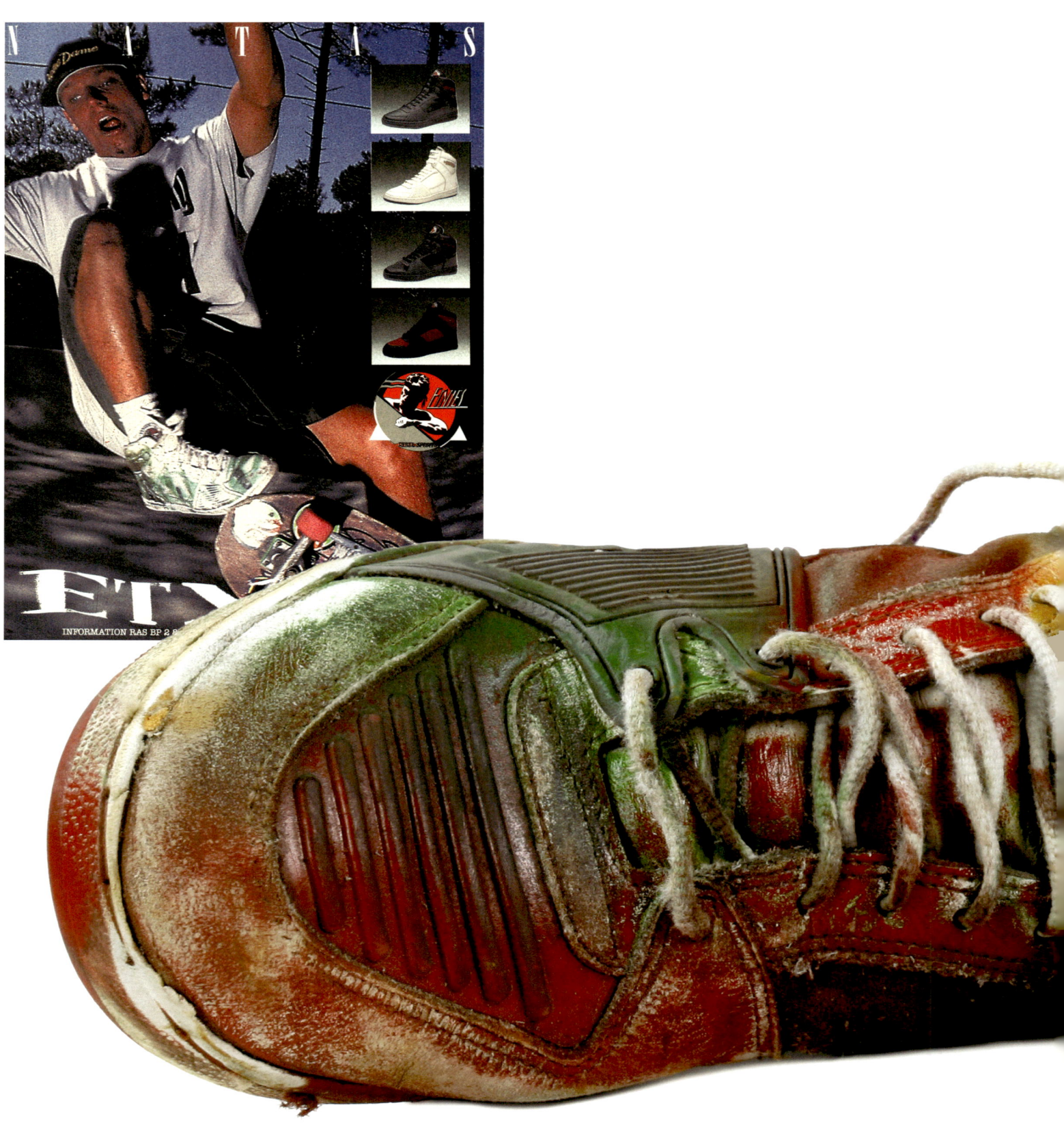

HERE COMES THE PAINT

Once the pro skateboarders dipped their shoes entirely in paint or painted them with markers around 1986, it all but started a movement among skaters worldwide.

Flipping the pages of late 1980s magazines reveals custom paint jobs on the feet of big name pros including Ed Templeton, Tony Hawk, Natas Kaupas, Jason Lee, Matt Hensley, Don Brown and Ron Allen, to name but a few.

To many professional skaters, art and riding a board went hand-in-hand: "Skateboarding has been the driving force behind everything I do. I wouldn't be anything without it," said Ed Templeton. "Especially when I paint or shoot photographs, my life as a skater informs my every action, even it it seems like it has nothing to do with skateboarding. The people and travel I experienced through skateboarding are the things that formed me as a teenager."

Favorite ornamentations included checkerboard patterns, or the iconic logo of the band Dead Kennedys. Skaters who preferred bolder strokes simply went for coloring as much area of the shoe as possible, mixing and matching layers of paint in the process.

"I started spray painting my shoes as far back as 1989. I rode for Airwalk for a short bit, and some of the colors I didn't like – or they weren't 'loud' enough for me – so I would decorate the shoes," Ed Templeton said. "Probably, I just had time on my hands, and would sit around drawing on the shoes." How about griptape or other custom paint jobs? "A little bit on the bottom of boards, mostly on the shoes. I rarely drew on a shirt. I never really did grip-tape art besides cutting the grip in different ways," Templeton said.

Speaking of griptape art, pioneer The Gonz also excelled in the level of detail and originality he brought to painting his shoes. Early on, adidas recognized the Gonz's potential and let the legendary skater design his first shoe in 1994. The collaboration continues until today, and adidas recently released a slip-on version of the classic Super Skate model, for which The Gonz provided the artwork.

THE SECOND SIGNATURE STARTS WITH A DOUBLE PAGE AD

SERIOUS SHOES FO

SERIOUS SKATERS.

THE VANS CABALLERO - AN ICON IS BORN

Started in 1989, the Steve Caballero signature shoe series by Vans is the longest running professionally endorsed shoe franchise in skateboarding. Currently, the highly popular "Half Cab" model is available in a revamped 2008 edition and remains the company's best-selling pro shoe of all time.

What's most surprising in hindsight is that when Vans first approached Steve Caballero about his own pro shoe, he was anything but excited about the idea.

"I didn't want it at first," says Steve Caballero. "They approached me with the signature shoe idea in 1988 with a pretty bad contract to follow. It catered to them mostly on sales and I felt that it was not a very fair deal on my part. So I decided to chill on the idea and just be paid a pro salary from Vans."

THAT WHOLE PRO SHOE THING

Finally, Steve met up with fellow Bones Brigade member Lance Mountain to hear his take on the royalty contract with Vans.

Caballero remembers Mountain saying: "We'll look at it this way, you could not do the deal, not get ripped off and make no money or you could do the deal, get ripped off, but make a lot of money at the same time."

A convincing argument, Caballero concluded: "I decided it was better to make the extra cash, so I signed the shoe deal in 1988 and my first signature shoe came out in 1989, the first high-top Caballero signature shoe."

AN ALL-TERRAIN SHOE

The first Caballero signature shoe featured a suede upper with a padded tongue and collar section, as well as a double layered ollie patch with double stitching extending into the toe area. And to provide the grip that skaters associated with Vans, the Caballero featured the classic Vans waffle sole with vulcanized side sections.

The Caballero also solidified the status of professionally endorsed shoes in skateboarding. With icons like Natas Kaupas and Steve Caballero backing the concept, it was more than just a fleeting trend. The fact that the Caballero shoe was a commercial slam-dunk for Vans also helped. "As shoe sales grew, so did the notoriety of the signature shoe and other riders started getting them".

Looking back, did Steve Caballero ever anticipate the magnitude of the trend he helped get started? "I had no idea what to expect at that time and never knew that it would be the next big thing after board sales," Caballero said. "I never knew it would even take precedence over board sales and that so many other shoe companies would pop up and give riders shoe contracts."

BUILD A VISION

Vision Street Wear (VSW) became synonymous with that classic 1980's "skater look" marked by big logos, bold pattern prints and loud colors on items of clothing as diverse as painter caps, berets, hip bags and sleeveless shirts. But in the footwear segment, Vision in 1986 cultivated a functional design that was everything the rest of the line was not: muted, understated and aesthetically pleasing without being flashy. A true classic, in other words.

The Vision Street Wear Suede Hi shoes had their shining moment in Powell Peralta's *Public Domain* and *Ban This* videos worn by Ray Barbee, a young amateur at the time who took the skateboarding world by storm with his nimble-footed street trickery and advanced technical skating. With their suede uppers, padded ankle section and signature rubber toecaps, the Suede Hi's offered a fresh take on the classic Vans high top – plus multi-colored sole patterns on select models.

With Vans still financially struggling in the aftermath of their early 80s foray into mainstream athletic footwear, Vision was able to dominate the skate footwear segment together with Airwalk for a solid two to three years between 1986 and 1989.

FROM A GARAGE INTO AN ENTERPRISE

Vision was started by Lou Ann Lee in 1973 in his California garage. The company would blow up into a multi-million dollar enterprise under the leadership of Lee's brother, Vision's VP of marketing Brad Dorfman. The classic Vision Street Wear Hi's possessed just the kind of urban, street-level aesthetics preferred by the new wave of street skaters.

For a moment in time, before skateboarding took a turn away from gigantic Ueber-companies like the one Vision had become, Vision shoes had the backing of an impressive pro team including the likes of Ken Park, Mark "Gator" Rogowski, Kevin Staab and Lee Ralph. Legendary street pioneer Mark Gonzales endorsed the shoes in an ad with the words "They work for me," scribbled in his by now emblematic handwriting. Freestyle pros Don Brown and Pierre Andre Senizergues even had a hands-on influence on shoe design: "I was involved with testing shoes at Vision [Street Wear] and brought that experience on board when I started designing shoes for Etnies with Pierre," Brown remembers.

So why the fall from grace? Basically, by 1988 Vision had grown too big and fashion-oriented to keep in touch with the onset of a new wave of street skating.

WEAPONS OF CHOICE

While pool skaters had already opted for heavier, sturdier shoes as early as the mid-1970s, street skaters and freestylers kept cruising along comfortably in thin, canvas-type shoes. This all changed when Rodney Mullen adapted the ollie manoeuvre to street in 1984, and the wear and tear from skidding across griptape reduced the lifespan of shoes drastically.

The impact of the street ollie on skateboard footwear may be illustrated best by looking at the shoe choices of Rodney Mullen himself.

The Converse Weapons HighTop basketball shoe became a frequent choice for Mullen as well as street skating pioneers such as Natas Kaupas, who could be seen sporting the weapons in his 1988 *Transworld Skateboarding* interview. For skaters around the world, the Weapons presented an inexpensive choice of a sturdy shoe that was widely available in "regular" sporting goods stores.

"It seems like a lot of shoe advancement was going on at the time that street skating was coming into its own," says Rodney Mullen. "I think perhaps the skaters' need was more pronounced, and companies listened. The push and pull from both sides eventuated. Fashion had a role, sometimes positive, sometimes not..."

Soon enough, the shoe racks at skate shops offered a wide number of skate-specific high tops that implemented design features of basketball boots. These technical improvements appeared just in time for the revolutionary advancements in street skating towards the late 80s. So did the evolution of footwear directly influence skateboarding? "Sure, but the flip-side is potentially more accurate," says Rodney Mullen. "It was symbiotic and synergetic. Both were carts, and both were horses."

AN AWESOME LIGHTNING BOLT

Jim Van Doren's Awesome Shoes are a chapter of skateboard footwear history that remains widely clouded in mystery today. Jim Van Doren is, of course, the brother of Vans founder Paul Van Doren and the two had started Vans together with Gordon Lee in 1966. But somewhere down the line, namely in 1985, Jim Van Doren left Vans.

According to Paul's son, Steve Van Doren, a court had asked Jim Van Doren to leave the company in the aftermath of the failed – and highly costly – attempt at making athletic shoes under the Vans brand name in the early 80s: "He wanted to be Nike."

The split came at a troubled time for Vans. Financial woes had started in 1984 and continued getting worse. Unable to pay sponsored riders or advertise their shoes and undergoing chapter 11 bankruptcy proceedings, Vans had their hopes set on several business deals that ended up getting foiled by the Black Monday stock market crash in 1987 – the same year Jim Van Doren's Awesome Shoes were launched.

THE "HONEY COMB" SOLE

Awesome Shoes at first sight presented a spitting image of Vans low tops and the iconic #38 model. The only notable difference lay in a lightning bolt stitched across the shoe's upper in place of the curved Vans logo, and a slightly modified pattern on the waffle sole; namely a "honey comb" sole for lack of a better term.

If you pay close attention when flipping old skateboard magazines of that period, a lot of shoes that appear to be Vans at first sight turn out to be Awesome Shoes, especially in British skateboard magazines.

In the end, the tide shifted for Vans. In 1988, an investment company called McConval-Deluit bought the company. Soon afterwards, Vans was able to pay their riders again and launched the successful Steve Caballero pro shoe in 1989.

Around the same time, Jim Van Doren's Awesome Shoes were discontinued and remain a hushed up body in the closet of skateboard footwear history. Steve Van Doren later took over the Vans family business and the company today is once again a striving multi-million dollar operation with deep roots in the sport.

THE VARIFLEX SYSTEM

Way before Powell Peralta Skateboards set out to become the number one company in the board sports world, Variflex raised the bar for how big a skateboard business could grow. Founded in 1977 in by Raymond H. Losi and son, Variflex quickly emerged as a leading manufacturer of skateboard equipment. Prominent team riders included Alan Losi, Lance Mountain, John Lucero and Jeff Grosso.

Backed by their reputation for making pro-level skateboards, Variflex released a skate-specific shoe in the mid-80s. And not to be stating the obvious here, but the similarity to the Vans Skate-Hi model is rather obvious. The only noteworthy difference lay in the Variflex shoe's characteristic soft rubber sole, which blended an M.C. Escher-esque 3D-version of the Vans waffle pattern with inset miniature suction cups in the style of vintage Makaha Radial shoes.

SCOOT SKATES

During the mid-80s, the company's commitment to skateboarding gradually phased out, as products focussed on complete boards like the Wiz, Dead End, Space Junk and Street Lite models sold at chain stores, while the shoe line was discontinued. In 1995, Variflex began marketing Scoot Skates, best described as skateboards with an upright handle reminiscent of the apple-crate scooters from Back to the Future.

While this invention fell short of becoming a record seller, the inline skate designed and produced by Variflex during the early 90s turned out the biggest success in the brand's history, sending sales soaring from $58 million in 1992 up to $100 million in 1995. Other successful ventures included snowboards, helmets and trampolines.

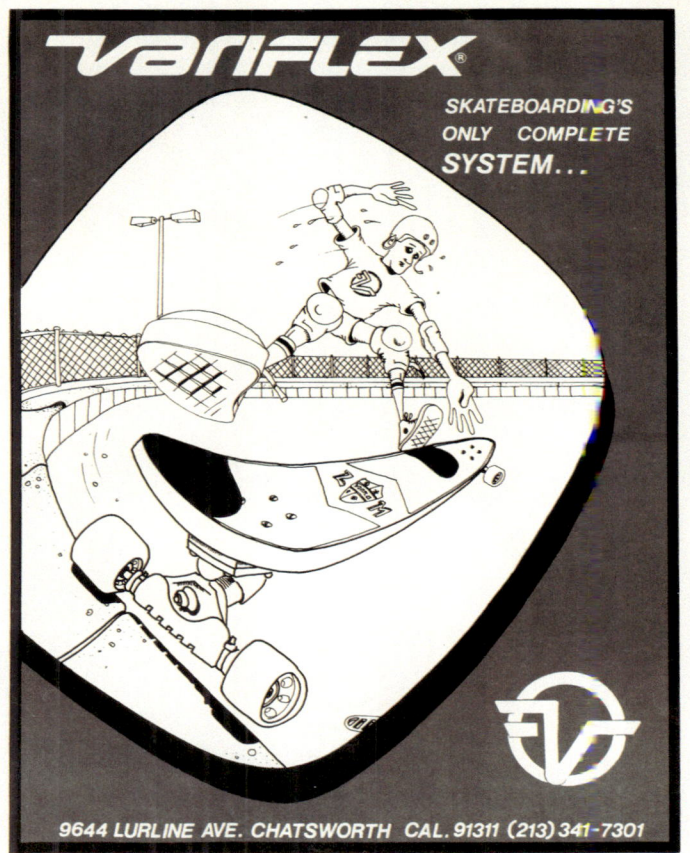

HERE TODAY, GONE TOMORROW: PACER HOGS

Pacer Skateboards are early predecessors in a long lineage of UK skateboard companies supporting their scene with products designed and built for the local skate community. Did we mention that UK board companies such as Blueprint, Landscape or Heroin are still dominating the market to this day, outselling US brands in many places? Just wanted to throw that in there.

As the mid-1980s skate boom hit the British Isles, Pacer emerged as a local manufacturer of hardware including wheels, trucks and accessories. So why not make your own shoes? In 1989, Pacer introduced the Hogs skate shoe, easily recognizable by their logo depicting a wild hog – very zany and wild in that colourful 80s kind of way, indeed.

The shoes themselves offered yet another variation on the ever-popular Chuck Taylor's mainly set off by an ollie pad and a much lower price point at around £24.99 (Chucks were pretty expensive in Europe since they needed to be imported from the US).

Despite the ollie patches on the side, Pacer Hogs allegedly fell apart within a week or two, with the thin soles being the first to go. As skateboarding flat bottomed again around 1991, so did Pacer and the legacy of Pacer Hogs lasted a mere two years.

Were they missed? Far from it, as a visitor in a skate nostalgia forum on the Internet summed it up: "Pacer Hogs? What rubbish!!!"

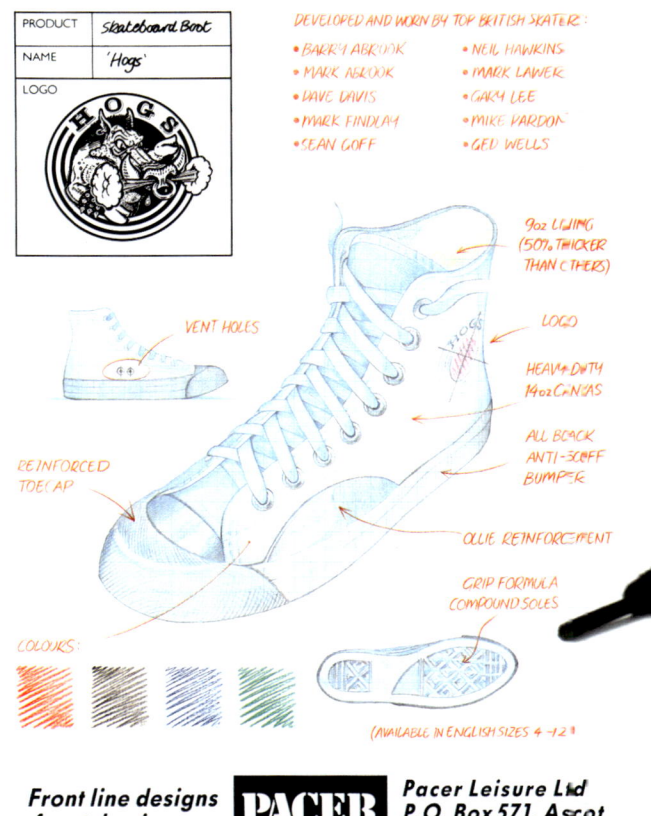

WIN!

PACER HOGS COMPETITION

Hogs are the hot new skate shoes from Pacer. Designed by skaters for skaters for maximum feel and control. Hogs are worn by top skaters like Mark and Barry Abrook, Neil Danns, Sean Goff and Davie Phillip. Now's your chance to join them!

IDENTIFY THESE SKATERS AND WIN A PAIR OF HOGS SKATE SHOES

These skaters ride for Pacer Hogs: Barry and Mark Abrook, Neil Danns, Dave Davies, Mark Findlay, Sean Goff, Neil Hawkins, Mark Lawyer, Gary Lee, Shane O'Brien and Davie Phillip. So who have we printed pictures of? Shouldn't be too difficult for you to work out. Write the names of the skaters in the pictures down on the back of a postcard or envelope, together with your name, address, SHOE SIZE and colour choice (red, green, blue or black) and send it to:

Pacer Hogs Comp
R.A.D. Magazine
40 Bowling Green L
London
EC1R 0NE

The first ten c
of the ba

Closi
comp

JUMP ON THE BANDWAGON

Mainstream companies find themselves on shaky ground once they make a direct offering to the skateboard crowd. The way to make it, is by being discovered by skaters. Otherwise, efforts can easily backfire, as history has proven again and again. Even companies initially regarded as cool by skaters get nothing but the cold shoulder.

Non-skate brands mostly try to get in at times when skateboarding is at the top of its game, when it's popular and everyone wants a piece of the pie. By 1988, skateboarding had once again grown into a global phenomenon and a multi-billion dollar market. Skating had also long since developed into a highly exclusive subculture and lifestyle in its own right. And through thick and thin, skaters had cultivated a common distrust towards "outside" companies trying to feed off skateboarding's image and culture, a distrust that also applied to core companies that had grown too big for their britches.

HARLEY DAVIDSON SKATE-SPECIFIC SHOES

One of the most striking examples of a short-lived stint into skateboarding was by iconic motorbike manufacturers Harley Davidson. Harleys and biker culture have always struck a chord with skateboarders. Even long before professional vert skater Jason Jessee first graced the pages of skate mags riding a Harley in the 80s. When chain wallets became a staple accessory of skate clothing in the 90s, one of the go-to brands was Harley Davidson. And even today, skaters gravitate towards the legendary brand – the Emerica skate team even did an entire "Wild Ride" US-tour on Harley bikes in 2007.

But when Harley Davidson started advertising their "skate-specific" shoes in skate mags, their motorbike street cred didn't quite make the leap into board sports. Big sports companies wanted to be part of the game, including L.A. Gear, who sponsored international skate competitions but never took hold.

HUGE LOGOS FOR A HUNDRED QUID

Upstart manufacturers launched skate-specific lines, including UK shoe brand Troop, started in 1988 by Clive King with Mike Rhodes as a designer. Their SPX brand was aimed at skaters with what looks today like an over-blown caricature of a skate sneaker: Huge logos around the back upper and sole sections, crazy flair like rubber capsules and Velcro straps. In the end, 100 Pounds for a pair of sneakers meant breaking the bank for the average skater, and the ads featuring obviously bailed tricks shot at weird angles didn't help, either.

Shoes became a touchy subject even for respected surf/skate companies. Take Jimmy'Z, the company launched by highly influential designer Jim Ganzer, whose work inspired a whole legion of follow-up companies. While their clothing line sold like hot cakes at surf and skate shops around the world, Jimmy'Z foray into skate footwear bombed tragically.

HARLEY-DAVIDSON USA

IXSPA 2000® is pleased to introduce the first licensed Harley-Davidson® Active Footwear line for "boarders." This line is geared towards members of today's generation that like the nostalgic, sneaker appeal and the "hot" look of Harley-Davidson®

The reemergence of Harley-Davidson® motorcycles has made their licensed sneakers the in-fashion look for footwear. If you would like to own a pair of Harley-Davidson® sneakers, just hop on your board and cruise over to your local skateboard or footwear store.

Harley Sneaker
Split suede upper with gum rubber outsole.
Black/Harley Orange
Black/Blue
Black/White
Suggested Retail: $42.00

Sportster®
Full grain leather perfed body upper with solid rubber wing outsole.
White/Black/Orange
White/Black/Blue
Suggested Retail: $75.00

Outsole design of Sportster & Heritage

Heritage®
Full grain leather textured elephant hide pattern solid rubber wing outsole.
Black/White
White/Black
Suggested Retail: $85.00

Available at Champ's California stores and all Harley Davidson […]
If there is not a store in your area carrying these items, send check […] ble to:
G.F.I. Holding Company, Inc., 14 Washington Rd., Building 7, Princeton[…] 326-6777.
State tax applied as required by law.   All orders subject to a $[…]

SKATING. O RADICAL DA RAINHA.

O novo Rainha Skating tem a sua cara: cano alto, cores vibrantes e estilo arrojado. E tem as qualidades da Rainha: o couro resistente, a lona reforçada e a borracha amortecedora, que juntos encaram todas as manobras. Com um Rainha Skating você entra de sola... e sai com ela inteirinha. Por isso, você vai ver que logo mais, só vai dar fera com ele. Rainha Skating. O pisante chocante e arrepiante da Rainha.

SHOES FROM BRAZIL

Ever since the early 1970s, Brazil has had its own, self-sufficient skate industry. After all, local manufacturers could draw on excess supplies of raw materials and offer their goods at affordable prices compared to what expensive import gear sold for at the shops – if it was available at all.

Since most manufacturers operate solely in Brazil and neighboring South American countries, company names such as Rainha, WT Radical, Condor, Kick or Alva shoes (that's right, Alva!) remain largely unheard of anywhere else in the skateboarding universe. But to Brazilian skaters, they offered a way to get by and keep rolling when times were tough.

"To buy and import American shoes is very expensive for the average Brazilian," said Rodrigo Petersen from Curitiba, Brazil. "That only creates a high demand for certain shoes or styles. The next best thing was to buy a Brazilian version, which did a lot of good business for local brands."

INSPIRED FOOTWEAR

While the Brazilian scene relied on local shoe manufacturing, designs were heavily influenced – or sometimes followed to the letter – by what was happening in California. "They were all knock-offs of popular American skate shoes that were out at the time," Rodrigo Petersen said, adding: "Brazil is a third-world country, and people couldn't afford to pay for American skate kicks, so the next best thing was to get the Brazilian versions."

PERSONALIZING YOUR STYLE

"I think we started making our own shoes between 1975 and 1977," said Beto Alva, the former owner of Alva Shoes. "Back then we were already making our shoes from canvas, in a cut similar to the old Vans. That was the beginning of personalizing that style."

"In principal, ALL the brands copied the classic Vans shoes, like the Skate Hi. That was pretty much the absolute shoe in Brazil for a long time," said Philipp "Moski" Marx, an avid skate collector living in Reutlingen, Germany, who was born and raised in Sao Paulo, Brazil. "The only difference would be that shoes like the Mad Rats would replace the Vans 'wave' logo with a 'double wave' logo to form an 'M' for Mad Rats."

Before anyone jumps to quick judgments about the apparent plagiarism in the Brazilian scene, Moski points out: "You have to remember that all the companies were created out of necessity. And Brazil and the US didn't always have the best trade relations and still don't. But still, people wanted to get their hands on the popular skate stuff."

A PASSION FOR SKATEBOARDING

You wouldn't know it by looking at all the gifted skateboarders to emerge from Brazil – but skateboarding has had more than a rough start in the land of Samba and Caipirhinha: "Basically, Brazil was a military dictatorship up until 1984. So there was a heavy trade embargo and at the time there was, like, only one Mercedes in all of Sao Paulo," Moski said.

Beto Alva explains: "It took until the 90s for our borders to be opened to free trade of all kinds by president Collor. Before that, we were depending on notorious smugglers."

Despite the initial economic disadvantage, skateboarding in Brazil enjoyed great heights of popularity quite early on. By 1993, skateboarding was already the number four most popular athletic activity among the country's youth, right behind surfing, volleyball and soccer.

"And for some people, skateboarding worked exactly like soccer," Moski explains. "You could come from a poor background and then get good enough to get sponsors in Brazil and eventually make it internationally like Sandro Dias, Alex Carolino or Bob Burnquist."

One of the main advantages of the Brazilian scene was the rich abundance of legally skateable terrain, mostly concrete skate parks. "You can't really build wooden ramps due to the high level of humidity there, they would just rot," Moski explains. "So everything was built from concrete."

MIXED FEELINGS

Overall, the local Brazilian brands received a mixed reception. On one hand, they posed the only financially viable option for many skaters. "I wouldn't say the [Brazilian] shoes were more popular, but they were definitely more affordable," said Rodrigo Petersen, who is pro for Listen skateboards and Nike SB. "Brazilian skaters had to ride whatever they could get and a lot of Brazilian pros were forced to ride for local shoe brands in order to get paid to do what they love."

Although many manufacturers would copy what was popular on the international market, other Brazilian companies started doing their own thing, Moski recalls: "Some companies like Urgh! and Lifestyles didn't copy other people's stuff. They would make their own product for their own scene."

NEXT GENERATION

The strategy of producing shoes locally under license has also proven successful for international shoe manufacturers. Nike SB has recently given Rodrigo Petersen and fellow Brazilian Nike SB team members the opportunity to create their second series of custom-made Dunk high tops.

To this day, the saga of Brazilian skate companies continues, with brands like Crail trucks and the relatively new shoe company Qix Shoes, launched in 2005, carrying the torch of local enterprises that support their scene with affordable products while sponsoring a pro team and keeping skateboarding alive through thick and thin.

Made in Brazil - The Nike SB Custom Series 02

A TALE OF TWO ALVAS

Dog Town skate legend Tony Alva can be credited with many achievements in skateboarding. But the "godfather of skateboarding" never had his own shoe company. At least not in the US. In Brazil, however, the Alva Shoe brand had been a staple of the scene since 1977. But why call a shoe brand "Alva" when Tony Alva had nothing to do with it?

"Many skaters here were tagged with the name of a famous skater as an expression of respect. I myself had the nickname 'Beto Alva' because my style was very similar to Tony's," the Brazilian Alva explained.

Given his own reputation as a talented skater in the Brazilian scene, Beto Alva soon realized that his nickname could be turned into an asset in the market place. "When I started distributing my own [skate] products, I didn't even have my own brand. The shop owners would only say that the products were from [Beto] Alva. So in my case, I was able to turn this amenity into an advantage."

BACKYARD SCENE BUILDING

The beginnings of Alva Shoes mirror those of count- less skateboard brands around the world. "We started in a backyard and together with Marcio and Yura from Mad Rats [shoes], we learned the craft in our basement," said Beto Alva. "Thanks to the growing demand we were forced to turn the whole thing into a registered business. That's when we started producing in Franca [São Paulo] und Novo Hamburgo [Rio Grande Do Sul]."

Demand increased exponentially, because Alva Shoes and other local manufacturers could offer price points that were affordable to local skaters.

At the height of his company's fame and glory, Beto was able to establish communications with his namesake in Los Angeles: "I contacted Tony Alva in order to work together with him."

But as it would turn out, the joint venture came at an unfortunate time. "The market crashed, since president Collor almost plunged the whole country into the abyss, and Alva Brazil, like so many other companies, went under."

thought we didn't have a shoe?

Think again. **Eric Koston** Model shown. **310.517.0059**. Spurs optional.

THE 4 NINETIES

BIG PANTS - SMALL WHEELS - LOW CUT SHOES

Big changes on an international level marked the onset of the 1990s. The world, as we knew it, was getting ready to never be the same again as the old order came crashing down. Socialism officially died an inevitable death. This opened the doors to skateboard culture in all the countries now enjoying open access to Western goods including pop culture.

Skateboarding had gone global. And if they're skating on Stalin's statues, the sky is the limit, right!? We are going everywhere! Rodney Mullen's doing casper flips on Moscow's Red Square. We're going everywhere! Time to grow, time to invest!

Let's face it: Everyone is touched on some primal level by the sheer awesomeness of a 12 foot air on a giant vert ramp, right? But to grasp the intricacies of a 360° kickflip on flat ground or a quarter pipe – not to mention the trial and error involved in finally nailing it – takes more capacity on behalf of the spectator. Bottom line: Big airs are more media and crowd-friendly.

When street skating replaced vert as the skater's top choice of terrain, skateboarding lost that easily accessible mass appeal. It was once again time to ditch the spotlight and undergo a period of refinement and soul-searching.

Companies expanded production capacities and shipped out shoes, boards and hip bags at an unprecedented scale. And then skateboarding went the way of Socialism and plunged into a shallow grave. The masses turned their backs on skateboarding once again, just like in the 60s and early '80s.

SUDDEN DEATH

"Could anyone have seen it coming?" the industry asked itself as truckloads of unsold hip bags made their last dusty voyage to be buried in the Arizona desert. Had there been warning signs? Any way of telling we'd hit the downward end of another cycle? Maybe the death of vert skating had been an indicator. After all, vert had been the biggest crowd magnet and supreme artistic spectacle that the masses could relate to.

The new technical type of street skating demanded for more agility in the ankles. Which meant even lighter, even lower-cut shoes. Since these were hard to find in stores, next generation skaters took the Exacto knife to their shoes and simply cut their high- or mid-tops into super low tops.

HOW LOW CAN YOU GO?

As shoes shrank, pants and T-shirts blew up during the "Big Pants, Small Wheels" era of street skating, mostly defined by going not too fast and testing out how many times you could flip your board. Not always pretty to look at, but skateboarding had faded from mass popularity anyhow. So those who stuck with it didn't care what anyone had to say about their goofy-looking pants and get-ups.

It was in this period that the classic skate shoe designs of today were drafted, with the Etnies Lo-Cut model presenting a classic suede sneaker with padded ankles and a soft sole for that overall "skate sneaker"-look that has been often copied since then. DC Shoes took skate shoes to a more technical level by introducing advanced materials like Nubuck leather together with features like reinforced mid soles, air pockets, and plastic eyelets to encase exposed laces. Overall, DC succeeded in introducing to skateboarding the kind of technical features that before had been the sole domain of "athletic" footwear.

DOLLAR DOLLAR BILLS, Y'ALL

It was also in the 1990s that skateboard shoes commenced being the biggest gravy train in professional skateboarding. Whereas before the pros had pocketed most cash from their board sales, the rapid rise to riches of popular skate shoe companies also enabled the early shoe pros to soon trade their Honda Civics for spruced up Audis and Beamers. Where did the money come from? Well, the margins for selling skate footwear are tremendously high compared to other product groups. Especially if you did what Airwalk already figured out in the 1980s to cut costs of labor – produce in Asia!

The formula worked: Shoes made for a handful of dollars sold for big bucks. The success of shoe companies helped pull skateboarding out of its slump. Now there was money for new skate parks, magazines, tours and all that was needed to solidify skateboarding as a lifestyle and culture. New companies entered the re-charged market. Mainstays Airwalk, Vans, DC, Etnies and Duffs were joined by Osiris, Adio, Simple, and Hook-Ups.

UP IN SMOKE

Does anyone remember "puffy tongues"? In those hip-hop heavy days that were the mid-1990s, the main look out on the street consisted of baggy pants worn on top of shoes worn with their puffy tongues sticking out over the bottom of the pant legs. To achieve this effect, early adopters of this style cut off an extra tongue from worn-out shoes or even rolled up some socks, which they would stick into their kicks for extra tongue protrusion.

It didn't take shoe companies long to catch on and soon everyone and their mom was making shoes with tongues that took the whole puffy thing to the next dimension. Some shoemakers even put a weed stash pocket with a zipper into the tongues, remember that? The weed stashes turned out a big success in mainstream culture as well, as did a number of skate shoes that soon became standard regalia at clubs and on urban sidewalks around the world. Major splashes into the mainstream include the DC Shoes Syntax and Boxer models, as well as the D3 Osiris kicks.

INTO THE MILLENNIUM

While the world feared total technological shutdown due to the Y2K bug for the new millennium, skateboarding was facing a bright future. By the end of the 1990s, another wave of shoe companies entered the scene, most of them founded by skate pros, who left their sponsors to do their own things. Think names like Lakai, DVS, iPath and 88 Footwear here. Australian surf company Globe also started introducing functional shoes endorsed by a legit pro team.

Behind the scenes, a number of corporate take-overs lurked around the corner, with major surf brands getting ready to branch out into corporate mega-label conglomerates. Mainstream companies also wanted a slice of the pie. Throughout, skate footwear had not only matured into the most lucrative segment of the entire skate business, but had also managed to hold its own in terms of style and originality.

After a decade full of ups and downs and tremendous changes skateboarding had re-invented itself and was here to stay. There would no longer be peaks and valleys for skateboarding, no more dramatic die-down periods and draughts with collapsing businesses and companies. By the year 2000, it was clear that skateboarding would always be around, from the US, to Europe, Russia and Australia, all the way to China, where soon enough a growing share of skateboards and shoes would be manufactured.

(IF THE SHOE FITS...) TH!NK

THE BIG "V"

Now that street skating was king, Vision was having a hard time making the transition. After all, for years their pro team had consisted of 90% vert skaters, including greats such as Tom Groholski, Kevin Staab and Joe Johnson. Plus, street pioneer Mark Gonzales had gone into semi-retirement after leaving vision for Blind skateboards and proceeded to redefine street skating in the the highly successful "Video Days" video in 1990. Ray Barbee, who had single handedly made Vision's Suede Hi shoes famous in his video parts, by now had a sponsorship deal with the fully recovered Vans brand.

THE FALL OF GATOR

Additionally, Vision's poster boy Mark "Gator" Rogowski – the biggest rock star in skateboarding next to Christian Hosoi – was in trouble. When Gator fell under mysterious circumstances and impaled himself on a fence at the Muenster World Cup in 1990, the skateboarding public became aware that all was not well with the charismatic California sunny boy, who at the height of vert skating's popularity had earned more than $100,000 a year. Gator also estranged his large fan base by punching a police officer at a contest in the US the same year.

When Gator re-invented himself with a new name, "Gator" Mark Anthony, and appeared skating a pool naked in an ad, even die-hard fans were outraged. Skaters went as far as burning their Gator spiral graphic boards in disapproval.

The back story of Gator's fall is chronicled in the 2003 documentary *Stoked* directed by Helen Stickler. A most revealing scene depicts Gator's frustrated attempts at street skating, which end in a temper tantrum with Gator screaming: "Fuck! I suck! FUUUUCK!!!"

Gator's career finally came to a grinding halt in May 1991 when he turned himself in for having killed a 20-year-old woman. In a heavily publicized trial, the fallen skate super star was sentenced to 31 years to life in prison for rape and murder.

TRYING TO GET BACK IN

While Vision Street Wear succeeded in creating a series of highly functional shoes oriented towards street skaters, they lacked the image – the perceived "realness", if you will – to regain the acceptance of what was now exclusively a hardcore market that coveted authenticity over brand pull.

Inevitably, Vision's ads went from double-page spreads to small black and white blurbs in the backs of magazines. Around 1993, Vision disappeared from the limelight, with short flickers of media presence and talk of a comeback in 1995 and 1999.

But here's good news to anyone looking to score a pair of OG Vision Streetwear kicks: In 2007, US footwear retailers PayLess Shoe Source acquired the rights to the Vision Street Wear brand – they also own Airwalk – and the Suede Hi is back as part of a complete re-launch. The new website says "Legends Never Die," and what more proof could anyone ask for?

TO FIT AND SURVIVE: SKATE RAGS

In the Hall of Fame of skateboard industry pioneers, Mr. Larry Balma deserves special mention. The Orange County skateboarder and former commercial fisherman founded *Transworld Skateboarding Magazine* in 1983 as a clean, sports-oriented alternative to the more rugged *Thrasher* magazine. Balma also built a considerable portfolio of successful skateboard brands out of Climax distribution in Oceanside, California.

Larry Balma's company Skate Rags Clothing enjoyed a reputation for functional garments and product innovation. And with little fanfare, the brand released its own series of footwear in 1990 – which as it turns out never hit the shops in the US.

What happened? "The shoes were produced by another company through a licensing agreement," explained former Skate Rags manager Joe Bowers. "These were the same people that produced wallets for Skate Rags and licensed products for companies like Ocean Pacific. They designed the shoes themselves and produced them overseas."

Only a small amount of Skate Rags shoes hit the streets at one point. "I'm almost sure that the only order that ever got delivered went to Titus [distribution] in Germany," said Joe Bowers. "We had some prototypes in the US, but I hardly think the shoes were ever available domestically."

Former Skate Rags distributor Titus Dittmann remembers: "We had the license for Europe and developed our own products [under the Skate Rags name]. Many products were available in Europe only, not the US. But when it comes to the shoes, I'm not sure whether we bought them somewhere or produced them ourselves."

A SOLID CHOICE

From a design perspective, Skate Rags shoes presented a number of key refinements on the classic basketball boot construction. Their striking resemblance to Vision Street Wear shoes indicate that Skate Rags kicks might have been manufactured at the same factory in China, but that can only be speculated.

Skate Rags shoes introduced an ingenious new lace saver construction, which instead of opening sideways with a vertical Velcro strip – as featured on the Airwalk VICs and other models – relied on a flap of suede fabric that would fold up from beneath the lower lace inlets, held in place on top by a Velcro strap above the ankle. In practice, this construction proved far more advantageous to Airwalk's sideways lace savers, known for their tendency for losing their grip and getting clogged with lint and dirt after a few weeks of intense wear.

For some time, Titus distribution went to great lengths promoting Skate Rags shoes in German magazines, until another licensee stepped in. "The store chain 'Street One' ended up suing me, because they had older rights on the brand. As a consequence, we needed to stop the entire production under license and stopped the entire sale of Skate Rags products," Dittmann said, adding: "Larry Balma then ended up selling the Skate Rags brand to Street One for a low price, since working with the brand in Europe was no longer possible."

PRODUCT PATROL

VELOCITY

The Disaster was a great shoe, but Airwalk's new Velocity goes one better. This is one company that knows skaters' feet. The Velocity features a durable, comfortable upper and the famous Airwalk sole. One great attribute is the tough double-stitched, shell-like front cone, which is good for kneeslides. On most shoes, the uppers wear faster than the sole, but not on these puppies. The price is steep but the shoe is deep.

CRUELTY-FREE FOOTWEAR

As the 90s rolled around, many skaters were no longer the happy-go-lucky freewheeling freaks portrayed in Hollywood movies. Maybe youth culture on a whole was getting more political again after the 80s had been a decade marked by limitless consumerism and egotism, who knows? Might be a bit of a stretch. But notably more pro skaters started voicing political opinions or going public with their lifestyle choices and beliefs at the turn of the decade.

DON'T SKATE MY FRIENDS

This was especially the case for vegetarianism and its lactose- and animal-protein-free cousin, veganism. Pro skaters like Claus Grabke and Mike Vallely openly took a stand against eating meat or animal products in interviews and with board graphics like Vallely's "Don't Eat My Friends" deck.

And eating meat was far from their only beef – wearing animal products was also entirely out of the question. So for a leather-free alternative, Vallely and Grabke could be seen sporting Converse Chuck Taylors on almost every magazine photo from those days.

STRAIGHT EDGE INFLUENCES?

Cultural anthropologists might be quick to point out at this point that the whole vegan thing may have spilled over into skateboard culture from the Straight Edge movement in hardcore music. Remember X's painted on the back of your hand, a staple at concert attended by youth of all ages? Or three X's tattooed on fingers? No promiscuity, no alcohol, no tobacco, no drugs? No meat! Bands like Minor Threat, Gorilla Biscuits, Youth of Today, SNFU?

Whether or not this was where Claus Grabke got the three X's he'd sign on autographs or Mike V. found inspiration to shave his head – hard to say. The fact remains that veganism in skating was definitely gaining momentum and Chuck Taylors would not be the only option in footwear for long.

A young skater named Ed Templeton from Huntington Beach became somewhat of a spokesman for the movement – although he never pushed his beliefs on anyone – leading by example:

"I stopped eating meat around 1989 or '90. But I got started a bit on the wrong track. I simply left the meat out of my meals and sustained myself on 'sides' at first. But as I found out more about the whole subject, I found that it's totally unhealthy to just leave out the meat and stuff yourself with more cheese instead. Plus I was really annoyed by the fact that cheese and milk products were produced just as unfairly as meat. So in 1990 I decided to go vegan."

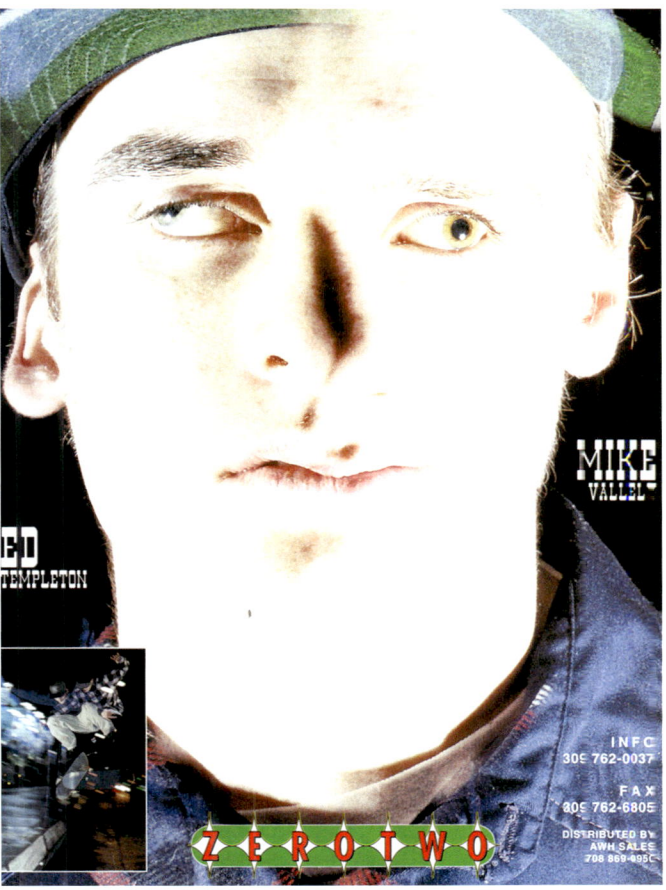

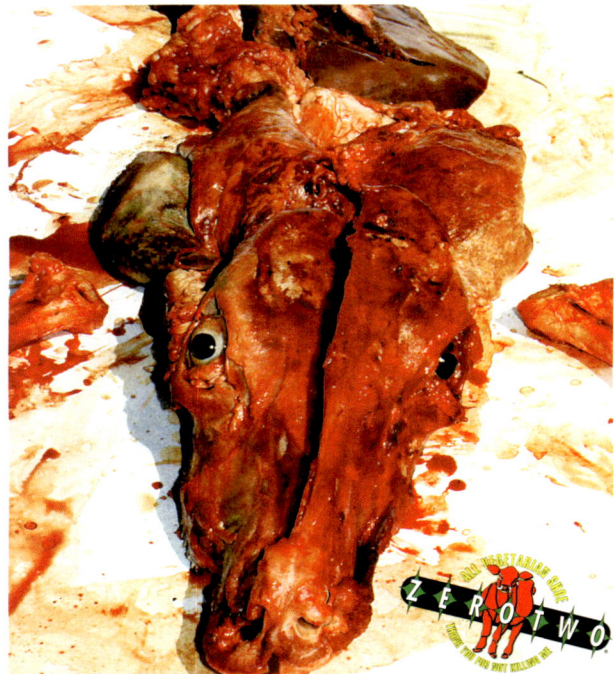

ZERO-TWO: VEGAN SHOES?

Many pro skaters adopted a vegan lifestyle in the late 80s, and many were outspoken about their choice in magazine interviews and videos. So it was about time for vegan skaters to create their own style of shoes and educate the masses. After all, a widely held belief in the skate community might be summed up something like this: "My shoes aren't made from dead animals. They're SUEDE!" But suede actually is a type of leather with a napped finish. And leather comes from animals. Period.

The first skate company to bring home this uncomfortable truth was Zero-Two Shoes in the year 1990. Their ads could hardly have been any more graphic, depicting the bloody remnants of a slaughtered cow stripped of its hide.

Zero-Two Shoes made the history books as the first all-vegan skateboard shoe company. Animal products in skate footwear were not only limited to the usage of leather, bone used in glues was also an issue. So were animal oils in soles, to which Zero-Two replied with the slogan: "There are no souls in our soles."

The shoes themselves were high-tops available in any color you wanted, as long as it was black. Their cut was reminiscent of a Chukka Boot, made more durable with movable Ollie Guards that could be attached anywhere on the side of the shoe for protection from ollie damage and concrete abrasion. In keeping with their vegan philosophy, Zero-Twos were made entirely from synthetic materials with an extra grippy soft sole in a waffle pattern.

Endorsing the message of cruelty-free footwear was an all-star vegan team consisting of Ed Templeton, Mike Vallely and Brian Lotti. But as it turned out: "The company didn't last because it was a joke and as soon as Ed and I figured it out we bailed," said Vallely. Templeton agreed: "The guy who made that company was not even a vegetarian, nor did he see his shoe as a skateboarding shoe!"

INTERMISSION: NON-PC-HUMOR!

With all that eco-consciousness around, World Industries founder Steve Rocco apparently couldn't help but dish out his own signature blend of non-PC-humor in a TV commercial for his DuFFS shoes brand.

In a spoof on a vintage documentary, the audience is shown the true, horrible origins of DuFFS shoes, demanding the "slaughtering of hundreds of steers, which in the tanning stages are processed with the finest bleaches and dyes… which we then dispose into natural waterways – destroying wildlife."

All that juxtapozed next to images of slaughtered cattle, dead fish and acres of scorched tropical rain forest. Take that vegans! Rocco's ad ended on the catchy slogan: "DuFFS - comfort that demands destruction."

In 1997, Sole Technology Inc. targeted the low price segment with a new shoe brand named Sheep. Initially, Sheep shoes were intended to counteract pressure from high street retailers offering their own, cheaper brands of shoes.

SKATE LIKE WOLVES, WEAR SHEEP

In order to keep prices low, the shoes were made from canvas and rubber, without any animal products like suede or other leathers involved. The plan backfired, however, as import duty for Sheep shoes turned out to be significantly higher than for suede or leather shoes. Nevertheless, vegan skaters became very fond of Sheep and the company was able to enlist big name professional Ed Templeton as their headline pro rider. "Sheep was awesome. It was fun working with Yogi, the art director, and approaching it a little more artsy," Ed Templeton said, adding: "My first signature shoe was with Sheep."

Templeton commenced to enlist some other fellow vegan and vegetarian skaters on the team, including Brian Anderson, Matt Field, Frank Hirata, Mike Manzoori, Rick McCrank, Sergei Trudnowski and Charlie Wilkins. Despite the star power on the team – and the highly acclaimed *Life of Leisure* video – the numbers didn't add up for Sheep and the brand was discontinued in 1998. "It came just at the moment that skating was growing quickly, and I don't think the market for that company was growing with it," Ed Templeton said, adding: "Sheep just morphed into Emerica."

SYNTHETIC KICKS

The discontinuation of Sheep shoes and Zero-Twos left some serious (vegan) shoes to fill. After all, the two brands had enjoyed a solid following among vegan skaters. Ed Templeton puts it in perspective: "Both were very specifically marketed in a world where specificity wasn't needed."

What had yet to be done, was to create a vegan shoe that resonated well with vegan skaters without losing its mainstream and commercial appeal.

Although never explicitly marketed as an entirely vegan shoe option, the DC Shoe Company's highly popular Syntax model introduced in 1996 was just that – cruelty-free and synthetic footwear. The Syntax was the unofficial pro model shoe for vegan skateboarder Moses Itkonen from Vancouver, Canada. Outside the skate market, the DC Syntax became a staple among club goers around the world and the company's biggest seller at the time together with the Clocker and Plug models.

Highly durable and resilient, the Syntax model still frequently pops up whenever people discuss the top skateboarding shoes of all time. Follow-up vegan-friendly shoes by DC Shoes included the Deuce and Substance models, also made from synthetics.

Vegan skaters riding for other companies also pushed their sponsors to pursue synthetic shoes. In 1997, Emerica introduced the canvas Jamie Thomas pro shoe, on which Thomas himself had a major influence in terms of design and material, making sure his signature model remained entirely free of animal products.

This summer ALL the fleebinistic skaters will be seen riding in Zero Two convertibles.

Hi-Top or Mid-Top
We've made it easy for you.

Zero Two is the durable skate shoe that's actually designed to be worn either as a hi-top or a mid-top. You make the call! We've stitched the ankle support so the shoe holds together, even after you've taken the scissors to 'em.

INFO/MAIL ORDER 309 762-0037
FAX HOTLINE 309 762-6805

DISTRIBUTED BY AWH SALES
INTERNATIONAL MAIL ORDER
209 275-1171

CUT YOUR SHOES

Now, why on Earth would you take a carpet knife to your brand new shoes and convert them into low tops?

Driven by the demands of ever more complicated technical flip tricks and ledge moves, street skaters in what would be known as the "Big Pants - Small Wheels" era opted for wearing the lowest cut shoes they could find. And if what was available wasn't low enough, the old exacto knife came out to convert a bulky high top into a fresh, new school looking shoe just like that.

"I remember everyone would cut off the tops of their shoes, then take the padding out and fold them over on top, sealing the whole thing with Duct Tape," says Pierre André Senizergues.

While this presented a rather advanced technique of turning shoes into low tops, a lot of skaters simply cut off the shoes and let the chips - or rather, the inside filling materials - fall as they may. As a result, a pair of brand-new shoes would look three weeks old in a matter of days, with inside padding spilling out all over the place - much to the horror of moms and dads around the world who had to foot the bill.

Every type of shoe was fair game for getting the knife. While Airwalk Enigmas, Vans High Tops and Airwalk Prototypes presented some classic choices for rapid lowering action, even already low kicks such as Vans Chukka Boots were "lowered" a few more inches. It was nuts.

"Yeah, the shoe companies couldn't keep up with the whims of the skaters so we took scissors to our high tops," Mike Vallely said. "I guess as skating got more technical the need for a lighter and less constricting shoe made sense."

FUNCTION BEFORE FASHION

Soon enough, footwear companies noticed that the low cut shoe craze was more than just a fleeting trend, but really the shape of things to come in terms of what street skaters wanted.

But even when companies came out with new styles of shoes for the new flippity-tech-skating demographic, the cutting off persisted. This was mostly for two reasons:

a) skateboarding had died down tremendously in the early 90s and the average skater was simply too broke to afford snazzy new low tops at full price points.

b) Many skate shops still carried full stocks of a variety of late 80s high tops that never got picked up, which they now offered at low prices.

Given the choice between paying $60 for a new pair of freshly released low cut skate shoes or getting three pairs of old Vision Street Wears, Airwalks or Vans for the same price, a lot of skaters ran the numbers and brought out the knives.

Another option for low cut shoes lay in adapting classic sneakers such as the Puma Clyde and the adidas Gazelle and Campus models for skateboarding. These shoes not only enjoyed some underground chique since the Beastie Boys had worn them in their 1992 *Check Your Head* video, but also offered extra low price points at around $20 for low cut shoes.

The whole craze ended as suddenly as it had begun when low cut shoes became established as the norm around 1993. Much to the relief of parents worldwide, the defiling of skate shoes had come to an end.

THE HALF CAB

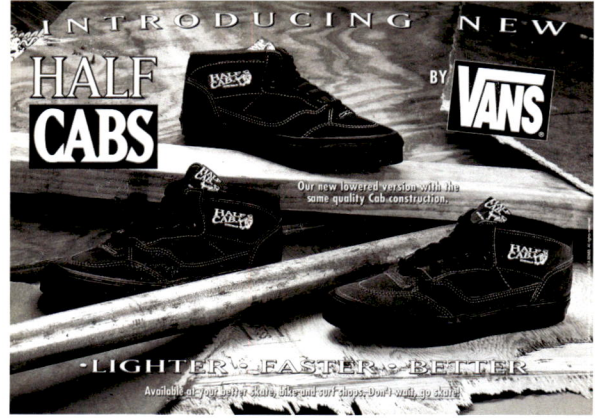

The timing for the release of the HALF CAB was perfect: "In 1991, I noticed that a lot of street skaters were cutting my shoe halfway down and wearing them that way," Steve Caballero comments. "So in 1992, I gave Vans the idea to make a lower cut shoe and call it the 'HALF CAB'. They said yes because the shoe was selling so well as a high top."

The rest is pretty much history. Lowered a few crucial inches compared to the original – all the while retaining the original design created by Caballero himself – the shoe became an instant classic. Its direct influence on the design of skateboard footwear to this day can hardly be overstated.

Only two years after its launch, the HALF CAB served as the design blueprint for Mike Carroll's first pro model in 1994. And ever since then, countless companies have produced their own shoes in the stlye of the HALF CAB.

BACK AGAIN

Over the past few years, the HALF CAB has made an impressive comeback. Vans voted it „Shoe of the Year" in 2007 and according to Steve Caballero, it was booked by Vans for Spring 08 as the best selling shoe in their hardcore stores and market.

For a 2008 re-release edition, Vans has created a HALF CAB edition replete with the signature bats from Steve Caballero's iconic pro model on Powell Peralta Skateboards, as well as the famous Dragon graphic printed on the insole.

THE MOST COPIED SHOE IN SKATEBOARDING?

"As the times changed, so did shoe designs," Steve Caballero says. "Now it's come full circle again with bowl and park skating being very popular and that's why the HALF CAB has made a strong comeback."

What makes the shoe such a timeless classic?

"As for the characteristics, it would have to be the whole shoe as a whole, from the white side rubber on the vulcanized sole, to the suede upper patterns, to the white stitching," Steve Caballero says. "It's just a clean looking shoe, with not many bells and whistles that actually performs well for a skate shoe. The Vans gum rubber sole has a lot to do with it as well because of how much grip it has. I think that really played a big role in making the HALF CAB a shoe people wanted to skate in."

And despite changes in tastes and styles, Vans continued carrying the shoe as part of their line-up throughout the years. "The shoe has always been in their catalogue as a classic shoe, so that hardcore skaters were still able to get them."

In conclusion, Caballero says: "I just wanna give a big shout out and thank you to anyone who has ever sported, been given, traded for or bought a pair of HALF CABs. It's because of you that this shoe has stood the test of time, thanks for all your support, it means a lot to me and I appreciate it very much!"

A LOWER CUT FOR A HIGHER TECH

THE LO-CUT: A CLASSIC IS BORN

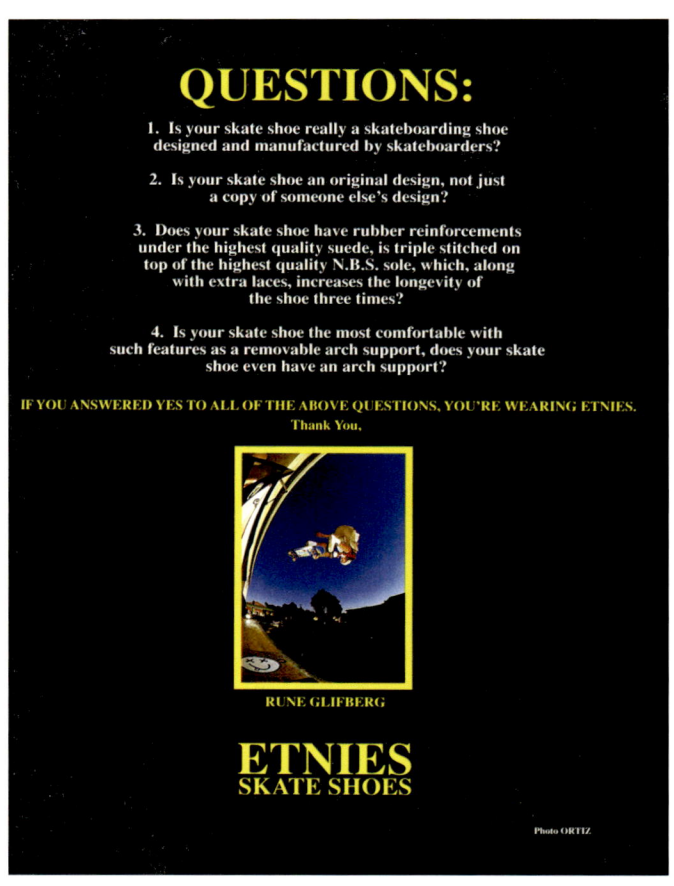

One of the most iconic shoe designs in skate history, the Etnies Lo-Cut broke with many long established conventions when it first hit shelves in 1993. "Making a low cut shoe for skateboarding was pretty much against the grain at the time, because everyone had ankle protection in mind when they saw high top shoes," said Don Brown, of Sole Technology, who created the Lo-Cut together with the founder of Etnies USA, Pierre André Senizergues.

"I guess there was a lot of influence from bigger athletic firms back then, all of which had high tops," Brown added. "You would think that a higher shoe would protect the ankle better, but a low top will give you more flexibility in the ankle, which builds it up and makes it stronger."

Little known fact: The Etnies Rap model had actually been a direct steppingstone in the creation of the Lo-Cut. Don Brown remembers: "I would see our team riders come to the warehouse with their high top Raps cut off, like everyone did in 1992. They would cut the inside rubber out of the upper part, fold them over and duct tape them in place to make low tops. So we knew we had to make a low top shoe for them."

Taking the feedback from his team riders, Don Brown crafted a basic design for a low cut and showed it to Pierre André Senizergues, who perfected the design into what would become the first modern low cut shoe.

Street skaters everywhere instantly embraced the Lo-Cut and Etnies hit the $1 million benchmark in sales that year. "Looking back I think it gave a new direction to skate footwear and it was pretty pioneering on a design level," said Don Brown.

THE SAL 23

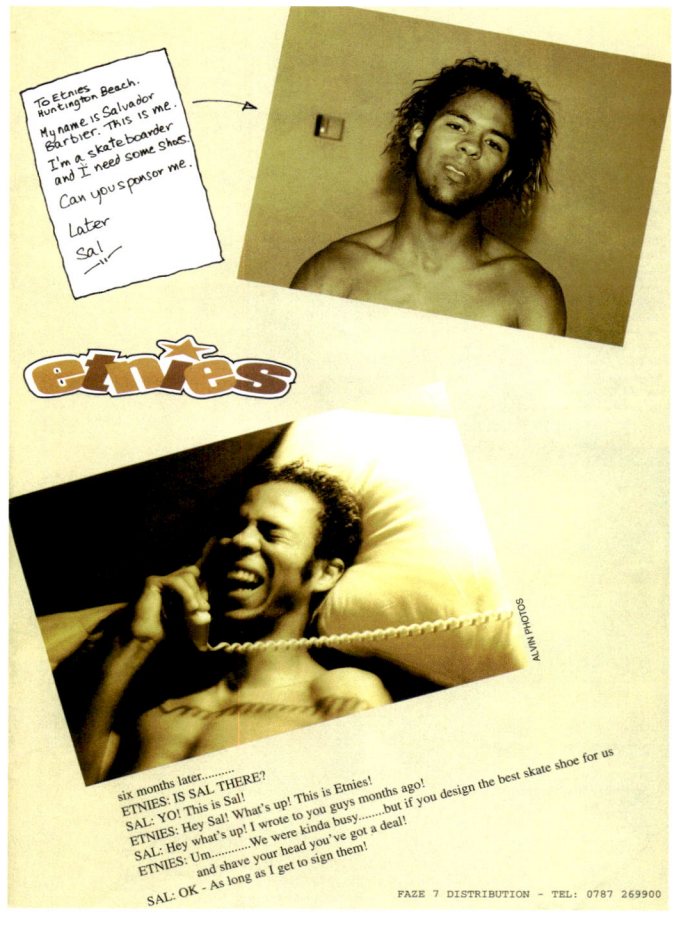

The Sal 23 model for Salvador Lucas Barbier (SLB) remains the best-selling Etnies pro shoe of all time. Pierre André Senizergues vividly recalls his first encounter with Barbier at an industry trade show in San Diego in 1991, where Etnies was debuting their unconventional Rap model, an all suede shoe with eccentric colorways. "We had bright red and blue, so they definitely stood out on the streets," Pierre André said.

"Sal walked into our booth, went straight for the Raps and said 'These are dope!' Right then and there I said to myself 'This guy's got it, he definitely knows what's cool!'"

Before long, Sal Barbier officially joined the Etnies pro team. According to Pierre André, SLB's feedback played a major role in many design decisions, especially during the rise of all-suede, low cut shoes with triple stitching in crucial places. So it is to no surprise that the Sal 23 follows this successful formula.

TWENTY-THREE

For added flair, the shoe featured the enigmatic number 23 stitched into the upper heel section, which caused speculations in the skate scene. Next to Michael Jordan, the number has been attributed to the secret Illuminati society in sci-fi author Robert Anton Wilson's books. Sal Barbier even founded the Twenty-three Skateboard company in 1995.

What is the connection? "I think that Sal will have his own story about this, but he had been using the number in school, and it was also a nod to [Michael] Jordan,'" said Pierre André.

Frequent re-releases of the original have been highly popular among modern-day skaters. In 2008, Etnies teamed up with In4mation, a Hawaiian-based skateboard and street wear store to release a cross-branded Etnies/In4mation Sal 23 shoe. The new shoe's insole also features the logo for Sal Barbier's skateboard store in Hollywood called SLB.

STOMPIN' IN MY AIRWALK ONES

In 1993, Plan B's second video *Virtual Reality* took technical tricks to bigger obstacles at more speed. And one of the main shoe choices of that era was the Airwalk One model, released in Fall 1993. The One became an iconic shoe of its time worn by the likes of Pat Duffy and Danny Way, as well as Tony Hawk.

In terms of design, the Airwalk One built on the successful Mid-cut "Heater" model released by Airwalk as early as 1989, as well as the highly popular mid-cut "NTS" (short for "Not The Same") model that came out in 1992. Another popular Airwalk model at the time was the "86" – basically the One's vulcanized twin.

KIDS HOOKED ON ACID HOUSE MUSIC

The enthusiasm for Airwalk Ones received a heavy blow when "ravers" – kids hooked on acid house music and all-night parties – picked up Ones by the hundreds and incorporated them into their outfits together with just the kind of balloony pants that skaters had just abandoned. As the One's signature white stripe became a staple of rave culture, skaters started leaning towards shoes in a similar cut, but with solid colorways, like the Airwalk Jim shoe.

ELEPHANT STRENGTH SHOES: SALMAN AGAH

One of the most influential street skaters of the early 90s, Salman Agah broke down the barriers between skating "goofy" and "regular" by showing the world that basically any trick can also be done opposite-footed, or "switch stanced."

In 1993, *Thrasher* magazine named Salman Agah their Skater of the Year and Vans awarded the pioneer with his own signature model. The shoe came packaged in a box embellished with a series of elephants engaged in a trunk-to-tail round dance.

The Elephant logo on the tongue was indeed an apt symbol – these were strong shoes, nearly unbreakable, mainly because of the prominent soft rubber ollie pads surrounding the entire toe area of the vulcanized outsoles on both sides (of course – they're meant for skating switch stanced).

Street skaters at the time nicknamed the shoe the "camel toe" in a humorous take on Salman Agah's classic camel board graphics on Real Skateboards. And if you watch closely, the first Salman shoe was a popular choice among skaters in the first Girl Skateboards video, *Goldfish*.

You can actually sign a petition on the Internet to make Vans bring the first generation Agah model back. "Those shoes were the sh#t," the petition reads, and at a time when footwear companies are resorting to the classics for new ideas, the Salman Agah may have a lot to offer.

A MAJOR CAREER BOOST

For Steve Caballero, the success of his signature shoes provided a tremendous career boost. When Vans hired a new CEO in 1993, Caballero called for another sit-down. "At this time, since my shoes had been such a huge success for Vans, I was able to negotiate a new contract with a better royalty deal".

"That was the time the Lo-CAB came out, which was an even lower cut design [than the HALF CAB]. I'd have to say the CAB 4 and 5 models were the peak of my shoe sales and I sold the most at that time because of its mainstream distribution."

SKATEBOARD ICONS TO THE RESCUE

Around 1995, it became apparent that Airwalk's throne was shaking. With a lot of the new shoe companies such as DC Shoes and éS enjoying great success with their focus on pro shoe models, Airwalk finally turned out two signature shoe models in 1995.

Good news was that the flailing giant had a number of trump cards up its sleeves, including big name pro riders such as Jason Lee and Tony Hawk, who were still under contract.

Allegedly, the main reason why Tony Hawk and Jason Lee received their own pro shoes was their loyalty to the brand. After all, Tony Hawk had been the first pro rider Airwalk had ever sponsored. Both Tony Hawk and Jason Lee were given direct design influence on their pro-models, with Tony Hawk's vert skating background clearly reflected in the toe section of his shoe, while Jason Lee brought in added pizzaz with blue suede as a material.

Jason Lee's shoe was loosely based on the highly popular Airwalk Sorry model, preferred by both Pat Duffy and Danny Way at the time. And although Jason Lee's shoe initially sold well, by the third pay check, the excitement had already worn off, as Lee told *Transworld Skateboarding Magazine*.

Tony Hawk Series

A tribute to one of the best skateboarders ever. The *Tony Hawk* signature shoe. Now available at a finer skate shop near you.

PHAT LACES AND PUFFY TOUNGES

In terms of additional flair, there's only so much you can do to spruce up your sneakers. Painting on your kicks is one option, puffing up the tongues is another. Sooner or later, all efforts towards standing out from the rest of the pack end up at the laces. And next to opting for crazy colors and patterns, what else is there to do but making them extra "phat"?

"Phat laces" of course have a history outside of skateboarding. One that goes back to the early days of hip-hop and breakdancing. The old "Beat Street" and "Wild Style" days. Back then, extra large laces in garish neon colors were all the hype, mostly because they created insane strobe effects when your feet windmilled through the air! The other option was to wear your old school sneaks "with no shoe string in 'em," like Run DMC. But that could be dangerous.

So when skateboarding culture as a whole took a turn towards a more urban overall feel in the early 90s, old school sneakers and fat laces made a comeback. Wearing the two together signaled that you not only were in touch with the latest skate fashions, but that you also had roots – like, deep – in hip-hop culture.

Before long, skateboard footwear companies abandoned the "Regular Joe" laces of the 80s in favor of fatter shoestrings. And with skaters becoming ever more sensitive to color-coordinating their outfits – like fitted baseball caps – most companies have been including an extra pair of laces in different colorways.

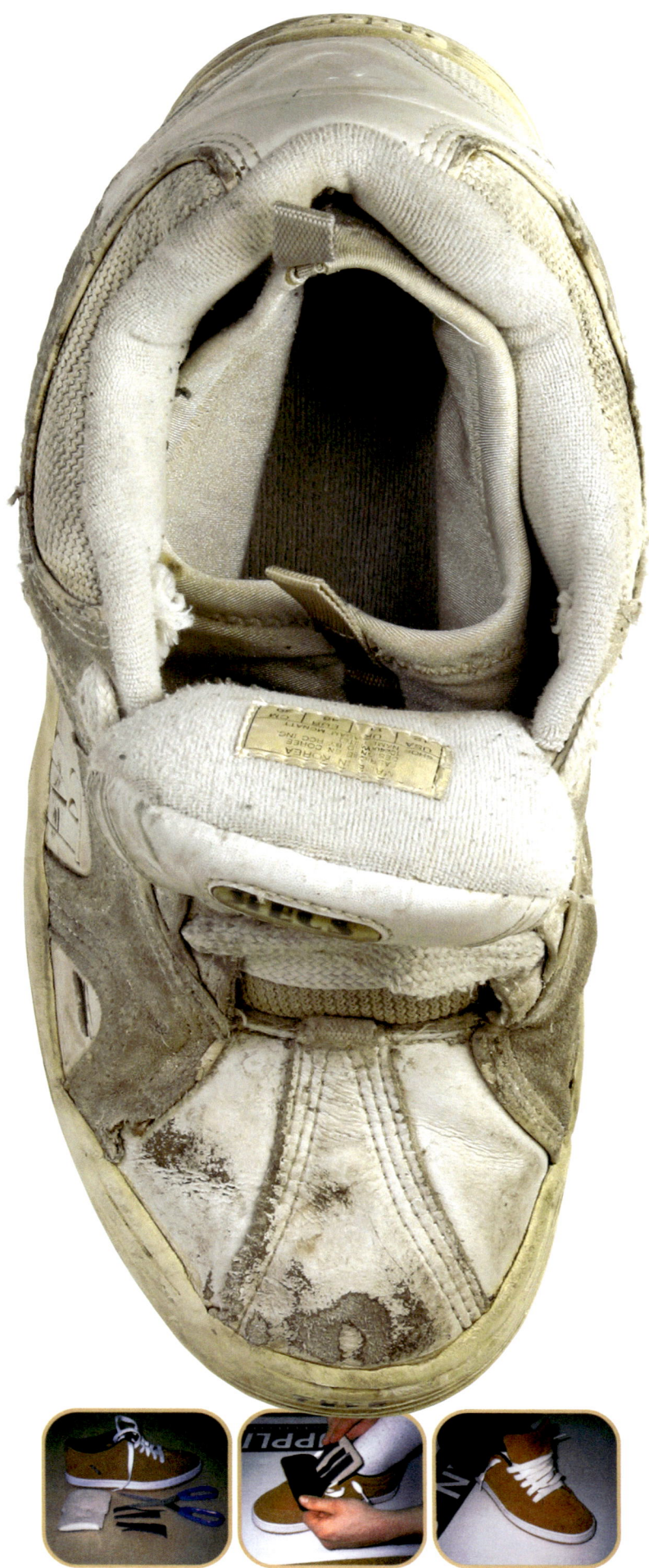

PUFFY TOUNGES

How about stuffing a folded sock under the tongue of your shoes to make them look more "puffy"? Skateboarders in the early 90s were "puffing" up their tongues with anything they could get their hands on – socks, kitchen sponges and, for a more refined version, the severed tongue of an old shoe, held in place by griptape. No slippin'!

Sometimes someone would bail at the local skate spot, and not one, but two cut off tongues would come tumbling out of a single shoe.

As moronic as they may sound today, Puffy Tongues are a phenomenon best viewed in the context of their own time. For once, hip-hop exerted a heavy influence on the stylistic and musical preferences of skaters in the early 90s.

In order to be "fresh," you needed to wear your shoes loosely with the tongues protruding visibly from under the cuffs of your baggy jeans or cargo pants.

Additional research revealed that puffed-up sneakers had already been sighted as early as 1981 on Washington DC projects basketball courts, namely a combination of rolled up "jelly roll" socks with Puma Clydes. One technique consisted of cutting the stitching at the level of the first lace hole to widen the shoe, then "rolling" the sock around the arch of the foot several times, holding it in place with a safety pin. You could also simply fold the socks under the tongue with the laces worn loose.

THE PUFFIER YOUR TONGUE

Footwear manufacturers soon realized the large demand for puffy-tongued shoes and have been making their kicks puffier right out of the box since then. For proof, just compare the tongues on, say, the HALF CABS with the first Muska signature model on Circa. That's evolution.

Speaking of Muska, this was also the time when stash pockets built into the tongue became popular, often concealed by overlapping material to provide a hiding spot during police searches. Stash pockets proved a big hit with "urban"-minded skaters – they are still around in select models today – and a considerable status symbol: The puffier your tongue, the bigger your stash. Puts a whole different spin on the term "rolling fat"…

Right when the trend was dying down, the ultimate gadget hit the shelves: Inflatable air cushions slipped under the tongues for adjustable phatness.

THE MAN WHO SOLE'D THE WORLD

Former professional skateboarder Steve Rocco started his own company World Industries in 1988 by giving the established "Big Five" skateboard brands a good kick to the shin. Nothing was sacred, no one was safe. Rocco's guerrilla tactics included drafting competitor's team riders, running controversial ads featuring violence and pornography and creating ironic takes on the competition's board graphics.

Soon enough, the former menace had become an industry magnate in his own right, and by 1994 Steve Rocco was at the helm of his own full-fledged skateboard empire. So why not start a shoe company?

Rocco started DuFFS together with professional skater Rodney Mullen, who contributed his extensive technical expertise to designing the shoes. Throughout his career, Mullen would also make decisive contributions to the design of skateboard trucks and skateboard decks.

As the first DuFFS ad revealed in signature Rocco irony: "Rodney Mullen spent hundreds of hours agonizing over rubber outsole compounds, split leather configurations and N.B.S. ratings in order to bring you the most advanced skate shoe ever produced. The results: all that could be decided on was this nifty logo."

They did finally decide on a sole for their all-suede, low-cut shoes. Easily recognizable by their own distinct waffle sole pattern, DuFFS had come up with a pattern that somewhat resembled corn on the cob, thus the name "Cobnobbler" for one of the early models.

STIRRING THINGS UP

Never known to shy away from the occasional dose of controversy, Rocco kept things interesting with elaborately produced video commercials that included a visit at the "DuFFS factory" – depicting Nazi guards towering over forced laborers – and a documentary style piece on the highly pollutant shoe production process.

The DuFFS team featured all stars such as Willy Santos, Ronnie Creager and Steve Olson next to Kareem Campbell, who broke new ground with his KCK model released in 1995. The KCK presented a departure from the established all-suede deck shoe formula towards a bulkier cut shoe that leaned more towards a tennis or basketball shoe.

With hits like the KCK or Matt Hensley's Gambler model, DuFFS enjoyed a solid following in the skate scene. However, Steve Rocco allegedly sold DuFFS the minute DC Shoes arrived on the set, deciding "to graciously step aside for the new champ." DuFFS continued under new leadership and was finally discontinued in 2004.

The End? Not quite – in March 2008, a new company named DuFFS 93 Ltd. purchased the global rights to the DuFFS brand and is working on a re-launch at the time of this writing.

HARDER, BETTER, FASTER, STRONGER - DC SHOES

DC Shoe Co.

Danny Way
SIGNATURE MODEL

DEALERS INQUIRIES
CIRCUS DISTRIBUTION
800-886-8225

To speak of the DC Shoe Company is to talk in superlatives. The footwear brand from Vista, California went from barging onto the scene in 1994 to establishing themselves as one of skateboarding's "Big Three" shoe firms in the blink of an eye. Revenues were already about $7 million in 1995, more than double the previous year's.

At a time when pro tours consisted of weeks of sleeping in the tour van, DC Shoes flew their entire dozen-strong pro team across the world on their elaborately staged "Super Tours." When it was considered okay for pro skaters to film their entire video part on the same picnic table, DC Shoes built the "Mega Ramp" for Danny Way's 1997 highest air world record. And when street skating seemed to be facing extinction due to increasing prosecution in the public realm, DC launched the Rob Dyrdek Skate Plaza campaign to keep things alive at a grass roots level.

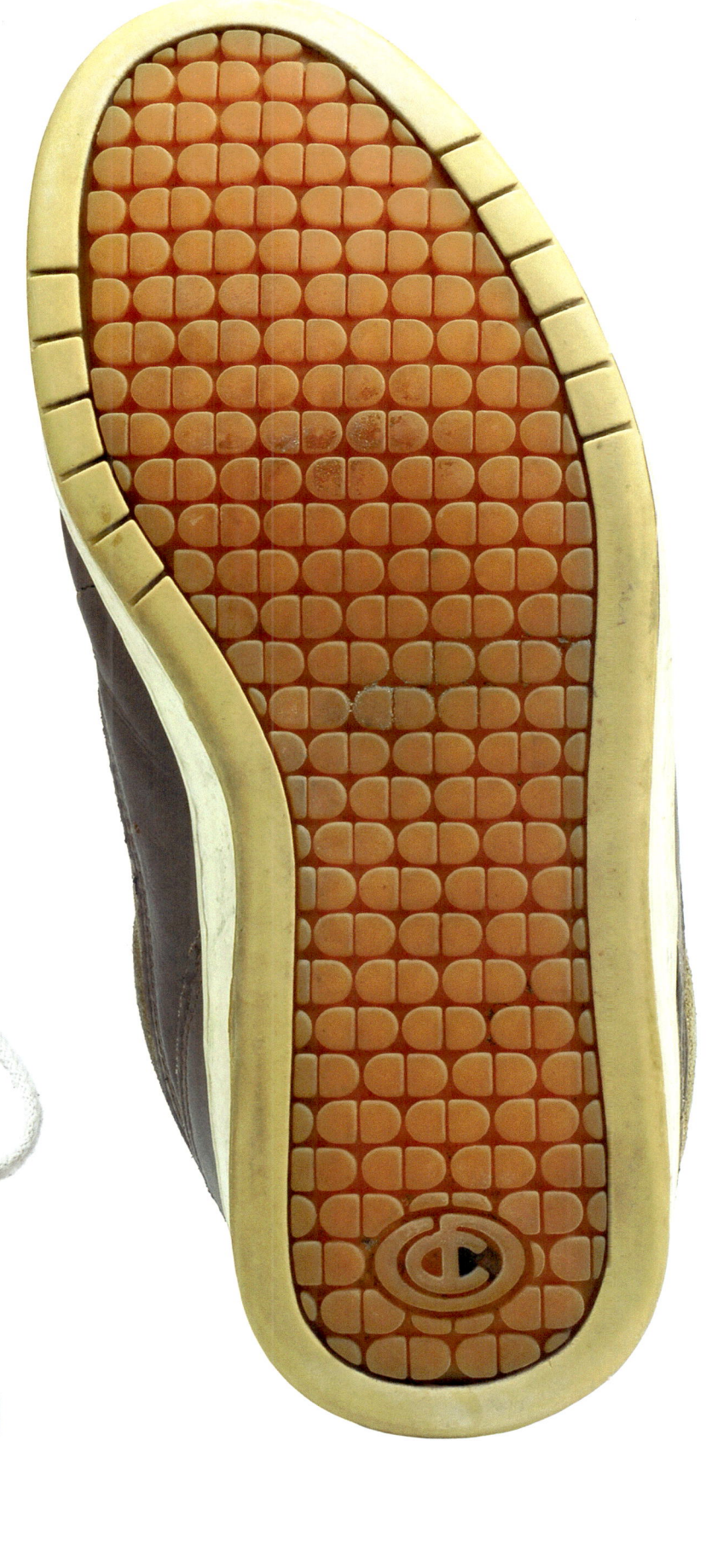

COMING IN HOT

Straight out the gate, DC Shoes made a name for themselves by doing things their own way. Pro shoes were already a major force in the skate industry at the time, but no one had yet based an entire company on a line-up of signature shoes. DC's first edition of pro models consisted of Danny Way, Colin McKay, Rob Dyrdek and Rudy Johnson, who needless to say are some of the most influential skateboarders of all time.

On the business side of things, designer Ken Block and Danny Way's brother Damon built the company out of Droors Clothing - reflected in the letters "DC" in the company name - with a startup financial boost from Merrill Lynch financial services.

DC Shoes received help in getting things off the ground from Pierre André Senizergues of Etnies fame, who handled production and manufacturing of DC's first collection. "It was my intention to help them because Damon's brother is a skateboarder and he was going to push the company," said Pierre.

Under the banner of one of the most widely recognized brand logos in skateboarding - the "Star Logo" created by DC artist Dave Kinsey - DC Shoes continued to break new ground in many aspects. Over the years, their strong initial pro team was expanded into what might have been the best company pro team of all time, including riders such as Rick Howard, Mike Carroll, Caine Gayle, Moses Itkonen, Keith Hufnagel, Scott Johnson and Carl Shipman.

In terms of shoe design, DC can be credited with taking skateboard shoes into the realm of performance-oriented athletic footwear with a wide range of industry firsts including:

- **Elaborate materials.** DC Shoes pioneered the use of novel materials such as Nubuck leather and entirely synthetic uppers as seen on the Syntax model. Standouts also include the H2 Zero shoe, a water resistant shoe with an upper made of wolverine.

- **Athletic features.** Reinforced midsoles, shock-resistant air pockets, breathable venting, encased laces, laceless shoes – you name it, DC Shoes brought it to skateboarding.

- **Laser etching.** In search of interesting new finishes, DC introduced laser etching of patterns into the shoe's upper, featured on collaborations with renowned artists and designers.

- **Limited edition craze.** With their 1998 limited edition shoe in collaboration with New York City store Supreme, DC brought the sneakerhead phenomenon into skating.

A major force behind DC's rise lay in the fact that club fashion wholeheartedly embraced the Syntax and Boxer models around 1996, sending sales skyrocketing across the world, especially in Europe. Throughout the 1990s, sales growth at DC Shoes was in the triple digits. In the year 2000, the company's annual revenue reached $60 million.

Over the years, DC Shoes have also won the hearts of numerous celebrities and rock stars who have worn the shoes on stage and in films, while some even collaborated on limited edition shoes. Here is a list of celebs that have been touched by the power of DC Shoes (name drop alert!): Goldie, Beastie Boys, Primus, Red Hot Chili Peppers, Sonic Youth, Rage Against the Machine, , as well as actors Brad Pitt, Jennifer Aniston and Adam Sandler, to name but a few.

INTO THE FUTURE

The new Millennium proved an important turning point for DC. While long-time team members Rick Howard and Mike Carroll had moved on to start their own company, Lakai Limited Footwear in 1999, it was time for a new generation of pros to shine. In 2000, Stevie Williams and Josh Kalis received their first pro shoe models, while riders like Anthony Van Engelen and Brian Wenning carried on the torch.

At the same time, the company successfully branched out into sports such as snowboarding, motocross, rally car racing, surfing and BMX, while staying true to its skating roots. In Spring of 2004, DC Shoes agreed to be acquired by surfboarding and apparel company Quiksilver, Inc. and Ken Block and Damon Way remained in charge of running DC as a wholly-owned subsidiary.

Since then, DC has kept pushing the envelope of what is possible on a skateboard with new editions of Danny Way's Mega Ramp that culminated in the historic jump over the Great Wall of China in 2005. The Mega Ramp has since then become a fixture at the X-Games, and Danny Way has since upped the ante by backflipping and 360° flipping the monstrous ramp, while adding on to his high air record.

In February 2008, the company launched dcskateboarding.tv as a new audio-visual forum to display the skills of their team – entirely free of charge to visitors. And with more and more skate plazas popping up, DC Shoes make sure that skaters will always have a home.

Overall, it is this ongoing commitment to skateboarding that has helped DC Shoes achieve a growth that is unparalleled in the history of the sport.

DUKES SHOES

Everyone primarily knows World Industries as a skateboard hardware company. But at one point in World's history, the company from El Segundo, California was home to not one, but three shoe companies: Axion, DuffS and Dukes Shoes.

The headline pro on Dukes was Jeremy Wray, who designed the shoes with an eye for functionality and resilience. Joining him on the pro team were Pat Chanita, a rookie at the time, and later Chad Knight of H-Street/Evol fame.

Aimed primarily at the function-before-fashion set, Dukes shoes faired well initially and even stayed under the umbrella of World Industries – or Dwindle Distribution – after owner Steve Rocco sold DuFFs shoes.

Dukes folded in 1998 due to falling demand, pressure from new brands and the overpowering ascendancy of the Big Three shoe brands.

SIMPLY THE BEST

Simple Shoes from Los Angeles are possibly the single most understated skate shoe company of all time. With their low-budget quarter-page ads in the back sections of magazines and total focus on the shoes themselves instead of hype and fanfare, Simple's name summed up their entire concept: simply shoes – that's all.

In the years after their launch in 1991, the all-suede OS Sneaker – a strikingly classic skate shoe at a time otherwise marked by overly technical footwear – would be their only shoe model for a long time. Nevertheless, Simple Shoes enjoyed a solid following among skaters who wanted a sturdy, well-constructed shoe at an affordable price. Simple shoes were also endorsed by a fluctuating team including upcoming street skaters such as Richard Mulder and Daniel Castillo, and for some time even skate icon Mark Gonzales.

Believe it or not, Simple Shoes are still available today and are now part of the sustainability-driven Decker Outdoor Corporation, together with brands such as UGG boots and Teva sandals.

HOOK UPS - KICK ASS SHOES

Professional skateboarder Jeremy Klein pushed the limits of street skating as one of the most influential figures of the 90s. He also left a lasting legacy by introducing Japanese animation style cartoons, video game characters and martial arts to skateboard culture.

Building on the success of his iconic 1991 "Dream Girl" graphics on World Industries - depicting a stylized Japanese "Manga" character - Jeremy Klein started his own clothing company, Hook-Ups, out of Birdhouse Skateboards in 1994.

At first, Hook-Ups was mostly a medium for Klein to play around with Japanese animation designs and to "hook up" his friends Jim Greco and Willy Santos with free stuff. But Hook-Ups soon became far more than a hobby. The graphics filled a huge demand for Japanese animation styles. And not only were the shirts literally flying off the shelves, the company also did well when Klein decided to introduce Hook-Ups Shoes in 1995.

With ads built around video game scenes - such as the Street Fighter II rendition that showed Klein getting kicked in the face by martial artist Mine Tran - and the most elaborate packaging of its time - Hook-Ups Shoes became yet another outlet for Jeremy Klein's lasting influence on skateboarding.

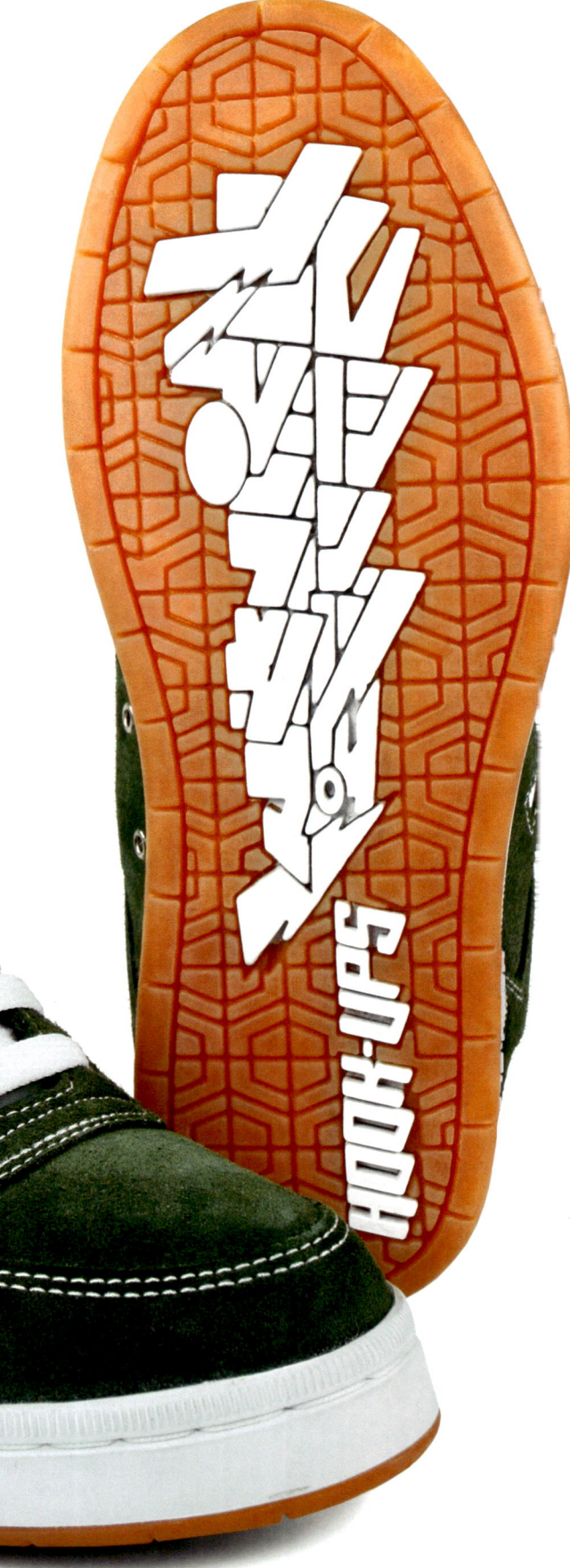

MINE TRAN CAN KICK YOUR ASS.

HOOK-UPS
SHOES FOR KARATE & SKATEBOARDING

SPECIAL POLICE

HOOK-UPS PO BOX 2820-161 TORRANCE CA 90509-2820

éS-PECIALLY FOR YOU

Skaters have always liked a touch of class combined with exclusive designs. To fill this niche in the skate footwear sector, Sole Technology in 1995 introduced éS Footwear.

"When we created éS it was to cater to the elite skateboarders, the Eric Kostons and Ronnie Craegers, and Chad Muskas and Aarto Saris out there," says Don Brown.

The launch of éS came right at the onset of the big 90s skate shoe boom. "At this point more competitors were coming onto the market, so it was really challenging to come out with something a bit more sophisticated," said Don Brown. "Our concept with éS was against the grain at first, with a bit more of an athletic design, while adding a lot more features to the shoe."

Aiming for a more advanced, more polished overall finish, éS introduced a number of new features like shock absorbing air pads and new materials to shoes like their Koston 1 model, which Don Brown co-designed. "That one made a big difference with its mesh upper and use of Nubuck [leather], which was really unique compared to what was out there at the time."

Other hit éS models include the Accel, originally released in 1995. Pierre André comments: "The success of the Accel is amazing. Since day one, it never stopped being a hot seller."

Other innovations include a secret stash pocket in the tongue of the original Chad Muska model, true to the company's motto of aiming at the high rollers in skateboarding.

« view point> east vertical identity> contour «color breakdown active»
«construction breakdown active»

contour « color breakdown <outer <inner <sole <sole
navy grey white grey

és footwear
po box 89 huntington beach california 92648
714 722 9669
714 722 9656
« source location data
«intentional use display: tom penny »

ronnie creager
eric koston
chad muska
tom penny
paul sharpe
bob burnquist
sal barbier
714 722 9669
catalog posters stickers

footwear
és

THE BEST SKATE SHOE OF ALL TIME? THE éS KOSTON1

Whenever skateboarders talk about The Best Skate Shoe of All Time, Eric Koston's first pro model shoe – the Koston1 released by éS in 1997 – is almost guaranteed to make the Top5. Designed by Eric Koston himself, this highly skateable and flexible shoe became an instant hit with skaters worldwide, even though it came at a much higher price point – especially in Europe – than shoes endorsed by less prestigious skaters/companies.

While the original release did not feature an air pocket in the shoe's heel, éS soon followed up with a history-making upgrade that did. This was a big deal, since Nike Inc. had held the exclusive patent on air systems in shoes for ten years at the time, after the technology had premiered in the 1987 Nike Air Max shoe. When the door opened, an updated Koston K1 became the first-ever skateboard-specific shoe with a visible air pocket.

"That was by far the best one in my mind. A lot of good times and radical shredding went down in those! It's hard to top an original," Koston recently said on the Crailtap website. Eric's former team mate Paul Rodriguez also feels a special connection to the shoe: "Probably fo nostalgia purposes and memories, the Koston 1 is my favorite shoe. It goes back to the time when I was coming up and it's connected to a lot of memories from those days, " Rodriguez said. "And they just brought it back."

In 2008, Eric Koston's current shoe sponsor, Lakai, brought back the classic Koston1's as a re-release. "We started talking about bringing Eric's original shoe back about a year ago," said Lakai's brand manager, Kelly Bird. "Our idea was to bring it back and really work on the tooling so it fit your foot better."

Was this possible because Koston owns the rights to the shoe's design? "You can't trademark shoe designs," Bird explained. "That's why every company makes pretty much the same ten shoes already. Not really sure what éS thinks about it, but the original design was his concept so technically I guess it's his intellectual property."

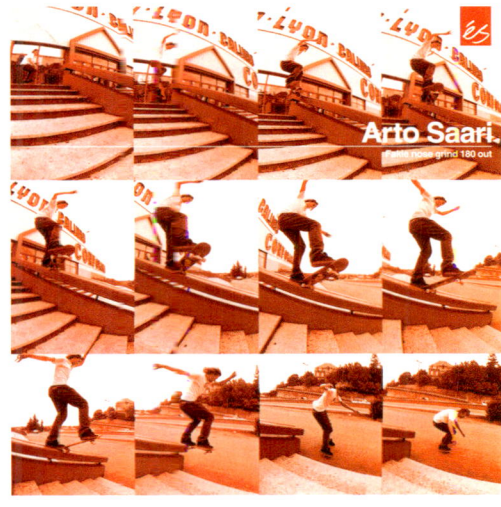

THE KIDS IN EMERICA

The Emerica brand was born as an answer to troubled times. Pierre André Senizergues had been designing and distributing Etnies shoes in the Unites States but when a European shoe conglomerate with American backers bought the Etnies brand name in 1995, Pierre André had to come up with something. Quick.

With Etnies possible gone forever, Pierre André started Emerica, derived from "Etnies America". He also started éS Footwear, as well as ThirtyTwo under the umbrella of Sole Technology Inc.

Emerica took over right were Etnies had left off, straight out the box, so to say. The situation did not last, though, and a few months later, Pierre André bought the rights to the Etnies name and has been producing both brands since.

The influence of the team has always been high: "Everyone who rides for Emerica is into different things. Some like high tops, some like low tops or people like Ed Templeton, with whom I designed a shoe, with want all-vegan, synthetic materials in a functional shoe," explained Sole Technology's Don Brown.

Ed Templeton fondly remembered the first shoe when he was asked about his all-time favorite skate shoes: "I would have to say the Templeton 1, and the current one, 'the Transit' with my name on it!" Templeton said. "I only can comment on my shoes because that's all I wear. I'm sure that my contribution to skateboard shoes does not come close to the 'best' category in most people's minds…"

What are the enduring design characteristics of a skate-specific shoe? "Skateboarding is one of the most innovative and intense activities, so you need the right amount of durability, flexibility and impact resistance without sacrificing any of the board control," said Don Brown. The formula seems to work and Emerica is still going strong today.

SHOE WARS

Actually, the otherwise usually quiet company made headlines in 2008 by bringing back Marc Johnson's premiere pro model, the Marc Johnson 1 under the moniker O.G. 1. People in the industry speculate that the move might come as a reaction to Lakai's re-release of the Koston 1, originally designed by Emerica's sister company, éS.

Emerica insisted in ads for the O.G.1 that it is "An Emerican Original" and announced a release of the classic for early 2009. After cross-branding and art shoes, re-mixes of classic kicks appear to be the next big thing in skate footwear.

ALL STAR SKATE SHOES

During the early 90s street skating boom, skaters started looking for more sturdy, low-top shoe. Once again, Converse delivered with a traditional classic: The all suede Pro Leather model.

The Pro Leather's were the preferred Converse for basketball-hall-of-famer Julius Winfield Erving II of the Philadelphia 76ers. Within the skateboard community the shoe was just called by Erving´s nickname "Dr. J's." Street legend Natas Kapuas used to skate them early on: "I bought all those shoes – Dr. J's, then the team series."

But despite the shoe's growing popularity, Converse chose to play it subtle in terms of advertising. Instead of launching an all-out skate-oriented campaign, Converse ran basket-ball-specific ads in *Thrasher* magazine in December 1994.

Another popular choice among skaters included the Converse "One Star", a modified version of the Chuck Taylor first produced in the 70s. The One Star was a low-cut suede sneaker with a vulcanized outsole and padding around the ankle. In the 90s, the One Star's popularity literally shot up over night, ready to be skated right out the box. In 1999, Converse released the EZ Chuck, also a low-top, but without the big star logo.

SUBTLE ENTRY

This below the radar approach would prove a highly successful way for major shoe corporations to target the skateboard market. As history would prove again and again, skateboarders on the whole tend to walk away when big corporations try to cater to them directly. At the same time, its perfectly okay when skaters "discover" a non-skate specific shoe such as the one called "Dr J" by the skateboard community and appropriate it into their outfits.

Converse added some subtle promotional power by sending free boxes of shoes to core skate companies such as L.A.-based Girl Skateboards. As Eric Koston reminisced about his early-90s shoe choices: "The 'Dr. J's' were probably my favorite. Probably because we used to get boxes of them sent to Girl back when we were all skating in them. Some of the best things in life are free, right?"

Koston's team mates Rick Howard and Guy Mariano could also frequently be seen skating "Dr. J's" in magazines and videos, making the iconic star-logo a staple at street spots around the globe. Mariano also became the first pro rider on the Converse skate team in 1995.

SUPERSTAR SKATERS

With legendary street skater Guy Mariano as a strong foundation, Converse continued to build their team over the coming years, adding riders such as Chany Jeanguinen, Felix Arguelles and Kenny Anderson to the line-up. Meanwhile, the Pro-Leather and Superstar models remained at the center of their team's shoe choices.

Soon enough, Converse applied their expertise in the footwear business to creating their own skate-specific offering. In 1998, Converse introduced the Cs-Pro1 and Sublime models, followed a year later by Kenny Anderson's pro model. While the skate shoes retained the iconic five-pointed star logo, they also offered a next-generation take on proven design features.

Converse flexed their production muscle with a re-modeled, skate-oriented sole featuring different durameter rubber in key locations, with harder rubber used around the heel and hypothenar areas for shock resistance.

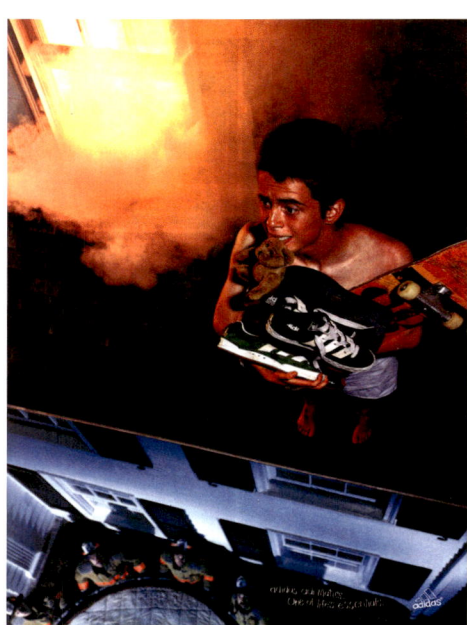

THE AGE OF PERFORMANCE

For the heads at adidas, the retro-trend of the early 90s was a wake-up call. In a short span of time, the brand had established itself in one of the most critical-minded scenes on the planet without the slightest marketing effort – time to step back into the game.

In 1996, adidas re-entered skateboarding under the umbrella of "Sport Performance", a division of products that included BMX, skate and other types of sports. The skateboard branch was spearheaded by legends Mark Gonzales and Lance Mountain and featured a colorful and creative team that made for a nice ironic contrast to the "performance" aspect. The irony was also part of the advertisement campaign, which made fun of the athletic orientation of the brand.

Gonz was the center of the team and a natural fit to the brand. Ever since he was a child, Mark had an association with the Performance part of adidas. His personal connection to the brand wasn't enough to metamorphose him into a prototypical adidas athlete. In an incident at an annual sales convention at the adidas headquarters, Mark gave a short demonstration of his creative approach to things.

The company had invited its star athletes to meet and greet the general public and its stockholders. As the Gonz was about to be introduced as an athlete, he skated out on stage with tennis star Martina Hingis on his shoulders. The audience was shocked, but not as much as the delegates of the company, who feared he was going to drop and "damage" their valuable athlete.

When he designed his first signature shoe on adidas, he suggested it to be made of wood: "I wanted wood to be placed inside the shoe and rubber around it to give it some soul," explained Mark. "So you have wood on the board and wood inside your shoe. It would be more natural; you could feel the soul of the tree." Unfortunately, adidas decided not to produce the wooden shoe.

The "real" Performance line consisted of rather technical footwear that wasn't popular enough to gain a strong foothold in skateboarding. "Some of the shoes were too advanced for the time or for the average skateboarder", says marketing communication manager Jess Weinstein. "It took some time before we learned that instead of reinventing the wheel, sometimes it's better to coast on a perfectly good set of wheels that work."

GLOBE: AUSTRALIAN SKATE SHOES

Skateboarding and surf culture are HUGE in Australia. Both sports enjoy solid roots on the continent and have been flourishing for decades now. Beyond its dynamic scene, Australia is also home to a self-sustained skate and surf industry. And since both sports evolved side-by-side in Australia – much like they did in the cradle of skateboarding, California – it's not unusual for companies to cater to surfers and skaters at the same time.

ADVANCED FUNCTIONALITY

From the start, Australian surf and skate shoe company Globe targeted both scenes. Launched in 1994 by former Australian professional skateboarders, the brothers Matt, Steven, and Peter Hill in Melbourne, Globe soon became one of the major companies in the Australian scene.

Early team riders included Australian powerhouses such as Tas and Ben Pappas, as well as Matt Mumford. In the US, Chet Thomas and Rodney Mullen became the company's signature pro riders, who exerted tremendous influence on the design of their pro shoes.

GLOBAL TAKEOVER

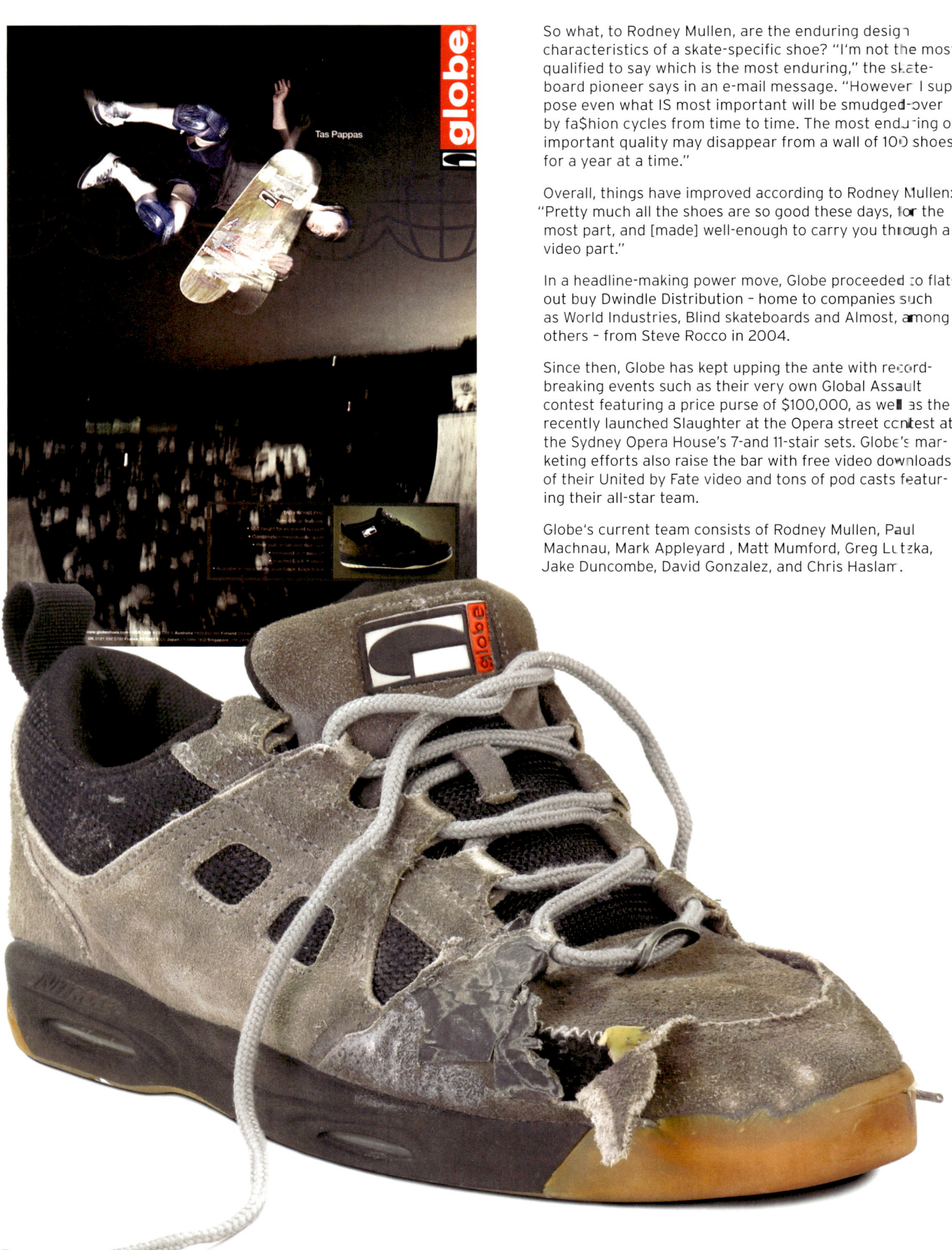

So what, to Rodney Mullen, are the enduring design characteristics of a skate-specific shoe? "I'm not the most qualified to say which is the most enduring," the skateboard pioneer says in an e-mail message. "However I suppose even what IS most important will be smudged-over by fa$hion cycles from time to time. The most enduring or important quality may disappear from a wall of 100 shoes for a year at a time."

Overall, things have improved according to Rodney Mullen: "Pretty much all the shoes are so good these days, for the most part, and [made] well-enough to carry you through a video part."

In a headline-making power move, Globe proceeded to flat-out buy Dwindle Distribution – home to companies such as World Industries, Blind skateboards and Almost, among others – from Steve Rocco in 2004.

Since then, Globe has kept upping the ante with record-breaking events such as their very own Global Assault contest featuring a price purse of $100,000, as well as the recently launched Slaughter at the Opera street contest at the Sydney Opera House's 7-and 11-stair sets. Globe's marketing efforts also raise the bar with free video downloads of their United by Fate video and tons of pod casts featuring their all-star team.

Globe's current team consists of Rodney Mullen, Paul Machnau, Mark Appleyard, Matt Mumford, Greg Lutzka, Jake Duncombe, David Gonzalez, and Chris Haslam.

Flipped, ripped and taped by Rodney "The Mutt" Mullen himself.

DVS - DOING THINGS YOUR OWN WAY

In retrospect, the year 1995 might have been to skateboard footwear what 1848 was to the Wild West: an all-out gold rush. Almost a dozen new shoe companies arrived on the scene that year, mostly founded out of the sheer realization that starting your own footwear label had never been easier.

DVS Shoes was launched in 1995 by professional skateboarder Tim Gavin and skate shop owner Kevin Dunlap. "We felt that there was room for a company that did things a little differently," said Tim Gavin. DVS Shoes set up shop in Torrance, California.

DIFFERENT, ENTIRELY

The meaning of the three letters 'DVS'? "It honestly doesn't stand for anything," Tim Gavin points out. From the very beginning, the initial commitment to doing things differently applied to the company's shoes as well as the team.

"We had guys riding for us that were a little different," said Gavin, pointing to the company's original line-up that included thoroughbred street skaters such as Sean Sheffey, Jeron Wilson and Chico Brenes instead of big name vert riders or contest-winning athlete types that were headlining the rosters of other shoe brands. "From the beginning we have focussed on providing quality and styles that appeal to skateboarders," Gavin explained. "My all-time favourite is actually my first pro shoe," Gavin said. "It's a very casual design that still lets you feel your board under your feet and also one of the better selling shoes that's been around for more than ten years now."

LISTENING TO YOUR TEAM

Although the popularity of skateboarding has been surging as of late, appealing to a mass audience is not an option for DVS. "I see the market headed for a complete 360°," Gavin says. "A lot of brands made the wrong decision by catering to the big box accounts, and we have kept focussed on the core market, the true skaters."

At the same time, DVS have kept their healthy scepticism towards new gimmicks and trends. "You see a lot of vulcanized shoes on everyone's lines these days," Gavin says, "but I think that the casual style of a skate shoe is definitely here to stay."

Pro model coming soon. 818 700 2538.

Daewon Song

These shoes were skated by Mr. Daewon "Skate and Create" Song!

EVOLVING SKATEBOARD FOOTWEAR

Tony Magnusson's influence on skateboarding can hardly be overstated. With his company H-Street – and their groundbreaking video releases – the Swedish vert pro helped open the doors for the revolutionary progress of skateboard manoeuvres in the late 1980s and beyond.

When H-Street folded in 1993, Magnusson rounded up a number of his former riders and started Evol Skateboards. On the business side of things, Magnusson was joined by designer Brian Reid, Tony Chen and Dr. C.S. Chen, and together formed Alias Distribution.

In 1995, they launched their own line of shoes under the moniker Evol Casuals. The technically advanced, highly functional shoes became an instant hit and sold well at stores all over. Evol Casuals also enjoyed backing by an all-star skate team, with most riders recruited from Evol Skateboards, while others skated for rival board sponsors.

And this potential for conflict with other board companies was, in a nutshell, the reason for Magnusson and cohorts to pull the plug on Evol Casuals despite its success. In December 1996, Evol footwear rose from the dead under a new name: Osiris Shoes.

THE CULT OF OSIRIS

The original Osiris team consisted of pro skaters Adam McNatt, Tyrone Olson, Gershon Mosley, and Dave Mayhew. The first shoe collection focussed exclusively on four signature pro models. Throughout the years, Osiris owner Tony Magnusson would make the interests of his team riders a priority.

While other shoe companies paid their riders shoe sales royalties only once a year, Magnusson would have the checks in the mail each month and involve his skaters in the design of their shoes.

D3 – A LATE BLOOMER HITS IT BIG

Designing shoes in close cooperation with the team would prove a highly successful strategy for Osiris. Head Designer Brian Reid remembers the genesis of the D3, Dave Mayhew's pro shoe and one of the most successful designs ever: "The D3 is basically a spawn of the relationship between Skateboarding, Hip-hop and Athletic footwear," he said. "There were three people involved: myself as designer, Dave Mayhew as the professional skateboarder and Tony Magnusson as developer," Brian Reid said.

In 1996, the shoe was rather unconventional in all its bulky grandeur, with large plastic lace loops, extra puffy tongue and brightly colored lining added to the sole and upper. "I had a shoe called the Guru that basically is the foundation of the D3," Reid explained.

"Dave and I were really into Hip-Hop, we had the oversized shirt and pants, the baggy skater look was in full effect," Reid said. Looking at what was out on the skate shoe market at the time, Reid and Mayhew decided that all shoes were too thin and looked too much alike. The two also wanted some of the comfort provided by Cross sneakers or basketball shoes, which they wore after skating.

But the shoe was far from a big hit. After six years of below average sales, Osiris was getting ready to drop the D3, when all of a sudden, sales skyrocketed. Practically overnight, the D3 – and the updated version, the D3 2001 – were everywhere.

Sported by skaters and club kids around the globe as well as musicians including Limp Bizkit front man Fred Durst, the D3

became the best-selling shoe in company history and remains the number one best-selling pro model skate shoe of all time.

For the D3's pro rider Dave Mayhew, however, things did not go smoothly. Far from it. "Dave had suffered a serious ankle injury during his skateboard career, and [his board sponsor] enjoi was starting to have some key people depart. Dave Mayhew wanted to go back home to Madison, Wisconsin," Brian Reid said.

"California in Dave's eyes was too fast and superficial," Reid added. "Dave made a good living of the California skateboard dream, and went home. We parted ways, but Dave Mayhew is one of the most humble, talented skaters we have ever worked with."

THE BIG 180°

Osiris continued to progress and evolve their brand. Technical puffy-tongued shoes such as the D3 and accessories like the Osiris backpack with built-in audio speakers had secured the company a solid following among skateboarding's hip-hop segment. With Chris "Dune" Pastras of Stereo fame as their new team manager, Osiris commenced to re-invent their brand by branching out towards skateboarding's punk rock/stretch denim set.

Steadily evolving, Osiris has also successfully branched out into other sports such as Motor FX and martial arts, while Tony Magnusson's son Cheyne carries on the family tradition of excellence in board sports as a pro on the Osiris surf team.

TIME FOR SOME AXION

As a professional skateboarder and owner of various companies, Kareem Campbell brought a lot of style and creativity to skateboarding. Campbell's first pro model shoe, the KCK on DuFFs in 1995, had marked the beginning of a whole new direction in skateboard footwear design. When Kareem started his own skate shoe brand Axion Footwear in 1996, the whole industry was watching.

Axion Footwear broke down the pre-conceived barrier between shoes considered strictly for skateboarding and those meant solely for "chilling". Axion presented a significant break from the norm. Other manufacturers followed suit and dared to make skate shoes more athletic-looking and technically advanced than before Axion had opened the door.

Axion Footwear hit some rocky ground after parting ways with Dwindle Distribution in 2001 and was discontinued a few years later. 2007, the Axion brand name was bought by Newseas Company Limited and the brand is now due for a re-launch.

While other manufacturers relied on the proven formula of all-suede shoes in classic cuts, Kareem Campbell combined a multitude of influences – from sport to srtreet fashion - into a distinct line of shoes that turned out to be highly skatable. The team included Kareem together with Gino Iannucci, Caine Gayle, and Guy Mariano.

...AND AXION

AXION

RUNE GLIFBERG

CREST

axion (ăk'shən) *n*
1. The process of acting or doing.
2. Makers of sport specific footwear.
see *logo*.

RECS IN EFFECT

Recs came into the spotlight on the heels of an elaborate marketing campaign announcing the launch of the new brand with double-page ads several months in advance. Quite an investment, especially weeks before the shoes would actually hit the stores.

With their alien-material-lands-on-Earth theme (slogan: "extraterrestrial performance, superior intelligence") the ads for Recs clearly stood out from what the rest of the industry was doing. The first wave of teasers hit magazines with the tag line "Await Arrival" and the image of a mysterious flying object approaching our blue planet in October 1997.

SHOES FROM OUTER SPACE

A month later, alien-looking containers signalled the "Arrival" of the shoes on what looks like the jungle set of the movie *Predator*.

The final stage was the "Recruitment" of an all-star team consisting of vert innovator Mike Crum and technical street skating pioneer Adam McNatt. They were later joined by Pat Duffy and Fred Gall. All four had pro shoes, designed under the direction of head designer Rob Mars. Mars would also bring guest co-designers such as professional skateboarders Jamie Story and Quy Nguyen on board.

SPECIAL TECHNICAL FEATURES

Technically advanced and performance-oriented, the Recs line introduced a number of technical features including poly-urethane midsoles with shock-absorbent gel pads with PVC windows in the heel.

Despite their elaborate design, all-star team and advanced marketing, the Recs invasion burned out before the new millennium arrived. There were no further transmissions.

TOO MANY FISH IN THE SEA

The shoe boom had turned into a gold rush and a new breed of desperados wanted in on the action. Although newly arrived shoe companies had to face tough competition to stake their claim in an overcrowded market, two factors were working in their favor:

1. Never before had it been easier to start a footwear company.

All you needed was a suitcase filled with $5,000 in cash, the telephone number of a shoe manufacturer (read: sweatshop) and a plane ticket to Bangkok. Three months later, you'd have a container full of shoes in your back yard. Now, whether you knew how to sell those puppies was entirely your problem. But so far, it had been easy.

2. Plagiarism was at an all-time high, since outsourcing meant giving up your coveted design blue prints.

With a bit of extra cash, you could have the machines at the place that makes the hot big brand's skate shoes working for an extra shift over night, making identical shoes – with your company's logo on it.

Anything was fair game for the new breed of copy cat shoe companies – the more successful an original design, the more imitations would flood the market by various manufacturers. Favorites included the Boxer and Syntax models by DC Shoes, the Airwalk VIC´s and of course the low cut Etnies classics such as the Lo-Cut or the Sal Barbier, and the éS Accel.

Fortune hunters such as 2Fish, Bizo, German clothing brand Homeboy and a number of fashion shoe brands or even shoe store house brands entered the market with lots of ideas, few of them original.

The only noteworthy exception among the companies pictured here are Kastel Shoes, who actually sponsored a legit team of skateboarders including Jason Lambert and came with the solid backing of skate industry veterans. But just like all the other forays into skateboarding mentioned here, they reached an untimely demise.

Since then, the situation in the Far East has only gotten worse as far as intellectual property rights and plagiarism are concerned.

SKATEBOARDINGS FAVORITE CLOWN!

To the general public, skaters in the early 1990s with their "goofy boy" baggy pants and oversized shirts may have looked somewhat clownish. But dressing in a clown costume and pulling all kinds of zany antics on custom-made skateboards turned heads even within the skateboard ranks. This is exactly how Simon Woodstock, a professional skateboarder from San Jose, made a name for himself.

Woodstock soon became Skateboarding's Favorite Clown – and one of the most controversial characters in the game. Did he really have enough talent to be pro? Was he just riding the wave of zaniness started by *Big Brother* magazine? Or was he a conceptual artist using skateboarding as a medium for reflection?

Mark Gonzales had something positive to say on skatebook.tv: "Simon is wacky, his bull's eye board trick was the best." And if you watch YouTube clips of Simon skating on "regular" boards today, it's undeniable that the charismatic skater with the colorful hair jobs had "serious" skills galore to back up his pro status.

AND LIKE THAT, HE'S GONE.

After leaving his prior shoe sponsor Airwalk, Simon Woodstock received his first pro shoe on Vans in 1997. The tongue featured a flip-flop hologram graphic that, depending at which angle you held it, would switch from the red-white stripes to the white-on-blue stars of the Star Spangled Banner behind Simon Woodstock's (fully trademarked) name.

Soon after the release of his pro shoe, Skateboarding's Favorite Clown pulled skateboarding's biggest vanishing act and disappeared from the scene practically over night. What happened?

THIS STUNT DID NOT SIT WELL WITH ROCCO

Simon Woodstock had targeted skateboard mogul Steve Rocco with a controversial magazine advertisement for Woodstock Skateboards. The ad entitled "Contract Negotiations" and designed in the comic book style characteristic of World Industries board graphics. It depicted a caricature Steve Rocco bent over with his pants down on the receiving end of backdoor love from World Industries mascot Devil Man.

Arguing that the ad had been an entirely unprovoked personal injury, Rocco took legal action that would have crushed his opponents. Rocco commented in a recent documentary *The Man Who Soled The World*, "Simon Woodstock just basically started crying. You know, his life was down the toilet." But as a way out, Rocco proposed a settlement to Simon Woodstock and his business partner Rich Metiver. The two were to pay $100,000 to Rocco and leave the skateboard business forever. And that's what they did.

NICE SKATE SHOES

Judging by numerous examples in skate history, the average life cycle of skateboard shoe companies usually follows along one of two alternate paths: A spectacular launch sliding straight into imminent success – or – a slow or delayed start spirals into complete and fatal burnout. But to hold on and stay alive on the sidelines without causing much of a splash – yet without dying out either – is largely unheard of. That is what makes the history of NICE Skate Shoes (NSS) even more remarkable.

Launched in 1997, the New York company burst onto the scene with a selection of functional low top shoes. While the company would never draw much attention to itself other than the occasional rider switch or new shoe model, Nice Shoes maintained throughout the years.

At some point, NICE Shoes moved to California and regrouped with big things in mind. In 2006, Nice made a splash by giving skate icon Jeff Grosso a pro model. The current team includes heavy hitters such as Kristian Svitak, Brian Sumner, Buster Halterman, Chad Knight, and Tom Knox. NICE Footwear focuses on technically advanced shoes, featuring novel lace-protection technology together with heel shock absorption and split soles with a variety of grippy materials. The company has also come to embrace classic vulcanized shoe constructions with a functional, modern twist.

Quite fittingly, the current NICE Footwear website opens with an audio sample by Kanye West saying: "That, that don't kill me, will only make me stronger." To which the history of Nice Skate Shoes is a living testament.

WHAT IF

No matter how people might judge Nike's involvement in skateboarding during the late 90s, everybody remembers the "What if (all athletes were treated like skateboarders)?" campaign.

Launched in 1997, the play on mainstream athletes being prosecuted like skateboarders – featuring courtside "NO TENNIS" signs and "skate-stopped" running tracks – struck a chord with skaters and non-skate audiences alike. While the ads and TV commercials increased overall conscience for the daily blight of street skaters, one problem remained: the shoes simply weren't up to par. *Big Brother*'s Dave Carnie´s bad review didn't help, either.

JUST DOING IT

For almost a decade, Nike had dabbled in skate-boarding while keeping a low profile, sponsoring events like the 1990 Air Attack in Belgium, or the YMCA Summer Skate Camps in the US. While Nike had already successfully created a following among athletes of pretty much every popular sport, success within skateboarding seemed to be eluding the major label brand.

In 1994, Nike had landed a surprise hit among skaters with the GTS shoe, a casual tennis court shoe. Although it was never intended for skateboarding, the GTS was adopted heavily by skaters in San Francisco, New York and Washington DC.

Slap Magazine gave the GTS a thumbs up, saying "it should last a good 3-4 weeks of heavy shreddin'" while pointing out that in the "mid to late 80s, Nike Air Jordans were the premiere skate shoes of the world." The review also drew attention to the fact that this was a shoe by a "major label," hinting at reservations among hardcore riders towards everything corporate and mainstream.

A year later, Nike took their skateboard-related activities to a broader audience by sponsoring the first edition of the ESPN X-Games in 1995. While sponsorship for the event continued over the following years, Nike also tested the skate scene waters by running ads in conjunction with Footlocker stores in skate magazines such as *Thrasher* and *Transworld Skateboarding* in 1996. The verdict among hardcore skaters? The ads were whack!

athletes were treated like skateboarders?

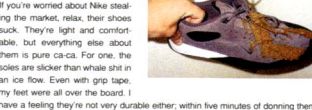

TREATED LIKE SKATEBOARDERS

What Nike needed more than anything else was a campaign that bridged the gap between the brand as the number one global sports equipment manufacturer and the core skateboarding scene.

The "What if" campaign created by a San Francisco advertising agency whose art director responsible for the campaign had skated since 1976, did just that. By depicting golfers getting "busted" by police while going after their favorite past time and tennis players climbing a fence on the run from the law, the TV commercials created an empathy for what skateboarders were going through in the streets on a daily basis.

Asking "What if all athletes were treated like skateboarders?" the TV commercials won numerous awards. By addressing a mainstream audience across a number of channels, they also turned Nike's "bigness" into an asset. Even police officers in the streets took it easy on skaters those days.

Among skateboarding's faithful, the campaign received mixed reactions, reflected in the comments elicited by the clips on YouTube. "Nike doesn't belong in skateboarding." Others commented: "Nike shoes suck..., but these commercials are so great."

No matter how great the ads, every campaign ultimately stands and falls with the related product. And the shoes, in the eyes of many skaters, just didn't cut it. The last straw was a magazine review in *Big Brother,* during which infamous skateboard-writer-at-large, Dave Carnie, defecated(!) on the shoes.

"If you're worried about Nike stealing the market, relax, their shoes suck," Carnie wrote, concluding that "the soles are slicker than whale shit in an ice flow." So while the campaign was well done, the shoes weren't what skateboarders wanted.

LEARNING BY DOING

A quick reflection on Nike's strategy is in order here. In 20/20 hindsight, Nike had already landed big hits among skateboarders in the 70s, 80s and 90s with the classic Blazer, Air Jordan, Dunks and GTS models without even trying. Why not bank on the proven success and simply re-release the classics?

Although the 1998 shoe release flopped, it provided important feedback. "We have to learn from our mistakes," said Kevin Imamura, communications manager for Nike SB, who joined the company in 2002. "That includes designs and new technologies. Whatever we learn works best, we use in our other shoes. If we don't use what we've learned, then we are wasting our time."

In the aftermath of "What If," Nike's skateboarding strategy split into two main directions: On one hand, the development of Nike's own version of a performance-enhancing, skate-specific shoe continued. At the same time, the company looked back to successful classics, unearthing Dunk model, which would become a cornerstone of Nike SB from 2002 onwards.

EASY DOES IT

The Dunk was featured in the "My First Sponsor" campaign rolled out in 2002, which was based on a new, more subtle concept. Center stage no longer belonged to advocating skateboarding or advertising a product. Instead, the personalities on the updated Nike skateboarding team, consisting of Reese Forbes, Danny Supa, Richard Mulder, Gino Iannucci and Todd Jordan - who also photographed the entire campaign - took the spotlight.

Behind the scenes, Nike had also made sure that everyone involved with the skateboard program actually brought a skateboarding background to the mix: "The concept was to let the riders pick someone from their life who had either influenced them or helped them get their feet off the ground on their way to becoming professional skaters," said Kevin Imamura.

While the riders and their families and friends figured prominently, logo and product placement were negligible at best. The Nike swoosh logo appeared in miniature in the background - on an apple or construction cone - while the shoes received no further mention other than being worn by the riders. With the new team and subtle brand message, Nike was on its way to winning acceptance in the skateboard scene. There was work to be done for the skate program - as Kevin Imamura remembers: "We were still calling it Nike Air, which didn't really mean anything." - but it was a start. Next step - Nike SB.

ADIO FOOTWEAR

When Hawk left Airwalk in 1998 after more than a decade to join a new skateboard footwear company, you can bet it was a big deal at the time. The company is California-based Adio Footwear – pronounced "audio" – started by Hawk's long-time friend, professional skateboarder Chris Miller, who also owns Planet Earth Skateboards.

From the start, Adio Footwear has put an emphasis on developing technically advanced shoes with a high degree of functionality for skateboarding. This was especially remarkable at a time when the majority of shoes on the market looked as if they had been produced at exactly the same factory.

Hawk's direct feedback manifests in many of the design features of Adio shoes, as well as his own signature line of Hawk Shoes. To Hawk, the enduring design characteristics of a good skate shoe include "soles that aren't overly-padded, Ollie patches, solid leather and good rubber soles."

Where does Hawk see his own contributions in terms of shoe design? "I skate vert, so I was always consider the durability of the top of the shoe, meaning the toe, laces and tongue," he explains. "Knee slides can destroy a shoe in a matter of days."

What are some of the landmark achievements that paved the way to modern skate footwear? "Impact-absorbent soles that still allow you to feel the board under your feet," Hawk says, adding: "Ollie patches and combining style with function."

True to the meaning of the company's name – from Latin "I listen" – Adio Footwear also sponsors a number of bands including CKY and HIM.

A SHORT-LIVED VITA

In 1998, Mark Oblow started Vita Shoes with long-time friend Natas Kaupas as head designer and recruited Jason Dill, Tim O'Connor, Reese Forbes and Danny Garcia to the team.

Next to those highly prominent riders, Vita made headlines straight out the gate with the return of Natas Kaupas to the pro ranks. The highly influential street skater also fulfilled design duties at Vita with his signature handwritten style and original graphics.

Natas also received hands-on influence on the shoes themselves: "After a little bit, Mark brought up the idea of designing a shoe," Natas says. "It was fun, I had to spec out the whole shoe and work with the factory. I quite liked it when it came out."

Vita shoes offered a blend between highly technical, yet muted and functional styles. Performance features included hidden lace loops to protect shoe strings against abrasion, as well as polyurethane ollie padding and mixed materials in the sole pattern. "With everything a real skateboarder puts his shoes through, I think skateboard shoes should be the gold standard of all athletic shoes," Natas said.

But despite the team's star power and the added design finesse by Natas, Vita Shoes ended up being a short-lived affair. Natas Kaupas and Mark Oblow moved on to work at Quiksilver as graphic director and skate team manager, respectively.

Does Natas have ambitions for starting his own shoe brand? "I never started a shoe brand [myself], I doubt if I ever will. I just believe in skateboarding."

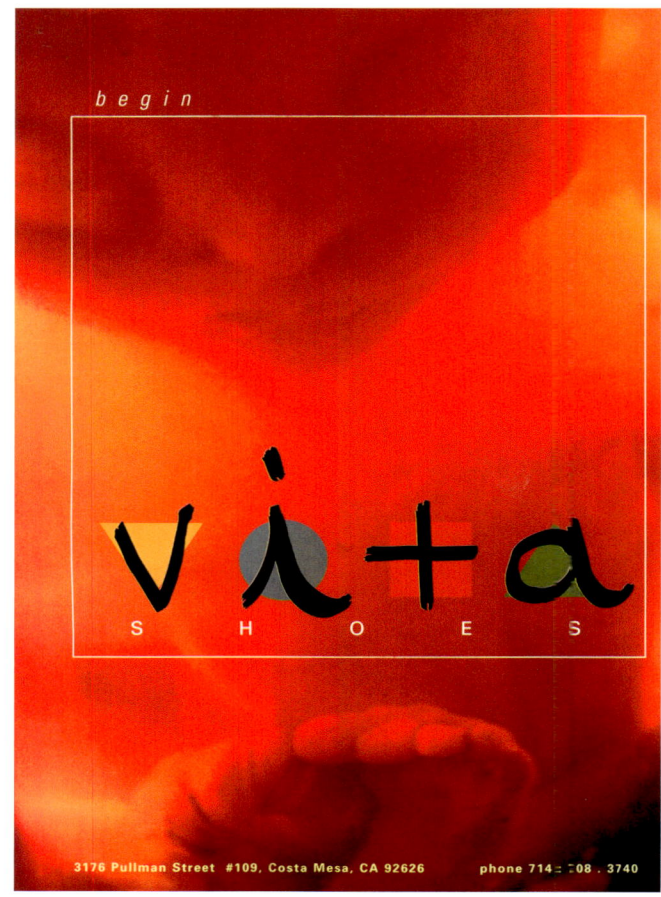

natas kaupas

signature shoe

jason dill
reese forbes
tim o'connor
danny garcia

vita
MANUFACTURING

SEND ONE DOLLAR FOR STICKER AND INFO
3419 Via Lido, Newport Beach, CA. 92663 phone 949.722.9492

COMMITTED TO SKATEBOARDING

In order to stand out, a new shoe company had no choice but going big. Like C1RCA, who signed two of the biggest names in skateboarding to their team – Jamie Thomas, who left Adio Shoes, and Chad Muska, who left éS Footwear when they launched in 1999.

"My shoe on éS was very successful and from that some people that I knew introduced me to some people from Four Star dist[ribution] and they gave me an opportunity to start a new shoe brand and then we started C1RCA together," Chad Muska said.

Both pros infused their shoe designs with their own ideas, and from the start, C1RCA stood for clean designs and functional as well as durable shoes. "I was completely involved from design to building the team to making the logo and name to sales and so on and some of the C1RCA stuff I did was pretty cool and ground breakin." Chad Muska explained.

In 2004, both Thomas and Muska left C1RCA but the company managed to maintain its strong standing due to the support of a new generation of team riders including Colt Cannon, Sierra Fellers, Peter Ramondetta, Tony Tave, Jon Allie and Adrian Lopez.

A NEW BREED

Adrian Lopez had actually been given the red carpet treatment when C1RCA brought him on board: "I was approached by Mr. Chad Muska himself," he remembers. "I was beyond flattered and knew that Raul, the founder of C1RCA footwear, and Muska wanted nothing but the best and I was down."

Lopez remembers the genesis of his first pro model shoe: "I took my first signature shoe at C1RCA very seriously. I never thought I would have the chance to make my own shoe, let alone several of my own designs." A bit later, the Lopez AL202 shoe even became the company's best-selling pro shoe.

SECRET STASHES

SKULLS ON SHOES

San Diego, California · circa 2005 PHOTO: SKIN©CIRCA 2005

What's the story behind all the skulls? "I have always been into skulls and darker feeling art work. I'm a Zero kid so it feels comfortable to be wearing the skulls," he said. What about the role of technical features in improving performance? "For me technology isn't going to solve the problem," Lopez said. "If you have an air bag for cushion then you lose feel but if you want feel then you get no padding. You just have to deal with it, skateboarding isn't meant to be painless."

As a household name in skateboard shoes, C1RCA continues to drive progression and innovation in both footwear design and its marketing activities. In 2006, C1RCA released their first video, It's Time, and started distributing the DVDs for free through authorized retailers and with some skateboard magazines. Other companies soon took up the concept.

ALIVE AND KICKING: SYKUM

Of all European footwear companies, many have long since kicked the bucket. German-based Sykum Footwear – slogan: "The first European skate shoe company" – is the only one still running. Founded in 1999 by Jochen and Armin Bauer, Sykum has been able to constantly advance the technology of their shoes while building a strong team of European skateboarders.

In 2008, the company based in Regenstauf, Germany, introduced an entirely new line of shoes, featuring updated versions of classics such as the IMPERIAL – now in its third edition – originally designed for street skater Dimitri Stathis. Besides the STEALTH mid-top sneaker designed for professional skateboarder Harri Puupponen, Sykum recently added a number of vulcanized shoes in a mixture of suede and polished leather to their collection.

Sykum's Velcro lace-up technology – basically using Velcro straps instead of conventional shoe laces – might just be the next big thing. The system first featured on the Stealth 3000 model. Why this number? "In the year 3000 Velcro will be ruling the world," they said. "Everybody will be drunk because water is getting rare and is way more expensive than alcohol so nobody will be able to tie their laces correctly anymore."

LAKAI: RIDER-OWNED AND AUTHENTIC

Quick pop quiz: Which two high-profile skateboarders left their sponsor Steve Rocco in 1993 to start their own company (Bonus question: and what was the company called)? If you answered Rick Howard and Mike Carroll – who started Girl Skateboards together with Megan Baltimore and Spike Jonze – give yourself some early Nineties trivia points.

While many voices in the industry predicted failure, the renegades continued to build their own vision of a skater-run company. And only six years later, critics had turned into believers in face of the successful portfolio of brands to come out of Girl Skateboards headquarters in Torrance. So when Carroll and Howard left DC Shoes – again, the biggest name in the business at the time – in 1999 to start their own shoe business the audience was watching.

Before the company was ready to roll out into the skate world, one thing was missing: A name. As legend has it, Mike Carroll at the end of a painstaking brainstorming session threw out his own nickname – "Malachi" (pronounced "Ma-la-kai") based on a character in Stephen King's "Children of the Corn" story – for consideration. And just as the name was about to get tossed out for virtue of being too long to fit on tongues and laces, Carroll came up with "Lakai," and that was that.

THE SHOES WE SKATE

While other new shoe companies struggled and strived, and many were lost by the wayside around 2003, Lakai experienced healthy growth and steady expansion of their team. Over the years, Lakai recruited promising upstarts including Mike Mo Capaldi, Alex Olson, and Vincent Alvarez. International team riders include Jesus Fernandez from Spain, as well as the "French Connection" J.B. Gillet and Lucas Puig (France) and the "Royal Family" Danny Brady and Nick Jensen from England.

THINGS COME FULL CIRCLE

The biggest new addition to Lakai's line-up was announced on 1 May, 2006, when Eric Koston joined the team, allegedly after Sole Technology had declined Koston part ownership of his former sponsor éS Footwear. In a play on "big time sports" such as tennis or pro golf, Koston's switch was announced in a spoof web video featuring the man of the hour at a press conference, fielding questions from the media and dodging flashlights.

And if the addition of Eric Koston hadn't been enough of a shake-up, "the video" surely was. With four years in the making, Lakai's video *Fully Flared* raised the bar for modern-day street skating when it premiered in November 2007. Featuring a full comeback part by Guy Mariano, the video won four awards at the 2008 *Transworld Skateboarding* Awards, and cemented Lakai's position as one of the most creative and respected brands in skateboarding.

In 2008 Lakai took the cross-branding craze in skate shoes to a new level with the "Lakai Racing Series." The shoes owe their name to being plastered with the logos of each endorsing pro's respective sponsors. A new angle from a pro's perspective: "The shoes that get us paid." Lakai also brought back Eric Koston's classic first pro shoe, the Koston1, as a updated re-release.

**PRESS RELEASE
FOR IMMEDIATE USE:**

"I'M BACK"

IPATH – THE NATURAL INFLUENCE

Skateboarding has always been about thinking outside the box. At a time when skate shoe companies were banking heavily on advancing the technical aspects of skate footwear, there was room for doing things in a more natural, greener way.

In 1998, professional skateboarder Matt Field – a dedicated vegan who had been part of the Sheep shoes team – created IPATH shoes as a platform for environmentally conscious shoe production with an undeniable Rastafarian influence. By introducing vegan materials such as hemp and organic cotton, IPATH steered away from the trend towards highly engineered, tech shoes.

Endorsed by positive skateboard personalities such as Karl Watson, Kenny Reed and Matt Rodriguez, and with visuals by artist Bigfoot, IPATH offered an entirely new take on skateboarding. The brand has continued on its sustainable path to this day and many other shoemakers have followed suit by offering organic materials and synthetic shoes.

THIS IS NOT THE NEW *D3 2001*

5 THE NEW CENTURY

BIG MONEY - BIG AIR - SUDDEN DEATH

Optimism abounded in the industry as the year 2000 rolled in, and why not? Skateboarding had ended the "old" millennium on a high note, especially in terms of shoe sales. And seeing Tony Hawk on television sitcoms and Andy MacDonald performing at White House receptions left no doubt about it: Skateboarders, collectively, had finally made it.

Some numbers to back this up: At the turn of the millennium, the United States were the center of skateboard activity with ten million participants, over three million of which resided in California. Based mostly in the Golden State, the manufacturing industry for skateboards and related products employed 15,000 people and generated 1.4 billion dollars in annual retail sales. At the time, an estimated 100,000 decks and 500,000 wheels were manufactured each month.

Showcase competition series like the "X Games", in which skateboarding appeared next to inline skating and BMX, attracted up to 275,000 spectators per event. In the year 2000, a total of 27.8 million viewers watched television coverage of the X Games on TV during the summer. Skateboarding was HUGE.

Just when it seemed like we could all go on forever skateboarding, living life and enjoying ourselves – and not struggling financially, either – one single day in 2001 all but derailed the course of history and set the world on a track from which we have yet to return at the time of this writing.

The 9/11 terrorist attacks entirely destroyed the World Trade Center in New York City, killing almost 3,000 people as the entire world witnessed the unspeakable events of this day unfold on live television. New York stock exchanges, the economic heartbeat of the Western world, closed for almost a week and reported historic losses immediately after reopening. The after-math of 9/11 made clear that in an increasingly globalized economy, everything is connected more and more closely. While airlines and insurance companies ranged among the most obvious sectors to be affected, the times of "business as usual" were definitely over all around.

The skateboard industry proved no exception. Although skating had historically fared surprisingly well in times of turmoil – consider the 70s oil crisis and the first Gulf War – skateboarding now followed the rest of the economy into a downward spiral.

One of the key concepts that the public at large became familiar with in these days was "consumer confidence." When a major downturn of unknown duration and proportion seemed imminent, people started saving their money and counting their pennies. The problem: If nobody buys anything, more and more people lose their jobs, and even less people will have money to spend. In Europe, the force of the economic blow became worsened by the introduction of the Euro as a common currency in over a dozen countries.

STAY AT HOME

One of the biggest trends initiated by 9/11 was called "cocooning." People stayed at home insulated by entertainment technology while shunning public places. Sales of cinema tickets dropped, as turnover of video games and home theater systems skyrocketed. And wouldn't you know it – the hottest video game of them all featured SKATEBOARDING! Released in September 1999, Tony Hawk's Pro Skater had already sold 5 million units by 2001, making it the most popular video game franchise of all time.

While cocooning exerted a tight grip on major parts of the population, the Tony Hawk game series spawned an entire new generation of beginning skateboarders – known as the "Pro Skater kids" among retailers. They would prove an important life line to the industry. Complete skateboards came flying off the shelves and shoe sales stabilized again for some companies.

Not all was smooth sailing. Skateboard hardware companies had it tough, since blank decks imported from China and "shop decks" sold by retailers at low price points intensified competition. Shoe companies were also struggling.

Victims of the squeeze included companies such as Axion, Nadia, (Airwalk-funded) Genetic Footwear, Memphis Footwear, Link, Aera Shoes, Power Skate Shoes, Epik Footwear, Axis Footwear, as well as Evos Footwear and Sens. A period of consolidation set in, and for a minute it seemed that skateboard footwear at large had shifted into the hands of the "Big Three" companies, namely DC Shoes, Vans and Sole Technology. "Big," as it would turn out, was exactly the shape of things to come in skateboard footwear.

BIG BUSINESS, MINUS THE BUSINESS SUIT

The fact that skateboarding was here to stay started to transpire to large multinational brand conglomerates. In 2002, the Element Skateboards brand was acquired by Billabong, who four years later began releasing its own brand of shoes. After reporting a total turnover of $100 million in 2003, DC Shoes was bought in March 2004 by surf company Quiksilver for a reported $87 million. And things were only starting to heat up.

In a much-publicized move, Stevie Williams left DC to headline the team of Reebok's DGK (Dirty Ghetto Kids)-branded shoes. Another power move into the skate shoe business came from no other than Pharrell Williams of The Neptunes together with Nigo, founder of Bape, who launched Ice Cream shoes, a brand marked by flamboyant colors and a team captained by Terry Kennedy of Baker fame. Nike returned with another direct attempt at establishing themselves in the skate market, successfully this time.

To top off the selling spree, traditional skate footwear brand Vans became part of the brand portfolio of the VF Corporation in June 2004 for the total sum of $396 million. In terms of footwear technology, the two biggest emerging trends consisted of a return to classic re-issues of formerly popular models and vulcanized shoes.

While shoe brands such as Sole Technology, Lakai and DVS remained skater-owned and operated, they were far from struggling. When Eric Koston left his longtime sponsor éS to join Lakai in 2006, rumors about contract royalties and part ownership in the company made it clear that the market for skate talent had reached pro athlete proportions.

represent.

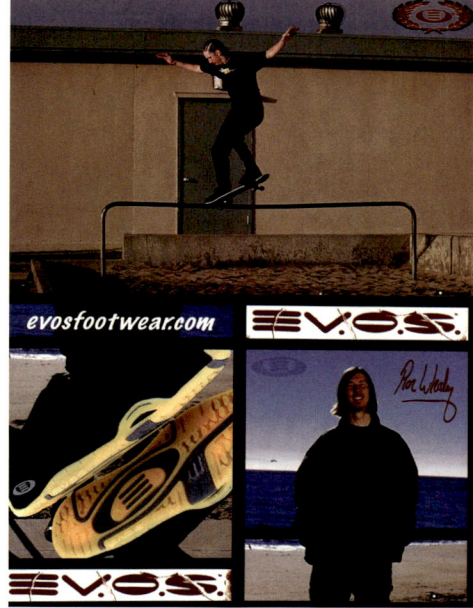

SKATEBOARDERS INVENTED THE INTERNET

The effects of the Internet on the skateboard industry can hardly be overstated. Here are some of the things that have transpired since the Web took over everybody's life in a matter of years:

Race for the best web presence. All companies are trying to outgun each other over the most elaborate presence on the Internet. Free video content anyone? Globe launches globe.tv, while DC Shoes follows suit with dcskateboarding.tv.

YouTube is the new sponsor me tape. Forget sending your tape to sponsors, let them find you on the web.

Those troublesome online downloads. Release a new skate video, two hours later it's all over online sharing platforms. With this in mind, most skate hardware and footwear companies have taken to offering their full-length company videos entirely free on the Internet, even as Podcasts for iPods.

Social networking – without leaving your home. Used to be you actually had to get out to meet people. But thanks to computerized networking sites such as MySpace and Facebook, everyone can find like-minded nerds in a second.

Online retail killed the core shop. The dark side of the Internet revolution brings increased competition to good old neighborhood skate shops by online re-sellers. Which is kind of unfair, since online sellers need not worry about renting store space or paying actual people to work with customers. Some retailers report kids coming into the store to try on shoes, only to buy them online.

Honest to blog. As it turns out, blogs are the new magazines. Just go online and post photos and random blurbs of typed conversations with an imaginary audience – and you're in business. The truth is that "real" magazines, as part of this development, tend to go OUT OF business, like *Big Brother* magazine, which gave up the ghost in 2004 and is now back in blog format.

In 2008 *Slap Skateboard Magazine* – the epitome of authenticity and dedication to skateboarding since its inception in 1992 – announced the discontinuation of their print issue.

Speaking of skate mags, one fortunate turn of events saw *Skateboarder Magazine* return as the Thinking Man's Skateboard Magazine in the year 2000, joined in 2004 by *The Skateboard Mag*, a long-overdue addition to print skate media launched by *Transworld Skateboarding* Magazine alumni Atiba Jefferson, Dave Swift and Grant Brittain.

BIG AIR

The cover of the *Skateboard Mag*'s first issue featured Danny Way skating his "Mega Ramp," on which he single-handedly ushered in a new era of skateboarding. Way's video part in the 2003 *The DC Video* turned the page with stunts like heelflip lipslides on the ramp's rainbow rail. The video premiere, held at Grauman's Chinese Theatre in Hollywood took skate festivities into the red carpet league.

The *Transworld Skateboarding Awards* established themselves as another red carpet staple, and their award for best video part is by now a renowned status symbol.

After upping his own record for highest air several times, Danny Way took his invention to the skateboard scene with the Big Air event that became a staple at the X-Games in August 2004. Outside the contest arena, Way continued to turn heads by becoming the first human to launch over the Great Wall of China in 2005.

While the sheer physical forces at work in these events are only comprehensible to Danny Way and a few select skateboarders who skate the Mega Ramp, the public at large received an impressive demonstration of how serious this level of skating really is when Jake Brown slammed 40 feet to the ground after a high air attempt gone awry at the 2008 edition of the X-Games. While Brown – bordering on a miracle – escaped the ordeal largely unscathed, reruns of the slam and Jake's shoes getting knocked off his feet - remained on the air for weeks.

Skateboarding on the whole, however, did not get swept off its feet, although the years since the new Millennium might have been the most rapid period of change. While skateboarding is progressing to unseen heights in large parts of the world, some cities – including Shanghai, where they just built the world's largest outdoor skate park – are only yet beginning to discover the possibilities. And just imagine a Chinese skateboard boom!

TALK SENS

SENS Footwear premiered their first line of shoes at ASR Tradeshow in San Diego, February 2000. The highly popular Osiris D3 model for pro skater Dave Mayhew finds its almost exact replica in the SENS Magma model – even down to details like the bulky lace loops, the plastic lining on the shoe's upper and the different-colored capsule inserts in the sole. Meanwhile, the "Hercules" model is a humble nod to another classic, the éS Koston 1.

Another SENS model, the S2000, apparently leaned close enough towards a competitor's shoe – namely the DC Shoe Company's popular Howard2 model – to give rise to the following press release issued in April 2000: "To clear any confusion, the San Diego-based shoe company Sens Footwear is not a subsidiary or in anyway affiliated with DC Shoe Co. The initial product line, which premiered at ASR, includes twelve styles in three to four colorways each."

Apparently, the acronym SENS is short for "Strategies for Engineered Negligible Senescence," which is science talk for strategies to prevent human aging, based on the findings of Cambridge researcher Aubrey de Grey. SENS got old after five years and was discontinued in 2005.

SKATEBOARDING'S SAVIOR?

Savier Inc. was launched in 2001 based in Portland, Oregon as a wholly-owned but independent subsidiary of Nike. The agreement between Nike and Savier implied that Nike would handle production of Savier products while contributing their patented footwear technologies – especially anti-shock features such as the Zoom Air system.

Meanwhile, the Savier brand would be developed by a team of eight employees led by Paul Fidrych, formerly at Burton Snowboards. Joining him at Savier headquarters in downtown Portland were Jeff Jewett and Rob LaVigne in marketing and Scott Roberts as product director.

The first Savier ads in magazines featured a barefooted Brad Staba with an old school skateboard hovering over his head like a halo – and no depiction of the actual Savier shoes. The rumor mill was spinning at full capacity and many skaters remained skeptical: What if Savier was just a Trojan Horse for Nike to win over skateboarders? Will the shoes even be skateable? But many critics turned believers when the first Savier shoes hit the stores.

DOING THE RIGHT THING

Highly functional, cleverly designed and durable, Savier shoes offered a legitimate alternative to established skate shoe brands with a high-quality finish and innovative features. Next to Brad Staba, the Savier team consisted of Brian Anderson, Tim O'Connor, Stefan Janoski, John Rattray and later Shaun White. Riders were given the opportunity to express their artistic talents with art installations in advertisements, most notably Brad Staba's video installations. In 2003 Savier also released Tim O'Connor's "The Story" model, which featured a short story on the soles of the shoes.

Highly efficient designs such as an all-rubber upper section proved highly durable, Savier advanced the materials of their shoes significantly. Their synthetic skateboard shoes were produced using only water-soluble glues and solvents while materials were entirely PVC free, including a synthetic leather called Green-Pro.

Despite doing the right thing in many aspects, Savier was discontinued in 2004: "Savier was not able to achieve its financial goals in today's challenging retail and economic environment," said the corresponding press release. Part of the team switched over to Nike SB, Nike's new skateboard shoe division. But given their high durability, Savier shoes could be seen at skate spots all over even long after the brand's demise as a reminder of one of the most ambitious projects in the history of skateboard footwear.

AEON - THE EUROPEAN INFLUENCE

The start of the new millennium marked a time of emancipation for the European skateboarding scene, who were tired of playing second fiddle to its American counterpart. The European skate industry made decisive steps towards independence with Aeon Footwear, a truly European shoe company launched by French skateboard enthusiasts Stephane Theng, Canel Frichet and Nao Nussbaum in 2002.

"Lordz [Wheels] was definitely the beginning, since we had all the European riders on the team," said Aeon's former team manager, benoit Copin. "And we were talking about a way to grow and do something really strong in Europe. So shoes seemed the way to go."

NO HALF-STEPPING

Aeon set a new standard for what could be expected from a European skate brand. The initial Aeon team consisted of all stars Henning Braaten from Norway, Alex Carolino from Brazil, Franck Barattiero and JB Gillet from France, and Florentine Marfaing of Germany.

While previous European companies often had to operate on a limited budget, Aeon went all out and took the team to Japan for their first tour. Aeon's advertising campaign in print and video formats oozed an aura of professionalism heretofore found only in the United States. But the European market proved challenging: "In the US you have an enormous number of shops in a market with the same currency and language, whereas in Europe, the languages differ as do the markets," said Copin.

Designer/co-owner Nao Nussbaum and designer Julien Desmettre kept advancing the technical aspects of Aeon shoes by introducing features like the AE-gel, extra light constrution and a host of skate-specific refinements. "I think the inspiration for design always came from the street, meaning all aspects of different sports footwear mixed with a strong background in skateboarding".

Ultimately the struggling European economy caught up with Aeon Shoes and operations were discontinued in June 2006. Was it worth trying? "A lot of shops were closing down all over France in 2006, so the money wasn't there for the production of the next shoe collection. It definitely wasn't easy to be a small European company, but I think in the end everyone had a good time, especially the team, and it was a great experience for everyone," concluded Copin, who now runs the Internet spot guide among other things.

19 - "88" SKATEBOARD FOOTWEAR

Some figures universally enjoy symbolic significance, like the number 13.

When 88 Footwear was established in 2002 by senior *Transworld Skateboarding* photographer Ed Dominick and pro skater Kris Markovich, the name had a sentimental basis. The year 1988 had been their favorite year in skateboarding.

THE NUMBER OF THE BEAST

But as some who have been to a European soccer match can attest, the number 88 has a demonic nuance, for football hooligans and skinheads. For them 88 is code for the eighth letter of the alphabet, HH meaning heil Hitler. The BNP [British National Party] uses it a lot as well," according to a July 2006 post on *Sidewalk Skateboard Magazine's* web forum. Whether this ambiguity was partially responsible for 88 having been discontinued is pure speculation.

"Unfortunately, the three years of operating 88 Footwear did not hit the projected returns that were expected of the brand. After struggling with less than expected revenues and profitability, we are forced to make a very tough decision. Alias Distribution will no longer fund 88 Footwear," announced Alias in a 2005 press release.

The company's demise came on the heels of their highly recommendable "Destroy Everything Now" video. Luckily, almost the entire team found a new home at Vox Footwear, founded by Ed Dominick and Art Director Nathan Peacher in March 2005. No misleading name here, and nothing but success since.

RISE WITH THE FALLEN

Jamie Thomas

"FIND IT IN YOURSELF TO RISE UP."

One of the most influential street skaters of all times, Jamie Thomas [The Chief] single-handedly redefined what is physically possible on a skateboard, taking the stair-count for gaps and handrails to the limit. Jamie Thomas was a headliner on any skate shoe company he joined. Jamie started Fallen, his own footwear company, in 2003 recruiting Billy Marks, Josh Harmony, Chris Cole among others.

THE SEARCH FOR A NAME

Fallen got off the ground with support from the owners of DC Shoes, who helped produce the shoes while Jamie retained the rights to the Fallen brand.

Thomas kept a hands-on approach from the start. The results are highly functional shoes that appeal to skaters in search of reliable performance rather than bling and flair. Backed by a solid team with Jamie at the wheel, the company has seen a steady climb, true to motto: "Rise with the Fallen."

THE MISSING LINK

Skateboard footwear is a lot like the restaurant business. Statistically speaking, about 30 percent of all newly opened businesses fail within the first year of operations. Roughly the same is true for skate shoe companies. While a number of key criteria influences the make or break of a new skateboard business, some failures still remain a mystery. Like Link Footwear, an ambitious skate shoe company that entered the spotlight in 2002. At first sight, it looked like they did everything right, especially regarding the usual stumbling blocks for skate shoe companies, which are:

1. LACK OF FUNDING AND POOR MANAGEMENT

Link Footwear had both. There's only so much an upstart company can achieve on a tight budget, but from the get-go, Link Footwear made a splash with their ads, their high-profile team and the look of their shoe samples. Sports industry giant adidas-Salomon, at the time the second-largest sporting goods manufacturer in the world, was footing the bill and provided distribution and manufacturing infrastructure.

2. NO INSIDE SKATEBOARDING KNOW-HOW

Link Footwear had this to spare. After initial difficulties at getting the proto-type shoes for Link Footwear right, Salomon decided to draw on certified skate expertise in-house. This was easy, since they had acquired Cliché, the original European skateboard company, in 2001.

3. LACK OF ADVERTISING/PROMOTION

When it came to Link Footwear, lack of advertising was definitely not an issue. More than a year before the first shoes began shipping to stores in August 2003, Link continued targeting all key skateboard media with monthly double-page ads - enough money to start a new company by itself.

4. NO ENDORSEMENT BY RESPECTED ATHLETE TEAM

Link Footwear started with an international team of respected riders including J.B. Gillet and Lucas Puig from France, Marcus McBride from the United States, Alex Moul from the UK and Cale Nuske and Andrew Brophy from Australia. While this line-up covered all major markets - Europe, the US and Australia - Link also had the foresight to add a Japanese team rider, namely Junnosuke Yonesaka from Tokyo.

5. BAD TIMING

Like any other market, skateboarding is subject to business cycles and fluctuation, so the difference between a hot seller and a failure can be a matter of mere months. While the launch of Link Footwear did fall into troubled economic times - mostly the aftermath of 9/11 and introduction of the Euro - this was only a temporary slump, not a full-blown recession. Granted, many months would pass between the first Link ads in mid-2002 and actual shoe shipments in August 2003, while many stores would never even get a pair of Links delivered at all.

Starting a new business is always a grand event, closing down happens reluctantly, without fanfare. In December 03, Link's demise was announced with hardly more than the occasional blurb on the Internet message boards that said: "Link Footwear is out of business."

NIKE SB - BACK ON BOARD

For Nike, the way to gaining new ground in the skateboard community was paved with an old classic – the Dunk basketball boot, initially released in 1985. Re-launched in a limited edition series under the title "Colors By" in 2002 – with colorways chosen by riders on the Nike skateboarding team Reese Forbes, Danny Supa, Gino Iannucci, Richard Mulder and guest artists including Natas Kaupas – the Dunk would become the foundation of Nike's future skateboard offering.

What made the shoe so attractive? "It all came down to what was the best shoe in the entire product line for skateboarding," said Kevin Imamura, communications manager for Nike SB. "And if you ask people, it's probably either the Jordan 1 or the Dunk."

Actually, both shoes share a similar history. In terms of design, the Dunk was a less technical precursor of Michael Jordan's first shoe, the Jordan 1, released later that same year. Almost instantly, Michael Jordan's tremendous star power together with the highly popular Air system helped his shoe outshine the Dunk in terms of popularity.

Much to the dismay of loyal fans, the Dunk was discontinued a few seasons later. Meanwhile, skateboarders started embracing the first edition Jordan shoe when it went on sale nearing the arrival of its successor around 1987. This made the Jordan 1 a contender for the No.1 most popular skateboard shoe of the late 80s.

So why did Nike choose to build their skate program around the Dunk in 2002? "The Jordan 1 would've been the easy choice, but by that time Jordan was really well established as its own brand and we wanted Nike SB to have its own identity," Kevin Imamura explained. "Plus, the Dunk is more flexible in terms of what you can do with it. It has no branding other than the Swoosh."

LOW, MID AND HIGH!

"I would also say the Dunk is definitely one of THE archetypal shoes in skateboarding in terms of its lines and construction," Imamura added. "It's the blueprint for the classic skateboard shoe, together with the original [Nike] Blazer model, the Vans ERA and the [Converse] Chuck Taylor."

With the Dunk as the new beginning, the Nike skateboard program was ready to take the next step. "The whole program started to grow very slowly and organically," Kevin Imamura recalls. "We had to make sure to get the product right. From there we made sure the ads were done by someone who actually skated and that everyone involved understood skateboarding."

What remained missing was a distinct name, as the Nike skate program still ran under the generic title "Nike Air." At the same time, their customized versions of the classic Dunk model – with an added Zoom Air insole liner and a thicker tongue – were shipped with the label "Dunk SB" on the box in order to distinguish them from other Dunk models. "So SB was already the product code on the boxes before we even had a logo or anything," said Kevin Imamura.

"Whenever we talked to the press or anyone about the program, we always made the point to call it 'Nike Skateboarding.' So since we already had 'Nike SB' on the boxes – and 'SB' meant 'Skateboarding' – we just decided to go with it at some point. It just all went together!"

SHOCK TO THE SYSTEM

For Nike Skateboarding, the year 2004 started with a bang: The company signed a multi-million dollar sponsorship deal with pro skateboarder Paul "P-Rod" Rodriguez, who left his sponsor to become the first skateboarder ever to receive a signature shoe from Nike. At the same time, further additions to Nike's skateboarding team included Chet Childress, Wieger Van Wageningen and Omar Salazar, and also Stefan Janoski and Brian Anderson, who joined the SB team from the defunct Nike-funded Savier Footwear project.

Resistance mounted as soon as word got out. The online message boards flamed up, criticizing P-Rod's switch. Users called the street skating prodigy "Paul Dollariguez," alongside comments best summed up by "007kid" in his post on the éS Footwear blog: "P-rod has mad skills but that doesn't matter worth a damn when you bail on everyone for the money." Nor-Cal company Consolidated Skateboards revitalized their Anti-Nike-campaign "Don't Do It", initially started in 1997, with full fervor. The battle lines were drawn, with little to no gray areas in between.

OVERCOMING OBSTACLES

How did Nike SB perceive the resistance in the skate scene? "Of course we felt it. That is just inherent to the brand and that will probably always be there," said Kevin Imamura. "The only way we will ever overcome this resistance is by supporting skateboarding and help it grow in the best way possible."
"By working with and supporting shops, events and other companies that are trying to help skating grow in the right way, everyone wins."

FOOT(WEAR) FETISH

One of the biggest rewards for core skateshops carrying the SB line stems from the fact that the re-vamped Nike Dunks have become the darling of obsessive footwear collectors, or "sneakerheads," willing to stand in line for hours for a pair of limited edition kicks.

Does Nike SB actually cater to this demographic with their frequent limited editions? "We're first and foremost a skateboard shoe brand, but at the same time we also realize that there is a huge following for the brand. So the limited editions are never our main focus but something we look at as a way to have fun and tell stories."

Telling stories, in this case, can mean a limited edition Dunk with colorways inspired by a classic 80s movie like *Ferris Bueller's Day Off* or *Thrashin* and even classic 8-bit skate video games like *Skate or Die*.

While Nike never explicitly advertises the source of their pop culture inspiration – especially since a Freddy Krueger-themed shoe giving a nod to the *Nightmare on Elm Street* movies resulted in hairy legal contestation – the sneakerheads do the math and present the shoe accordingly on the Internet. "Telling stories with our shoes is a way for our footwear to be more than just another colorway on the wall," said Imamura. "But even that has its limitations."

PRO SHOES

"When it comes to pro models the process it is very intimate and involved because it is representative of who they are as a person and designed for their type of skating," said Nike SB's designer James Arizumi. "I like to start out with a few casual meetings where we catch up on who they are and where they are at a specific point in time. I use that as a reference point and paint very broad strokes of how they see themselves and how the product would represent them best."

"I then work with them on finding out their current interests whether it be cars, furniture, music, their dog, specific types of design, anything and everything that will help me get a feel for their style and tastes," Arizumi explained. "I then develop sketches and loose concepts to lead them down the road on a specific aesthetic that they want the shoe to look like."

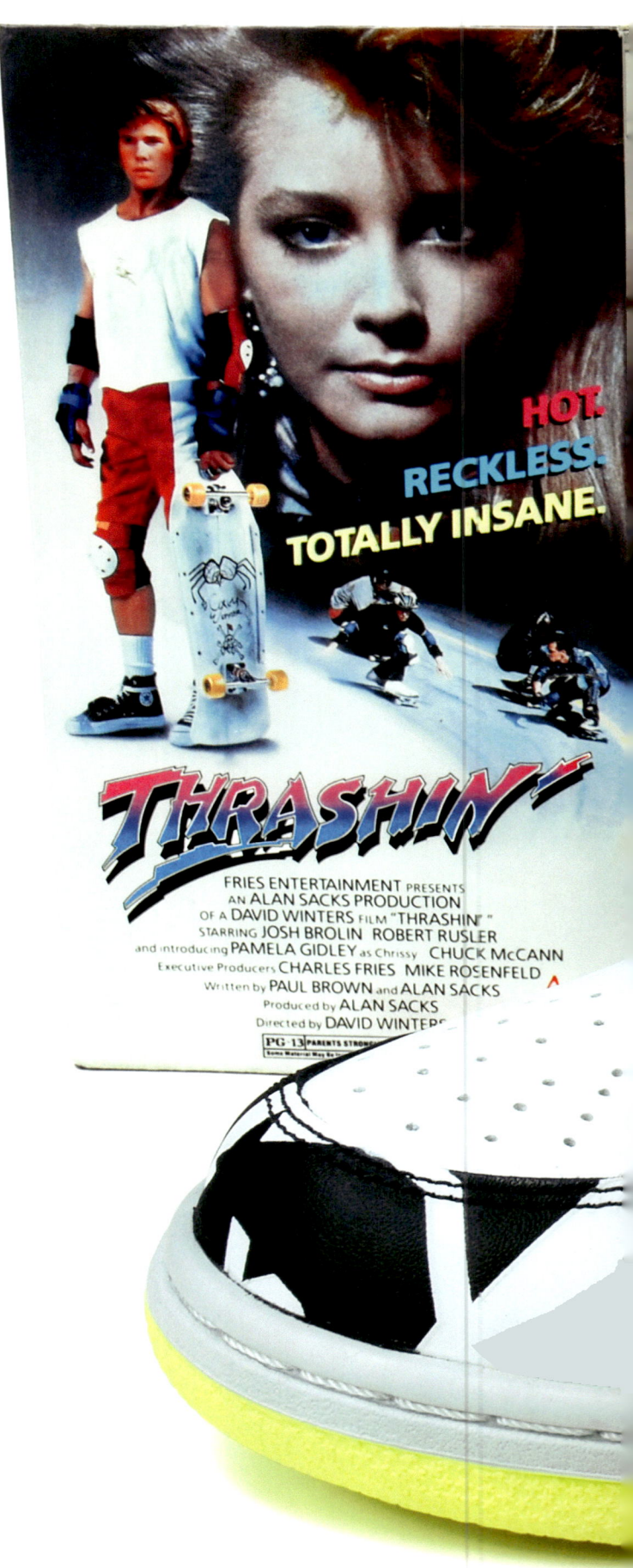

CONCEPT OF A HIGHTECH SHOE

Aside from constantly updated colorways, the shoe's design has received a few careful nips and tucks. The Dunk's cult status puts clear limits on how far efforts at modernizing the shoe can go. "You don't want to make them too different because people love and skate the Dunks for their own specific reasons."

"So as a result, we have taken two perspectives on skate shoes," Imamura explained. "One is to build on the classics like the Blazer and the Dunk. And then there is the perspective to go out and try something different, which is a reflection of Nike's heritage in pushing the technical advancement of footwear."

James Arizumi explained how the company conducts its shoe development. "First and foremost we listen to our athletes. We find out what their needs are and work on finding solutions to their problems. As a designer my job is to be a problem solver, focus in on a specific concern and develop a design concept to fill that need."

"I start with sketches and concepts, which are then turned into prototypes for testing," Arizumi explained. "I work with the engineers to construct the molds, develop materials, tweak airbags, work on midsoles and outsoles, and work on the patterns for the shoe." The next step consists of testing the prototype shoes at Nike's high-tech laboratory, the Nike Sports Research Lab NSRL, where the shoes undergo tests for abrasion resistance and flexibility, before being released into the streets on the feet of Nike SB team riders.

MAKE A BETTER SKATE SHOE

Nike's line of highly engineered, technical skate shoes started in 2003 with the E-Cue model that was "quite bold at the time," as Imamura admits, featuring a plastic mesh incorporated into the shoe's upper section for a highly unusual look compared to the rest of the market at the time. Development at the Nike Sports Research Laboratory continued over the years with offerings such as the URL and Angus models to what is now the Zoom Tre A.D. Released in 2008, the Zoom Tre A.D. (Advanced Design) features technologies initially developed running and soccer shoes.

"Now, do we think these will be our best sellers?" Imamura asked. "Maybe not, but you have to try to make a better skate shoe and get it as good as you can. The riders are constantly innovating, so it's unfortunate when companies don't do the same. But mostly, it would just get boring."

DEKLINE - A NEW CLASS OF SOCIETY

Founded in 2002 out of Tum Yeto, Dekline had been under development for almost two years by the time the first shoes hit the stores in Spring 2004. The wait paid off, and the shoe label based on the motto "ENJOY THE RIDE" has been on the upswing since.

Dekline's secret: A distinct, classic look with an emphasis on exclusive fabrics, basic colorways and print designs instead of bells and whistles or over-technical features. Masterminding the design department is August Benzien, a veteran in the footwear business who landed a smash hit with the Matt Hensley "Gambler" model on DuFFS shoes.

KEEP THE COLORS SIMPLE

Maintaining a sure eye for overall style, Benzien keeps the colors simple and bold while incorporating materials styles and suede or even tweed into shoes that perform well for skateboarding thanks to their grippy vulcanized sole. Dekline also contributed to the resurgence of high-top shoes, adding an ankle brace to the mix and putting the "high" back in high top with a boxing boot style.

The current team includes Patrick Melcher, Matt Ball, Jason Adams, Olly Todd, Adam Dyet, and with a European squad of Peter Molec, and the traveling Frenchman, Soy Panday. Frequent artist collaborations include limited edition models with Portland-based artist Bwana Spoons, whose "whale-agator" mascot is depicted on the side of the shoes in front of a dream landscape. The Dekline shoe created in conjunction with legendary artist Dalek even features laser-etched graphics for a unique finish.

Enter skateboarding's dynamic duo, Jason Lee and Chris Pastras – known as the original founders of Stereo Skateboards – who in 2008 received their own Rider's Choice shoes on Dekline. Cross-branded with the Stereo Skateboards logo, these seem like a sure fit.

ADIDAS "ORIGINALS"

The early millennium brought about slimmer silhouettes and many re-released shoe models. It was the death of bulky and technology-oriented footwear. With a history of classic footwear both in and outside of skateboarding, adidas took a logical step by returning to its "Originals".

In 2005 adidas abandoned the athletic approach that had defined most of its efforts in skateboarding throughout the late 90s. "We're no longer grouping skateboarding in as a traditional performance sport," says marketing director Jess Weinstein. Therefore, it was moved to a new division within the company – from "Sports Performance" to "Sports Heritage".

This change affected the list of professional riders, but Mark Gonzales remained as the team's grand master. The legendary streetskater was an original himself and embodied skateboarding's progress over the decades. He became the "Gonzfather" of a new team, largely recruited by longtime *Thrasher* photographer Bryce Kanights. Instead of superstars, the team is an individual crew of skateboarders, each with a distinct flavor: Tim O'Connor, Dennis Busenitz, Lem Villemin, Benny Fairfax, Nestor Judkins, Vince Del Valle and others.

CLASSICS RESURFACING

The "Originals" concept also meant a return to classic shoe models, modified in subtle ways to meet the challenges of modern skateboarding. Gazelles, Superstars or Campuses returned to skateboarding. "They were just well designed" said adidas designer Danny Kinley. "Plus, there was something about having to search them out. The thrill of the hunt, like searching for spots. When you found a fresh pair at a fair price in banging colors you were psyched. People miss those days and that's what keeps those shoes going."

These classic shoes weren't designed for skateboarding. Therefore, the biggest modification had to do with abrasion resistance, impact absorption and fit. "We want to avoid blown-out toes and heel bruises," says Kinley. "We want to give our shoes that special look and feel that only skateboarders can spot without blindly going down the puffy tongue road. adidas 'Originals' combine the knowledge from the past with modern manufacturing capabilities – traditional style with a grain of technology."

adidas Campus Vulcanized - Skated and customized by Dennis Busenitz

adidas Superstar "Gonz" Skate - Skated and customized by the Gonzfather himself

FIDEL SHOES - SHOES FOR EVERYONE

First off, Fidel Shoes are NOT named after Fidel Castro. And the company's founders also do not condone socialism, communism, or any kind of "ism" for that matter. "There is no [brand] philosophy, the creators of Fidel Shoes are against philosophy," said André Fernandes at Fidel Shoes.

Started in 2004, the Portuguese footwear company has made a name for itself in the European skate scene with a line-up of vulcanized suede low-, mid- and high tops in the style of a classic deck shoe.

At the same time, the brand does not want to limit itself to the skate demographic. "Fidel Shoes are used by skateboarders because of their comfort and good quality construction," André Fernandes explained. "But Fidel Shoes are not a sports company, and not aimed at anyone in particular."

Initially, the name Fidel derived from "Fidelity" which was the title of a Portuguese skateboard brand started in 1998. The brand's characteristic logo was marked by a dot in the middle of the name – read: FIDEL.TY – and as a tribute to the old hardware brand, Fidel shoes took the "L.I"-part of the emblem to create their own logo, which they labelled the "Falling Towers" logo. What does this (somewhat cryptically named) logo stand for? "The falling towers side logo represent the never ending war between humans," Fernandes said.

PRAY PAY OFF BABY

Fidel Shoes have also come up with their own labelling system. "We put the style name of the shoe on the back of the shoe, either printed or embroidered," André Fernandes explained. "Fidel is the only brand doing this." Style names include "PRAY PAY OFF BABY," "FONTANA SLEEZE," "GET YOUR SHOW DOWNS" and "CHEAP SOUL CRASH."

What all this means? Since the makers of Fidel Shoes insisted they don't subscribe to any fixed philosophy, it's probably best to assume that they're just out there having fun.

THE NEXT LEVEL: PAUL RODRIGUEZ

They say you can never surpass anybody by following in his footsteps. As the son of famous Mexican-American actor Paul Rodriguez Sr. – known for his work in a number of popular TV series and movies such as Ali, Rat Race and Bloodwork – young Paul Rodriguez Jr. could have easily sashayed into a career on the big screen. Like, almost by default. But skateboarding, of all things, turned out to provide an opportunity for Paul to blaze his own trail. "I didn't want to turn 40 and not have anything in my life that I created all for myself," he says. "Skateboarding is the one thing that led me away from acting. And create something for himself he did. He's what many believe to be "The Next Big Thing" in skateboarding.

PUTTING THE "P" IN "PROFESSIONAL"

Paul was discovered at an early age by skateboard legends Kareem Campbell and Eric Koston. In 2004, when he was merely 20, Rodriguez signed the biggest shoe contract in skateboard history with Nike SB. Paul "P-Rod" Rodriguez has not only climbed to the upper echelon of the pro ranks, but has single-handedly raised the bar on professional skateboarding. Out of all the athletes Nike sponsors, Paul Rodriguez is the first Mexican-American athlete to ever receive the honor to get a signature shoe. "Nike is definitely bigger than your average company and I think I get extra attention because of it." Paul said.

While other pros his age make headlines by getting arrested at contest parties or because of their drug exploits, Paul Rodriguez keeps it clean, professional, and lets his skating do the talking. "Some people, even some of my friends, just proceed to act around kids as if they weren't around," P-Rod said. "But I know that when I saw my favorite pros as a kid, how they acted definitely affected me. I guess that it's just part of my personality," Paul said. "I try to live my life not doing anything I would end up being ashamed about."

PERSONALIZED SHOE CONCEPTS

Paul is working closely with Nike SB designers on the creation of his third signature shoe, the Prod3, scheduled for release in summer 09. "I'm more involved with the feel of it, rather than the function and technology behind a shoe. They give me some designs to see which ones suit the way I want my shoe to feel," said Paul.

"It usually takes about a year until a shoe is finally done." Does Paul keep a collection of all his shoes? "I always try to have all the current shoes that are out at the moment. But I'm running out of space to put them, so at some point I end up giving them away."

Things are going well for P-Rod in his chosen career. In 2008, he opened a skate shop called Primitive in Encino, California and scored a history-making $100,000 first place at the Maloof Money Cup street contest. "I was fortunate to fall in love with skating and progress to a point where I could make a name for myself in an industry where my dad didn't have any connections. That means a lot to me. And skateboarding really is my one true love."

VOX POPULI, VOX DEI

After the demise of 88 Footwear, senior *Transworld Skateboarding* photographer Ed Dominick pooled resources with art director Nathan Peacher in 2005 to create a new shoe company. VOX Footwear is based on their vision of a rider-driven company producing functional skateboard shoes.

"The name VOX comes from the Latin word 'Voice'," said Ed Dominick. "The VOX tag line is 'This is your voice,' really meaning 'Skateboarding is your voice.'" With an all-star cast including Peter Hewitt, Justin Strubing, Nei Blender, Dan Drehobl, Emmanuel Guzman, JT Aultz, Adrian Mallory, Peter Watkins, and Darren Navarrette, VOX was able to hit the ground running and continue right where 88 Footwear had left off.

PURE SKATEBOARDING

Addressing an age-old problem in skateboarding – namely, broken laces – VOX developed Optional Lace Protection (OLP) to protect the bottom laces from abrasion during ollies and flip tricks.

When it comes to supporting the skate scene and promoting their team, VOX broke new ground by offering free video podcasts and their regular video magazine *Black&Blue* as a free DVD addition to magazines such as the *Skateboard Mag*.

And in order to make sure that skateboarders with a preference for high-end concrete skate parks will always have a place to go, VOX has partnered up with legendary park builders Dreamland Skateparks from Portland, Oregon. Headed by Mark "Red" Scott, the Dreamland crew has been building creative and challenging skate parks across the world for more than a decade now. The VOX Trooper Dreamland model is their official shoe, awarded in recognition of their contributions to park design and skateboarding as a whole.

SUPRA - TAKING IT TO THE NEXT LEVEL

Supra was founded out of KR3W Clothing with a pro team consisting of Penny and Muska together with Erik Ellington, who had left his shoe sponsor Emerica a year earlier, and with Jim Greco and Antwuan Dixon. The word "supra" is Latin for "above," reflecting the shoe company's exclusive style and top-shelf branding.

Supra Footwear's initial collection revolved around mid- to high-top skate shoes in the mode of a basketball high-top. Over the years, Supra Footwear has also come to embrace vulcanized outsoles in shoes such as the iconic Chad Muska "Skytop" pro model, which features an extra high tongue and wax laces. According to Chad Muska, it's his personal favorite skate shoe.

LOOK FRESH, FEEL GOOD

"I am always very involved with all my shoe designs," Muska said. "Sometimes I will sketch out an idea or design a concept in [Adobe] Illustrator and then work with our shoe designer Josh Erubaker in getting it spec'd out and ready for production. Then I help pick colorways and different materials.

"With Supra I like to help out as much as I can to put my style in the brand," Chad Muska said. "The most important feature for a shoe to me is that it has to look super fresh... so fresh that you may not even think its a skate shoe. But then you put them on and they are ready to skate right away!"

THAT EXCLUSIVE TOUCH

Artist collaborations and limited edition sneakers play a big role when it comes to setting off Supra Footwear. "Limited" to them often means "extra limited," for example Supra's silver, white and turquoise "413" model, released for their flagship store in Los Angeles, had been sold to only 11 retailers in the US at a restriction of 30 pairs each Continuously updated colorways – with elaborate patterns including zebra or leopard – and collaborations with designers are also key. "If it were up to me I would only make 100 pairs of shoes at the most of each color that I put out. . . just to keep things fresh and make people have their own identity," Muska said.

In 08, Supra introduced their trademarked Supratuf technology, bringing durable abrasive-resistant upper materials to a wide range of low to high-top shoes. Chad Muska also brought back the secret tongue stash from his first éS shoe model to current releases such as the Hawaiian-patterned Floral Skytop model, staying true to the roots as Supra advances into the future.

ELEMENT - FOOTWEAR WITH ROOTS

Throughout the 60s and 70s, it was almost a given for brands to manufacture the entire range of skateboard equipment. Companies such as Hang Ten, Hobie or Makaha would offer boards, wheels, trucks and also skate-specific shoes all at the same time. Once the early skateboarding boom had subsided, several decades of strict separation into specialized hardware and shoe companies followed. Never the twain shall meet.

The separation seemed almost insurmountable. Skate hardware companies had no luck when it came to running a successful shoe brand under their logo. In 2006 Element Skateboards became one of the first next-generation brands to rekindle this idea, introducing Element Shoes, their own line of footwear.

connect.
coming spring 2006

THE ELEMENT OF FOOTWEAR

Element's reputaion as an authentic board brand since 1992 was strong enough to see them through this new and challenging endeavor. One advantage of launching a footwear sideline out of an existing hardware business is that the the process of forming a team is a much easier task. The Element Shoes start-up roster boasted impressive names such as Darrell Stanton, Brent Atchley, Chad Tim Tim and Mike Vallely. "Element is the best brand I've had the opportunity of working with in my twenty-three years as a sponsored skater," said Mike Vallely.

ALL TIED TOGETHER

The foundation for the new shoe line is provided by Element's company philosophy, which is geared around the elemental forces of wind, water, fire and earth. Accordingly, Element's footwear offering is separated into four branches. The "Wind" line emphasizes light and flexible shoes with a lower profile for heightened board feel. The "Water" line is based on classic court shoes with a cup sole and full-length cushioning throughout the EVA midsole.

The "Fire" category is geared around resilience and durability, with added padding in the midsole and the shoe's upper for increased protection. The "Earth" line presents the most casual of Element's shoe line, with classic shoes in a compression molded rubber construction with a vulcanized sole, maintaining a high degree of skateability and chill factor.

LISTEN AND LEARN

With more than 20 years of experience as a professional skateboarder under his belt, Element team rider Mike Vallely brings a strong background to the brand, including hands-on knowledge in shoe design and development from former sponsors. Vallely has also channeled this experience into his pro shoes on Element. "I'm very involved in my shoe designs," he said. "Durability is always a big thing with me. If someone is going to spend good money on a shoe to skate in, I think it should last."

ELEMENTALITY

In line with Element's overall philosophy, the footwear branch also promotes elemental awareness, as well as support for skateboard art and culture. One of the latest initiatives included an auction of hand-painted "Ladybug" iPod sound docks by Vestalife. Proceeds of the auction went directly to the Elemental Awareness Campership Fund giving less fortunate kids an opportunity to go to Element YMCA Skateboard Camp.

To provide a forum for the cultural diversity that is unique to the skateboard scene, the company started the "Element Advocates" program. It displays the talents of the likes of skateboarder/musician Ray Barbee, environmentalist Todd Larson and Hawaiian tattoo artist Mike Leger. Current artist collaborations include a special edition Mike Vallely shoe for his band Revolution Mother.

Element Skateboards have proven that it is possible for a brand to break with conventional expectations and be creative. After all, skateboarding is more than riding a board - but a whole living, breathing culture, surrounded by the elements.

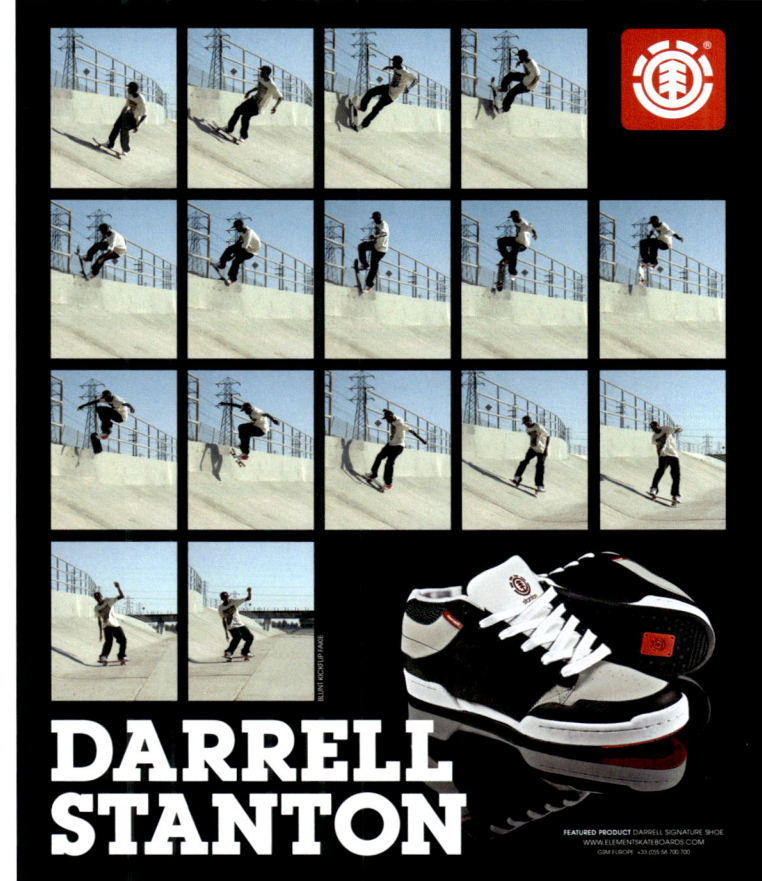

The Element Vallely signature shoe rocked by Mike V personally!

"I'LL BE BACK": SKATE-SPECIFIC CHUCKS

A proven maxim in product marketing says "culture beats strategy." In other words, when a product becomes embraced by a certain group or subculture as part of their everyday practice, it's destined to be a winner. And even more so than the smartest advertising and branding strategies could ever achieve.

This is actually great news for Converse, whose Chuck Taylor All Star sneakers have enjoyed a steady following among skateboarders for several decades now. Earlier in this book, Tony Hawk even maintained that their classic design makes Chucks THE quintessential skate shoe. "It is the simplistic nature of the Chuck Taylor that makes it a timeless design," said Brandon Brubaker, CONS Senior Footwear Designer.

The only problem, so far, had been their lack of durability. Here's where the 2009 re-launch of the classic Chuck Taylor in a skate-specific edition comes in.

"We've included a few features to make it a more durable skate shoe," said Brandon Brubaker. The new low-top version is revved up with performance-oriented enhancements such as extra-sturdy collar padding under the heel and with extra rubber padding in critical ollie areas.

The old classic also packs some new technologies: "The material in the tongue is memory foam and definitely provides a new level of comfort compared to the previous foam, or lack thereof," said Brandon Brubaker, adding: "This stuff is fresh! The padding molds to the shape of your foot after you rock them for a few days. We also added an insole with a stability shank to prevent ankle roll. We used high abrasion suede and canvas, and stitching for durability."

WHAT'S THE STORY BEHIND THE LOBSTER?

One of the most striking style features of the new Converse line is an embroidered lobster at the inside of the tongue.

"The lobster in the label is representative of the New England heritage behind Converse as a brand," explained Brubaker. "Skateboarding, as you know, is very much tied to that West Coast California vibe, and we wanted to be sure to represent the East somewhere in the product, in a subtle way, of course." Brandon Brubaker expanded on the brand philosophy: "We are trying to keep it true Converse - simple and clean."

Next to the updated Chuck Taylors, the new Converse skateboarding line features low-cut functional skate shoes, including the suede Pro Leather Skate. The shoe premiered at the Fall 2008 edition ASR trade show. Converse also unveiled their new skateboard team, consisting of Raymond Molinar, Sammy Baca, Ethan Fowler, and Anthony Pappalardo. The new collection is scheduled to hit stores in early 2009. Brandon Brubaker announced further innovation. "We are trying to push it without being overly technical. We are also working on some crazy new vulcanized soles that no one has done yet!"

GRAVIS IV SK8

For their latest line of skate-specific shoes, Gravis Footwear relied on the expertise of Arto Saari. Saari headlined the 2008 launch of the IV Skateboarding program (IVSK8) with The Viking, a signature shoe model. Arto Saari recalls seeing his first pro-endorsed skate shoe. "I think the first signature shoes I had were the Dyrdek DC kicks and the second were Jeremy Wray's Dukes. Kareem kick's were awesome too (DuFFs). I was freaking over them."

The year 2008 brought dramatic changes for Arto Saari. Before leaving Etnies for IVSK8, the highly acclaimed street skater from Finland had parted ways with long-time sponsor Flip Skateboards. "Life moves in recurring seven-year cycles. And since I had just reached the end of such a cycle, I thought it was time for me to make some changes in my life."

THE PROFESSIONAL TOUCH

In 2001 Arto Saari was honored with *Thrasher* Magazine's Skater of the Year Award at age 20. His pro shoes on Etnies, known for the signature pine trees logo and the number 22, were among the most skateable options in the entire Etnies line-up. The entire European Etnies team skated them religiously.

Why leave a winning team? "My contract at Etnies was running out and my time over there had come to its peak, so I decided to go and see what Gravis wanted to do with their shoes and in skateboarding," Saari said.

He is joined on the IVSK8 pro team by Javier Mendizabal, Steve Forstner and Dylan Rieder. "The team represents a diversity of styles and personalities, a philosophy we want to promote with IVSK8. All the guys are really gnarly and doing their own thing." Industry veteran Mark Oblow, formerly of Vita Shoes and Quiksilver, runs the show behind the scenes at IVSK8 as Creative Director.

The new IVSK8 Viking, created by head designer Kelly Kikuta, combines the winning features of previous Saari signature models: the flexible cup sole, high breathability and impact protection. The result is a completely re-designed whole. The low-top version is complemented by the Viking Hi, which introduces combination suede and leather uppers in a high-top construction for added ankle support.

When it comes to pushing the limits of skateboarding, how much can be attributed to shoe designs? "Skate shoes have definitely come a long way. If they directly influence the gnarliness of skating I am not sure," Arto Saari explained. "Jamie doing that 50-50 barefoot, Rowley doing some [of] the gnarliest shit in skateboarding with slip ons. I mean, I think it is still up to the skater to push the limits!"

Designed, tested and aproved by Arto Saari personally!

DRUNK VS. DUNK

One of the most outspoken voices for keeping The Swoosh (Nike) out of skateboarding belongs to Consolidated Skateboards of Santa Cruz, California, who launched their ongoing "Don't Do It" campaign in 1997, parodying the Nike slogan. The man behind the campaign, Consolidated owner Steve "Birdo" Guisinger, remembers his motivations: "Seeing as how they aren't skateboarders, we weren't into it because it was obvious to us that they were just trying to capitalize on its popularity. We felt – and still do – that skateboarding is not something you can buy your way into."

Birdo, who started Consolidated in 1992 and owes his nickname to his resemblance to the actor portraying *The Birdman of Alcatraz* in the classic movie drama, felt vindicated at first by Nike's withdrawal from their skateboard program after their unsuccessful campaign in 1997.

"If they were so down with skateboarding, why did they pull out?" Birdo also said that after Nike abandoned the attempt, "the [Don't Do It] campaign went into hibernation."

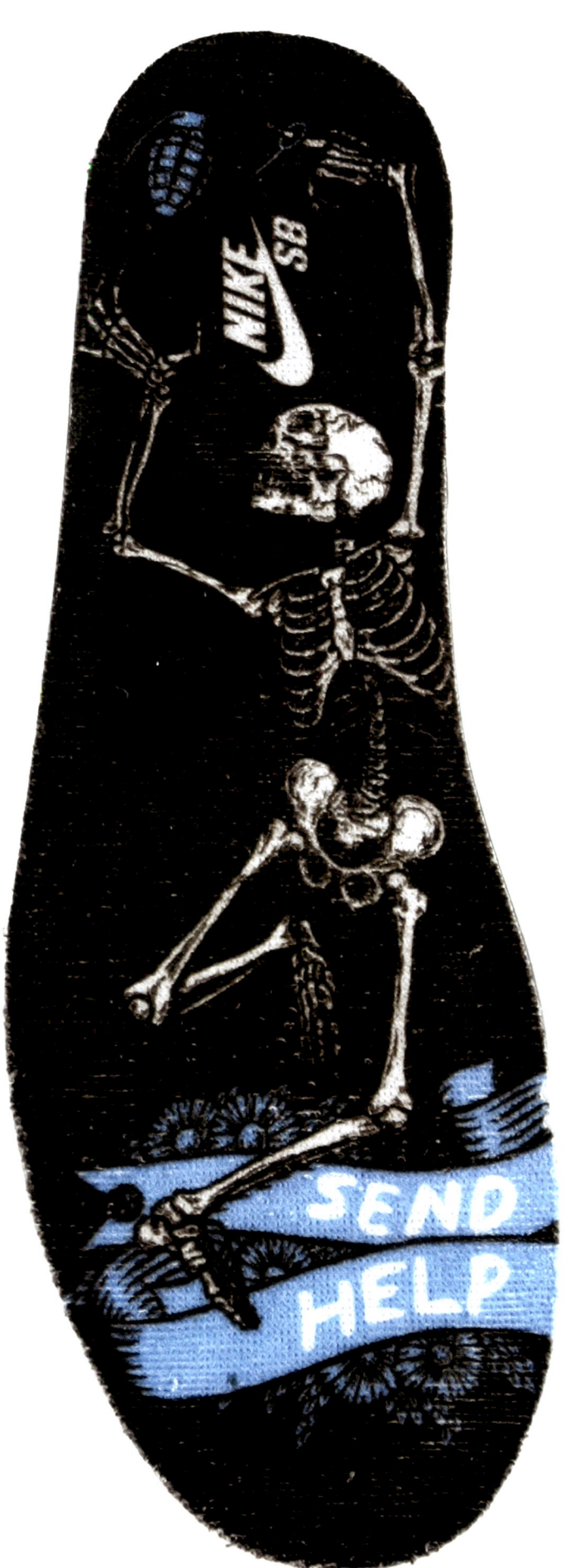

WOLVES IN SHEEP'S CLOTHING?

For four years, the resistance subsided, until Nike co-launched Portland-based Savier in 2001 as a wholly-owned but independent subsidiary of Nike. Birdo and the folks at Consolidated smelled a rat. In Fall 2001, Consolidated ran a magazine advertisement under the title "THE GIVE AND TAKE." To Birdo, reviving the Don't Do It campaign was all about piercing the veil of what was happening behind the scenes. "We wanted to expose Nike for just hiding behind another name. We wanted skaters to understand how it works," Birdo said. "In order for these corporate outsiders to stay in skateboarding, they need to take from – and put out of business – skater-owned companies." The reactions among hardcore skateboarders were positive at the time, Birdo remembers. "Skateboarders understood what it was about and what was at stake."

A HEATED BATTLE

When Nike came back with a skateboard team under the Nike brand name in 2002, Birdo's activism continued, but there were obstacles. This time around, magazines refused to run the "Don't Do It" ads. Asked about which exact magazines rejected the ads, Birdo said: "Almost all of 'em. They're like crooked cops. They don't want to lose the special treatment they get from Nike." Not deterred in getting the message out, Birdo created a page on MySpace.com for continuing the campaign.

Birdo admits that he underestimated Nike's re-entry into the market. "I didn't realize the extent of all the behind-the-scenes maneuvering they were doing with the core shops, magazines, company team managers, and more. Their entrance this time was calculated and very well thought out. When I started fighting again, I was like, 'Holy shit! Everyone has been paid off by them!'"

CAUGHT IN THE CROSSFIRE

While the battle of words continued, the paths of both companies crossed when Consolidated's art director Todd Bratrud agreed to design a limited edition artist series Dunk for Nike in 2006. Allegedly, the idea started when Nike approached Fobia skate shop in Bratrud's hometown in Minnesota about doing a shoe and they brought the artist on board. Fast forward to the actual shoe coming out: Big Drama in the house!

Two things about the shoe set off a storm of protest. "Some sales person at Nike said something about Nike and Consolidated collaborating, and then it turned into this whole big thing," Todd Bratrud remembers. Allegedly, a sales rep referred to the shoe as "the Consolidated shoe." Which was an undesired association from Consolidated's perspective, but the tipping point ended up being the shoe's colorway.

Asked about his first thoughts upon seeing the shoe, Birdo said: "Same colors as the Consolidated Cube [logo]." And Bratrud himself said: "I knew that these were the same colors as Consolidated's, but at that time they had a bunch of other meanings for me." Inspirations, according to the artist, had ranged from the "MAXX" comic book character to the San Jose Sharks hockey team to the "Bruiser" Airwalk Prototype shoe made famous by Mike Vallely.

But the damage was done, and Birdo took it rather personally. "Todd had told me that they wanted to call it the "Consolidunk" but he'd told them 'NO WAY! This has NOTHING to do with Consolidated.' This was just Todd, the artist, doing a shoe," Birdo said.

GOT OURSELVES AN ARMY

Birdo channeled his anger into a new ad campaign that ran in select magazines, proclaiming: "IT'S NOT A CONSOLIDATED SHOE!" In taking the brand war to a new level, Birdo announced the founding of the Don't Do it Army. To Todd Bratrud, the whole initiative is part of a bigger story. "I don't know how much of a battle it is between Consolidated and Nike, as it is Consolidated trying to keep skateboarding pure and keeping it skateboarding only."

EXPRESSING BEEF WITH A BANANA

Soon after the Don't Do It Army, Consolidated released their very own shoe, The Consolidated BS Drunk, advertised with an image of team rider Tanner Zelinsky vomiting off a curb. Featuring a banana in lieu of a Swoosh, the Drunk was shipped in a box that proclaimed an "ULTRA RARE COLLECTOR SERIES" of 600 pairs. In a spoof on the limited edition shoe craze, the Drunk's box also proclaimed: "suggested retail price on eBay: $269.98."

In 2007 Consolidated released the first Drunk collaboration shoe – the Osiris Drunk – as the start of a series of collaborations. Asked whether the Don't Do It "black list" included other major sport shoe brands, Birdo said: "Yeah, it's all the sporting goods companies that had no hand in building skateboarding, yet want to capitalize on its popularity." Birdo's final words on the issue: "Let love and passion for skateboarding continue to rule our industry."

THE GIVE AND TAKE

Don't you hate it when one of your favorite riders gets endorsed by a company you don't like or that isn't even a skateboard company? Usually it's cuz they offered him a lot of money to try and legitimize their company in skateboarding. So don't hate the skateboarder-he is just trying to feed his family.

These non-skateboarding companies see that skateboarding is getting popular and they want a piece of the action. When they pay riders, run ads, and sponsor events, they are "giving" to skateboarding. Though they appear to be giving, they are not "saviors." Their motives are to take more than they give. These companies aren't dumb, but they think we are.

So What do You Do??!!!

Just don't buy their products. You see, if you don't buy their products, then they can't take more than they give. And don't worry, since they're big companies, they'll keep paying the riders, and when one gives up, another will step in.

These companies know that lots of skateboarders already know this, so they try to hide really good, with different names and separate warehouses. But it's not that hard to figure out-just ask around. Skate shops usually know.

So let them keep giving. Maybe someday we can even say thank you.

CONSOLIDATED SKATEBOARDS

CONSOLIDATEDARMY.COM
P.O.Box 1279 SANTA CRUZ, CA. 95061 PHONE: (831) 457-8206 FAX: (831) 457-8219 CONSOLIDATEDSKATEBOARD.COM
SEND A DOLLAR AND A SELF ADDRESSED STAMPED ENVELOPE FOR A COUPLE STICKERS AND STUFF

ART ON SKATEBOARD SHOES

*introducing the NIKE Fish classic SB by Jeremy Fish

If the art fits, wear it! Ever since the late 1970s, art-minded skateboarders – and skate-minded artists – have been customizing their kicks. "It's a walking billboard, like a T-shirt, but for your feet," said artist and former professional skateboarder Andy Howell, adding: "And everyone looks down at people's feet when they are alone."

It was only a matter of time before shoe companies stepped things up by offering select skateboarders an opportunity to pen their own designs on limited edition footwear collections. adidas led the way with a Mark Gonzales-designed shoe as early as 1994, many years before the Gonz would stage art shows and performances. A few years later, renowned skateboard artist Ed Templeton put his Midas touch on 500 pairs of limited edition Emerica Templeton pro shoes by spray-painting them golden.

Does Ed Templeton think that skateboarding boosts creativity? "I think skateboarding draws creative people to it rather than boosting it. So if you find skateboarding, you will be around creative types, and that could be a learning experience. But that was when I started, I don't think it is the same today."

Etnies took things to the next level by staging an entire series of art shows entitled "This is Me," featuring artworks and customized shoe editions. In 2000, DC Shoes launched the ongoing "The Artist Project" with colorways and design twists by artists and musicians including Goldie, graffiti artist Kaws and Shepard Fairey.

SKATEBOARDING – A BREEDING GROUND FOR NEXT-GEN ARTISTS?

For his Artist Series DC Shoe, Andy Howell wanted the shoebox to reflect the packaging of toy figurines from his youth. "I came in with the idea of incorporating a box like this Doze Travella Figure I had, you know the door and the cellophane window so you can see the toy? I wanted to mimic the toy box, using the shoe as the figure. In a sense the box itself became the artistic focus almost equal to the shoe."

The final design of Howell's shoe actually grew organically out of layers upon layers of art. Howell explains: "My studio walls were covered with thousands of practice strokes and little sketches. People who had painted there with me had tagged and drawn on the walls." Finally, Howell took photos of the walls and handed them to former professional skateboarder Steve Saiz, who ran them through the computer."

BUT IS IT ART?

In discussing the collaboration between commercial shoe companies and artists, Howell posed the question: "How authentic is an artist who does an Artists Series Shoe? I celebrate it actually. I believe there is a new cultural movement happening for art and that is that artists are collaborating with brands, creating products for films or cars. It's very liberating for the creative mind, actually."

Jeremy Fish said that shoes are "not so much a canvas for art. It's just a shoe and I need to design the best one I can. It's a challenge like making any other product."

Collaborations between artists and skate shoe brands are now in the dozens with contributors as diverse as notorious New York street artist Neckface. While shrouding his real persona in mystery and never appearing in pictures – "My real face is my mask" – Neckface provided signature demonic imagery featured on Vans shoes including the Sk8 Hi, DD66, AV Era, and TNT models.

Classic skate artist Pushead of Zorlac fame and contemporary designer Jeremy Fish both created their own customized shoes on Nike SB. "First I picked a model to work with. I chose the classic Wimbledon because it was the most simple," Jeremy Fish explained.

To come up with the material for the elaborately crafted shoe, Jeremy Fish allegedly sent in an old woman's hat as a sample for the tongue and a vintage handbag for the upper material. "I use a lot of old Victorian style patterns in my artwork. I liked this pattern because it was wax-stamped on the material. So, as you wear it the pattern slowly fades away," Jeremy Fish explained. The heel of the Nike Fish SB also featured embroidered the artist's emblematic "Pink Bunny and Skull" artwork.

Nike SB's artist collaborations will continue, replete with accompanying art shows in several cities, said the brand's communications manager Kevin Imamura: "We have another series of shoes coming out for the next leg of the Heritage Art Show featuring Lance Mountain, Gonz and Neil Blender, for which Lance is creating his own Blazer model."

Over in Europe, Sykum Footwear teamed up with Portuguese street artist Mar, real name Gonçalo Ribeiro. "A friend of ours brought an old pair of our Imperial 2 shoes painted by his buddy Mar. We liked it so much that we had the graphics printed on the Imperial 3 shoe, released in a limited edition in Fall 2007," the Sykum crew said.

MORE AND MORE EXCLUSIVE

At the same time, some voices in the skate art scene are skeptical whether the trend will continue: "It's over now I think," said Jeremy Fish. "It's been done to death. Too many horrible shoes, and I think the craze has died down for now."

In search of ever more exclusive ways of customizing their artist shoe series, companies like DC Shoes are putting their artists to work on every single pair individually. This happened during DC's collaboration project with *Arkitip Magazine* for a joint exhibition at the Palais de Tokyo Museum in Paris.

Further gimmicks featured on skate art shoes include printed soles, customized art socks, booklets and poster art, miniature figurines and photo prints on the shoe's upper.

How do the artists themselves feel about the fact that most of their shoes will actually never be skated? "That's a choice," said Andy Howell. "I had a friend wear them every day I ever saw him, and some people are saving them in a plastic bag for eBay."

Meanwhile, skateboard companies are introducing artistic features into their "mainstream" shoe collections. Sold at regular prices, these shoes are proliferating art into the streets on a broad scale. In 2008, Element Footwear introduced "Connect Editions" shoes with matching board graphics in identical colorways. This bridges the gap between board and shoe designs – a hot trend in 2008. Some skaters even make sure to match their board artwork – for example Rasta colors – with their laces. The result: Art is everywhere in the streets, as it should be .

Jeremy Fish also pointed out: "Skate shoes, much like skateboards were designed to be used and enjoyed, destroyed and replaced."

COLLAB' WITH YOU LATER, SKATER

Multi-branded or "collaboration" skate shoes are everywhere these days. The crossover hype manifests in shoes jointly branded by board and shoe companies, like the Girl and Chocolate Lakai shoes, or the adidas/Krooked collaboration shoe. Rock bands and musicians are up in the mix, including Goldie with a shoe on DC Shoes, Dinosaur Jr. on Nike SB and Iron Maiden, Kiss, Bad Brains and Bad Religion on Vans. All shoes come replete with iconic album cover art and other gimmicks including printed insoles for a rocking finish.

DC Shoes continued the trend in 2006 with their "20-94" model in cooperation with hat makers New Era, of which only 114 pair exist. The name of the hand-stitched shoe reflects the years in which New Era and DC Shoes were founded, respectively. The 20-94 shoes fetched up to $350 a pair at stores, not to mention added value among sneakerheads on eBay.

A SPECIAL BIRTHDAY GIFT

Birthdays are always a welcome occasion to produce a limited edition collab' shoe, for example the 20th birthday of London's own Slam City Skates shop in 2006, for which Etnies put out a special edition Sal Barbier shoe, with the shop's birth year "86" replacing the iconic 23 on the shoe. That summer, Etnies also released a 20-year birthday edition high top of their "Rap" model for legendary New York City skateboard brand, Shut Skates. Legendary skate shop Supreme, which began the whole limited edition craze with a cross-branded Vans Old School model in 1996, recently created a series of Supreme Vans shoes, available in a number of colorways in the HALF CAB and Chukka Boots models.

One of the most polished joint offerings so far may be Element Skateboard's collaboration with San Francisco art collective Delphi, ran by long-time Element art director Matt Irving. adidas recently launched an exclusive Mark Gonzales shoe in collaboration with *Skate*, the high-end video game by Electronic Arts: The Mark Gonzales "High Score" Superstar Skate features a striking light blue and yellow colorway.

CROSS-BRANDING: WIRED OR EXPIRED?

By the way, video games such as *EA Skate* or the *Tony Hawk Pro Skater* franchise are literally cross-branding machines, letting players customize their own skate avatars with all kinds of clothing, shoes, wheels and decks from real-life companies. Not to mention all the rappers and rock bands that get to inject their songs into in-game soundtracks, and consequently the minds of millions of gamers worldwide. For a seamless connection into real life, adidas even invites players to shop at their own virtual adidas Originals store in Skate's fictional city of San Vanelona, where they can access limited edition shoes.

Mainstream companies have long since been placing their products in skate video games, especially consumer electronics such as the Sirius Satellite Radio featured in the *Tony Hawk Wasteland* game, or the T-Mobile Sidekick that serves as the main in

-game communication device in *EA Skate*. Speaking of communications, in 2008 WeSC released a limited Travel Edition of the Nokia 3250 phone that ships pre-loaded with WeSC's world travel guide. Girl Skateboards teamed up on limited edition boards benefitting the worldwide AIDS/HIV-relief organization Product Red.

The skateboard media have not only been covering the rampant cross-branding trend – they've jumped right into the thick of it. Since skate magazines are brands in their own right, the sight of a magazine's logo on a shoe actually benefits both sides.

Popular examples include special editions for *Thrasher*'s 25th birthday by Nike SB and Lakai, a *Slap* Nike SB shoe, Circa collabo shoes with *Thrasher* and *Kingpin* magazines and countless others. DVS Shoes even devoted an entire series to the people behind the lens: Their "Photographer Series" featured shoes designed by shutterbugs Gabe Morford, Mike O'Meally, Ben Colen, Atiba Jefferson, and Giovanni Reda.

FOOT(WEAR) FETISH – LIMITED EDITION KICKS

Passersby stop and stare when several hundred people, most of them dressed in baggy pants and hooded sweaters, line up around the block at Supreme skate shop in New York City. Most likely, the scene is a procession of footwear enthusiasts – or "sneakerheads" – anticipating their turn to buy a pair of limited edition shoes, for which Supreme has built a reputation around the world, together with a number of select stores in which collector's item sneakers are exclusively released to the public.

Inside the store, supplies will most likely be limited to one pair of shoes per shopper. After all, the rarity kicks sell for multiples of their retail price on the Internet, where a global community of sneaker aficionados follows the latest shoe releases on sites like sneakerfreaker.com. On a good day, a shoe bought for $120 at the store can auction for up to $1,500 on the web.

That's just the tip of the iceberg, as sneaker mania progresses to ever-new heights. During a charity auction on eBay in 2003, a customized pair of Nike SB Dunks went to an Australian bidder for $30,000. The proceeds were donated to the Skaters for Portland Skatepark Foundation and the Tim Brauch Foundation. A few weeks later, a pair of rare Nike SB "FLOM" (For Love Of Money) high tops - a shoe produced only 24 times and with only three pairs released through a public lottery - sold for $9,000 on eBay.

Now, to most folks these sums are outrageous. What, aside from the resale value, is the attraction of limited edition sneakers?

"For me, the attraction of collecting shoes was never about having a mass of shoes, it was always about quality over quantity," said sneaker enthusiast Roland Bieber of Germany. "I always wanted the rarest, hardest-to-find shoes. So I ended up owning shoes that even Nike employees didn't know about."

His shoe collection consists of 60 pairs, he said. "At its peak it was up to 100 pairs, half of them being samples worth almost as much as a vacation home." What are the features that make a shoe attractive to collectors? "Brand model, overall condition – like when it comes to old Air Jordans or Dunks – and whether they are a sample or prototype and the overall number in the edition," Bieber explained.

HARD-TO-GET

In reality, every shoe is "limited" to some extent. Footwear companies only produce a certain number of pairs per production run, whether it's 10 pair or 10,000. If the shoe stays popular, they'll make another edition. If not, the shoe might get discontinued, or a certain colorway will not be produced a second time. This is when things start getting interesting for collectors. Additionally, shoe companies as of late have been intentionally keeping numbers at an exclusive minimum: Nike released 300 limited edition styles in 2007 alone.

According to sneaker expert Bieber, the spread of production numbers in relation to value progresses as follows:

1 to 24 pairs = perfect
24 to 48 pairs = very valuable
50 to 200 pairs = high potential for increase in value
500 to 1,000 pairs = not bad, but little potential

Living in a Box-
The Collectors holly grail... collecting dust.

THE COLLECTOR'S CRAZE HITS SKATEBOARDING

The skateboard community has always had a knack for rare memorabilia. An avid collector's scene has been trying to get its hands on vintage skateboard decks, wheels and stickers for decades now. For some reason, shoes had failed to catch on among skate collectors. At the same time, a vintage Tony Hawk or Mike Vallely pro deck can easily fetch up to $6,000 on eBay, if it's in mint condition. But still, when it comes to spending $30,000 for a pair of sneakers, you're stepping into an entirely different league.

Historically, the craze for collecting sneakers first peaked in Japan, where avid shoe connoisseurs were already spending large sums of money in the 80s on rare kicks. Throughout the 90s, sneakerheads became a full-blown global phenomenon, especially thanks to the emphasis of sneakers as fashion statements in hip-hop culture.

The first skateboard footwear company to release an explicitly labeled "limited edition" shoe was the DC Shoe Co. In 1998, DC joined forces with New York City's Supreme skate shop to create a shoe aimed at the Japanese market. And for the first time, the sidewalks were flooded with shoppers waiting patiently for their pair of sneaks.

Although short-lived, Savier was right on the money when it came to appealing to sneaker collectors and hit home runs with a number of limited edition rarities, for example their Japan-only colorways that sent eBay auctions into the quadruple digits.

Sole Technology are also among the pioneers when it comes to limited edition skate shoes. Every year around Christmas time, owner Pierre André Senizergues brings back an old classic like the Rap or Sal models in limited edition runs to give to close friends and associates.

COLORS, MATERIALS, STORIES

How do the brands go about creating a concept for their limited edition offerings? "For us at Nike SB it's a way to have fun with shoes," Kevin Imamura said. Over the past few years, the brand had stirred up interest with limited edition colorways for the NikeSB models. Giving a nod to pop culture references such as movies, cartoons, video games and beer brands.

"We actually never name the shoes, that always happens after the shoes end up on the Internet and get tagged as the 'so-and-so' shoe. Even if the inspiration really comes from, say, the colors of a bubblegum wrapper, someone on the net will say it's something else. And the backlash over copyrights has made it tough, but we want to continue to tell stories with our shoes."

Materials provide a way to separate the real deal from imitations. With all the money being spent on rare kicks, it's no surprise that counterfeiting is rampant in the shoe collector's scene. According to an estimate almost 98% of all Nike SB Dunks offered on eBay are fake.

MADE FOR SKATE -
Hours of fun - A shoe with stories!

THERE IS A DARK SIDE

At the same time, almost none of these imitated shoes can hold up under close scrutiny and are easily recognizable as knock-offs because of their fabrics and stitching. Then again, if you already paid for your eBay purchase, it might be a tad bit late.

For the release of their *Nothing But The Truth* skate video, Nike SB released the "What the Dunk" model at a production run of 300 pairs worldwide. To give bootleggers a run for their money, the shoes incorporated actual fabrics used in the production of 31 different Nike SB Dunk models over a span of several years, including camo, tye-die and silver elements, along with with different blends of fabrics used on prior production runs.

Needless to say, given the immense production effort behind the shoe, the "What the Dunk" was practically impossible to imitate, and originals scored up to $1,500 on eBay. Even before the real shoes hit select stores around the world the imitations were already up on eBay, although with one fatal flaw: The shoe laces were still based on early sample pictures of the "What the Dunk," and Nike switched the laces last minute before the official shoe came out.

New technologies such as laser-etching of artwork, as seen on select DC Shoes, éS and Nike SB models, will continue to give bootleggers a hard time, while keeping the sneaker heads on their toes when it comes to scoring that extra exclusive, hard-to-get pair as the capstone for their collections.

THE
6 FUTURE

NEW FRONTIERS OR BACK TO BASICS?

What will the future of skateboard footwear look like? Will there be shoes that lace themselves up smugly to their owner's feet, like Michael J. Fox's kicks in *Back to the Future II*? That's how Hollywood depicted shoe technology in the year 2015.

Right now, for a large number of shoe brands moving ahead into the future means going back to the classics. As Nike SB's Kevin Imamura quickly sums up the current shoe market: "Vulcanized..." Meanwhile, a select few companies are willing to expend the time, energy and money to drive technical innovation in skateboard footwear ahead.

According to Tony Hawk, the future will bring "patterns and new aesthetics with the same level of function." Don Brown looks ahead optimistically: "I think the next few years are going to be really exciting, because the only way to stand out and make a difference will be by having different designs and technologies."

LAB-TESTED SKATE SHOES

DC Shoes have always been a driving force in pushing the level of technical innovation. DC Shoes can be credited with inventing the first-ever laceless skate shoe: The Solution pro model was introduced with a Velcro strip for adjusting the shoes instead of conventional laces. An idea that has of yet not been expanded.

Savier Footwear also introduced a hidden tie-up system for eradicating the problem of frazzled laces, together with a revolutionary "no glue and no stitching" construction for the upper shoe sections. DC Shoes introduced their Super Suede in 2004, a more durable material for the shoe's upper.

Etnies, éS and Emerica took the next by establishing their Sole Technology Institute (STI). Opened in 2003, STI is the first-ever research laboratory solely dedicated to the research and testing of skateboard footwear. Inside the 10,000 square foot hangar, six full-time employees are submitting new materials to tests of resistance to abrasion, cushioning capability and color fastness using high-tech gadgetry.

"The impact that skateboarding is taking on the body has progressed tremendously over the years, to a point where a whole generation will be out there with back, knee and ankle injuries someday," said Don Brown. "So Pierre had the idea of creating a lab to really investigate the mechanics of skateboarding, and now everything we develop goes through the lab."

During biomechanical test runs, skate team riders slip into motion-capturing suits, while their stunts on a number of skate obstacles are monitored by high-speed cameras, temperature sensors and an in-shoe pressure monitor. The lab also features a 4 by 4 foot force plate that can be placed on the floor to gauge impact.

"We found out that the impact is much more severe than anyone thought before," said Pierre André Senizergues. "Jumping off 20 stairs is like landing a parachute, and bailing out on a rail has an impact of 17 to 18 times the rider's body weight."

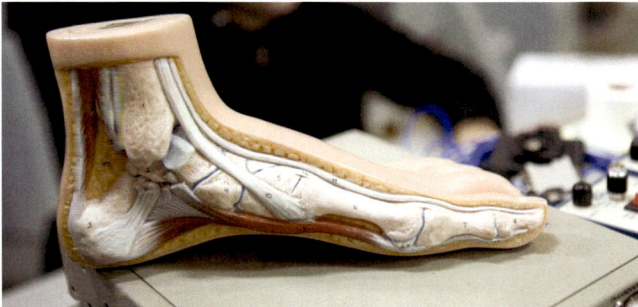

NEW TECHNOLOGIES

In 2003, Sole Technology premiered their first anti-shock system called System G2. "Through the testing we had done, we found out that air bags would disintegrate under pressure and we concluded that gel worked best to reduce the impact," concluded Don Brown. The STI team has also written a number of scientific reports published in major industry publications including the *Journal of Applied Biomechanics*. Further innovations include a vented tongue system and an FTI foam insole filter lining to reduce what is scientifically known as smelly foot syndrome.

LEARNING-BY-DOING

Another company known for their technical shoes is Nike SB. At their Oregon-based NSRL (Nike Sports Research Laboratory), the Nike development team has conducted tests on impact resistance as well as high speed film analysis since the early 80s. Rider feedback from their team also plays a large role when it comes to designing new shoes, picking materials and developing new technologies.

One of the first highly technical shoes in Nike's line-up was the E-Cue model. At the time, the shoe was highly unusual, but it provided the design team with important learning experiences that could be channeled into future technologies, said Kevin Imamura: "The E-Cue was the first shoe we did with a rubber toe cap, and we learned that it needed to be more flexible. So that helped us develop the Zoom Tre, which in turn showed us that incorporating certain flex groves into the sole together with Zoom Air pockets would also work. We took that [knowledge] and plugged it into the P-Rod2 shoe."

Beyond Nike SB's highly popular classic shoes, breaking new ground in terms of technologies has been a cornerstone of the brand's development. "For more than 30 years now, Nike has been trying to build a better shoe," Imamura explained. One key advantage lies in their ability to draw on technical developments from several branches of Nike footwear. "Nike has so much experience with footwear innovation that if we weren't pushing the envelope we'd be doing a disservice to the company's history," Imamura said. As an example for these synergy effects, Imamura cited the Zoom Tre A.D.

"This is our third technical shoe, and the sole incorporates FREE technology, originally developed for runners. It creates a really flexible shoe and simulates running barefoot, which also strengthens your foot. The fitted heel cup comes from a soccer shoe. And now that we have all that in the Zoom Tre A.D., we can plug those technologies into other shoes like Paul Rodriguez's third shoe."

MATERIAL VALUES

85% of the world's athletic shoes and consumer electronics are produced in the Chinese Province of Guangdong, thanks to the local government's highly accommodating conditions for international clients? A number of people in the skateboard industry care, since the entire planet's future is on the line here.

Nike has been implementing eco-friendly practices for a while now. "For example, Nike has been using water-based solvents since the early 2000s and has been doing things like collecting used shoes and recycling them since the late 90s," said Imamura

Sole Technology belongs to the leaders in skateboarding's new eco trend. "We are implementing all green practices, which is very dear to Pierre's heart," said Don Brown. "We use water based glues with no toxins and are doing a lot of reduction to eliminate waste, which has become a big part of the design. Overall, we are trying to reduce our carbon footprint as we get bigger and are trying to be more responsible and green."

In the early years of the new millennium, Sole Technology restructured its headquarters into a sustainable facility with 660 solar panels mounted on the roof to save an annual 97 tons of carbon monoxide. All packaging, shipping and sales materials for all their products also consist of entirely recyclable materials.

"I think that shoe design will be re-invented," said Pierre André. "We are seeing a major crisis in the environment as we are entering what is called the Eco Age. This will be another Industrial Revolution in it's own right. The first one was powered by the discovery of petroleum, but we know now that this will not last. So the new revolution will be a total reversal with alternative design and alternative energy sources without the use of petroleum."

Sole Technology also provides information on the energy and resources used during the production of each shoe on a label inside the shoe box. "It's like the nutrition facts on a food label, we want to be more transparent in terms of the real cost when you buy a pair of skateboard shoes, which is also the carbon footprint and not just the price of money you pay."

In 2007, Lakai launched The Lakai Recycled Program for applying excess shoe material that would otherwise be thrown away to the production of select shoe styles. These include left over upper materials and die-cut EVA midsole sheets in the production. By using a mix of new gum rubber mixed with reground rubber waste in their soles, Lakai reduces the usage of new materials by 40%.

DURABILITY
THIS INJECTED SYSTEM DELIVERS MAXIMUM DURABILITY AND COMPRESSES TO ABSORB SHOCK FOR ADDED PROTECTION.

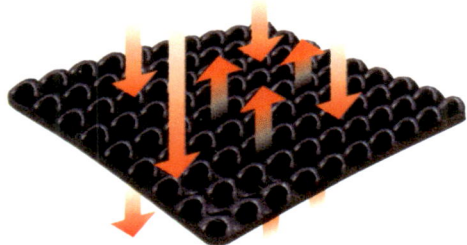

BREATHABILITY
THE TOE PIECE IS ENGINEERED WITH PERFORATIONS TO PROVIDE COOLING AIR FLOW THROUGHOUT THE ENTIRE FOREFOOT.

GRIP
THREE DIMENSIONAL INJECTED TPU SYSTEM IS DESIGNED TO SHEAR AND CREATE A REMARKABLY GRIPPY SURFACE.

SKATABILITY
REGIONALIZED APPLICATION OF GUM RUBBER FOR TRACTION, BOARD CONTROL AND ABRASION RESISTANCE. UNIQUE GRIDDED TREAD PATTERN WITH DEEP FLEX GROOVES (INSPIRED BY NIKE FREE TECHNOLOGY.)

THE SAME PROCEDURE AS EVERY YEAR?

Some skateboarders have found their perfect skate shoe in the vulcanized mid-top design. Others have found their perfect kicks in the low-top all suede skate shoe built on a cup sole. After all, these two design traditions form the main lines to which most skate shoes these days can still trace their heritage.

Chad Muska predicts: "Technical shoes died out and everyone went retro. But by the time this book will be released I think there will be a resurge of technical shoes that have a retro look."

Over the years, have skate shoes really broken any new ground? Have they helped skaters get better at what they are doing? "I think that we have come a long way from the Chuck Taylor's that I started skating in and skateboarding has come a long way from launch ramps and curb stalls," Muska said, adding: "Is the evolution directly connected? Of course… as products get better it allows the rider to get better."

Mike Vallely puts things in perspective: "I don't know that the skate shoe industry has really done anything groundbreaking. I mean, really I can skate in any shoes. Skate shoe design has made shoes last longer and be more responsive and comfortable, but I don't think skate shoes have actually helped skating itself progress."

Along these lines, even the most technically advanced shoes will only take you as far as your talent can reach. For proof, look no further than Jamie Thomas lipsliding a 12-stair handrail with no shoes on in 1995. Or Bastien Salabanzi flipping barefooted over a barrier into a steep bank at the Metz contest in 2008.

So technical advancements are all very well, but if the tricks aren't coming, the shoes will never be the only ones to blame.

phil zwijsen - frontside feeble • photo: bertrand trichet
WWW.CARHARTT-STREETWEAR.COM

EPILOGUE

WE KNOW - LET US KNOW - KEEP IN TOUCH

First of all, we would like to thank you for picking up *MADE FOR SKATE - The Illustrated History of Skateboard Footwear*. We hope you enjoyed the 400-page journey covering almost half a century of skateboard shoe brands, design ideas, technical developments, rider interviews and one or the other odd story we were lucky enough to uncover.

It's exactly these kind of stories that help *MADE FOR SKATE* stand out from standard works on skateboard culture, and we owe it to the contributions of countless individuals who believed in the book and supported us with their collector's item shoes, their memories and opinions and we wouldn't have been able to tell this story without your help. So thanks to all contributors listed below, and all contributors we've forgotten.

We hope we were able to take you back to some of your own stories. The times when you were actually walking and skating in some of these shoes. It's funny how many mental images can be unleashed by something as unassuming as a skate shoe.

At a time when we're constantly bombarded with new information and ideas at breakneck speeds and increasing intensity, it's nice sometimes to stand still and reflect on all the steps we've taken that got us to where we are today – and some of the shoes we took those steps in. Like Ferris Bueller said: "Life moves pretty fast. If you don't stop and look around once in awhile, you could miss it."

HISTORY CAN NEVER BE COMPLETE

At the same time, we are very much aware that any attempt at giving a history of the entire field of skateboard footwear can never be complete and final. There surely are some shoe brands out there that we failed to include or were unable to dedicate enough space to. And of course there are shoe models and designs that would have also been worthy of making the spotlight. We actually had way more shoes on our hands than could fit the pages of this book.

In the end, nothing written and presented here is set in stone. History is a living, ongoing process and we highly welcome your comments, ideas, criticism and feedback.

We'll add new stories on shoes to our website:

WWW.MADEFORSKATE.COM

This will be a frequently updated news source for new developments, articles and interviews, as well as a space to publish some of the materials we were unable to present in the book. The *MADE FOR SKATE* exhibition that started this whole venture will also continue.

DONATE YOUR SHOES - PRESERVE SKATEBOARD HISTORY

Maybe you even have a special historic pair of shoes you would like to donate to the museum as an exhibit. If your shoe has it's own, personal story - and they all do - feel free to write us about it. After all, the worst thing to happen to shoes that have any kind of value attached to them (even if it's only sentimental), is have your mom throw them away when she cleans out your basement.

YOU CAN CONTACT US AT ANY TIME AT:

INFO@MADEFORSKATE.COM

Thanks again for reading, we hope you enjoyed. If you're ever in Stuttgart, Germany, feel free to visit the Skateboard Museum.

Stay safe and remember what Ferris Bueller said!

FauxAmi

A BIG THX TO OUR CONTRIBUTORS

We would like to thank everyone who has supported the *MADE FOR SKATE* book with their contributions, time and input!

We would never have been able to tell the story of skateboard footwear without your suggestions, comments, photos and shoe donations. Most of all, we want to thank you for believing in this project!

INTERVIEWS AND QUOTES:

- Berto Alva
- James Arizumi
- Jochen Bauer
- Roland Bieber
- Kelly Bird
- Todd Bratrud
- Don Brown
- Brandon Brubaker
- Dennis Busenitz
- Steve Caballero
- Benoit Copin
- Ed Dominick
- Titus Dittmann
- André Fernandes
- Jeremy Fish
- Tim Gavin
- Mark Gonzales
- Claus Grabke
- Steve "Birdo" Guisinger
- Tony Hawk - 20
- Andy Howell
- Todd Huber
- Kevin Imamura
- Natas Kaupas
- Eric Koston
- Markus Koenig
- Adrian Lopez
- Lance Mountain
- Philipp "Moski" Marx
- Rodney Mullen
- Chad Muska
- Rodrigo Petersen
- Stacy Peralta
- Dirk "Shorty" Rassloff
- Marc Richards
- Brian Reid
- Paul Rodriguez
- Arto Saari
- Pierre André Senizergues
- Ed Templeton
- Mike Vallely
- Miki Vuckovich
- Jess Weinstein

CONTRIBUTING PHOTOGARPHERS:

- Grant Brittain
- Daniel Bourqui
- Wolfgang Burat
- Florian Böhm
- James Cassimus
- Tom & Rick Corombes
- Claus Grabke
- Jim Goodrich
- Daniel Josefsohn
- Bryce Kanights
- Christian Kline
- Daniel Mandell
- Wynn Miller
- Lance Mountain
- Cândido Neto
- O
- Chuck Saccio
- George Schwartz
- Swank
- Ron Stoner
- Bertrand Trichet
- Tobin Yelland

SPECIAL SUPPOTERS OF THE BOOK:

- Don Brown
- Partick "Bärty" Bruns
- Mo Cohen
- Brecht Cuppens
- Julian Duval
- Julius Dittmann
- Julia Froemel
- Lars Greiwe
- Birgit Gruber
- Kevin Imamura
- Martin Magielka
- Jascha Müller
- Philippe Lalement
- Stephen Luther
- Andrea Stoll
- Charlie Tidball

SPECIAL PROMOTERS:

Dirk Aerts
Marco Asim
Michael Brooke
Ron Cameron
Gabe Clement
Tony Chen
Brett Chittenden
Agra Ciapari
Anja Egger
Arne Fieh
Johannes Fürst
Michael Furukawa
Humphrey Gentry
Justin Gold
Florian Gottesmann
Martin Grüb
Jonathan Hay
Anika Heusermann
Rich Holland aka „Badger"
Brian Howard
Jörg Ihle
Jehle Werbetechnik - Karl Jehle
Ines, Rebekka, Hartmut, Ulrich
Ulrich Köhler
Arne Krüger
Martina Luger
Jörg Ludewig
Thomas Martini
Angel Martinez
Ruedi Mater
Paul Merrell
Charlie Morgan
Greg Nelson
Sebastian Palmer
Michael Paul
Beate Pietrek
Leticia Ruano
Brenda Springer
Marc Sülze
Axel „Starsky" Kleinhans
Martin Van Dooren
Kaspar van Lierop
Gary Warrett
Bjorn Wiersma
Woody
Günther Zott

FOR SHOES, LETTING US CRASH ON THE COUCH AND ANY KIND OF SUPPORT:

Christian Buttler
Michael Baldauf
Achim Bauer
Mathew Bauer
Thilo Benneke
Thomas Binder
Geka Blümlein
Mikesch Blümlein
Peter Bodenhaupt
Stefan Bodenhaupt
Bod Boyle
Ralf Braitling
Sascha Bruckhoff
Holger Carl
Aytekin Celik
Lee Charon
Neil Chester
Sean Cliver
Marije de Haas
Laurence Desarzens
Peter Ehlert
Hannes
Shepard Fairey
Pitt Feil
David Fischer
Marco Frey
Steven Fröhlich
Alexander Funk
Khan Furqan
DJ Kris Gärtner
Matt Grabowski
Florian Gubba
Florijan Hadzic
Felix Hälbich
Burkhard Hagelauer
Jonathan Hay
Frank Hellener
Markus Hensinge
Dirk Hermelingmeier
Marcus Hoch
Jennifer Huber
Erin Kirkpatrick
Fritz "Pommes" Klein
Klaas Kleinschmidt
Kosse
Robinson Kuhlmann

Robinson Kuhlmann
Timo Lieben
Lozza
David Luther
Dan Magee
Rick Marr
Alexander Martin
Stefan Marx
Jocks Sport -
Mike und Fam. Mazur
Marc McKee
Mos Eisley Crew
Axel / Frieder
Marc Münster
Michael Neuss
Wolfgang Nill
Gordon Nowak
Patrick Oelsner
Fola Osu
Brooke Pedersen
Sandra Petralia
Rolf Pfingsttag
Jim Phillips
George Powell
Aaron Press
Eric Rebmann
David "Shitbird" Rogerson
Christian Roth
Jörg Schaller
Daniel Schindler
Florian Schmid
Philipp Schmidt
Stefan Schorer
Marc Schwarz
Michael Seiler
Sieben Siebe Stuttgart -
Florian u. Sascha
Mike Sprunkel
Jay at Styledepartment
Lorenzo Taurino
Stefan Thomas
David Turakiewicz
Charly from "Trauma"
Marco Tremiliti
Nico van der Wel
Sergej Vutuc

Michael Wagner
Damon Way
Oliver Weber
Steffie Weis
Michael Wehrmeyer
Hanno Wellmann
Felix Wellmann
Gerd Witulski
Alexis Zavialoff
Marc Zeitzschel
Niklas Zingler

The makers of MADE FOR SATE would like to take this opportunity to extend some personal Thank You's.

Dirk Vogel would like to thank: My wife Tilley, my family and everyone who's helped me along the way and read my stories. Special thanks to Holger Smolinski, formerly at Gerich skate shop for all the support and Jörg Ludewig for getting me on board writing for Limited Magazine in 1993, which was the very start of my journey as a writer.

Daniel Schmid especially wishes to thank: My parents Elvira and Edi for always being there, no matter what (and for Sweden)!! My beloved partner Silvia for her help and support, for all the encouragement, patience and love. And thanks to Skateboarding, the mother of all good things -.--.-

Jürgen Blümlein especially wishes to thank: My parents Dieter and Renate Blümlein my grandmother Emma Ehlert for their support. And of course my wife Martina for her love and patience and my daughter Lisa for her lovely everyday smile!

...And all the friends and people who supported and helped us and the Skateboard - Museum along the way.. You know who you are ;)

We tried very hard to include everyone who's helped us along the way in this list. In case we have forrgoten someone, we are very sorry. Please let us know and we will honor your support on the MADE FOR SKATE website. And who knows – there might be a second edition of the book so we can fix this horrible mistake!

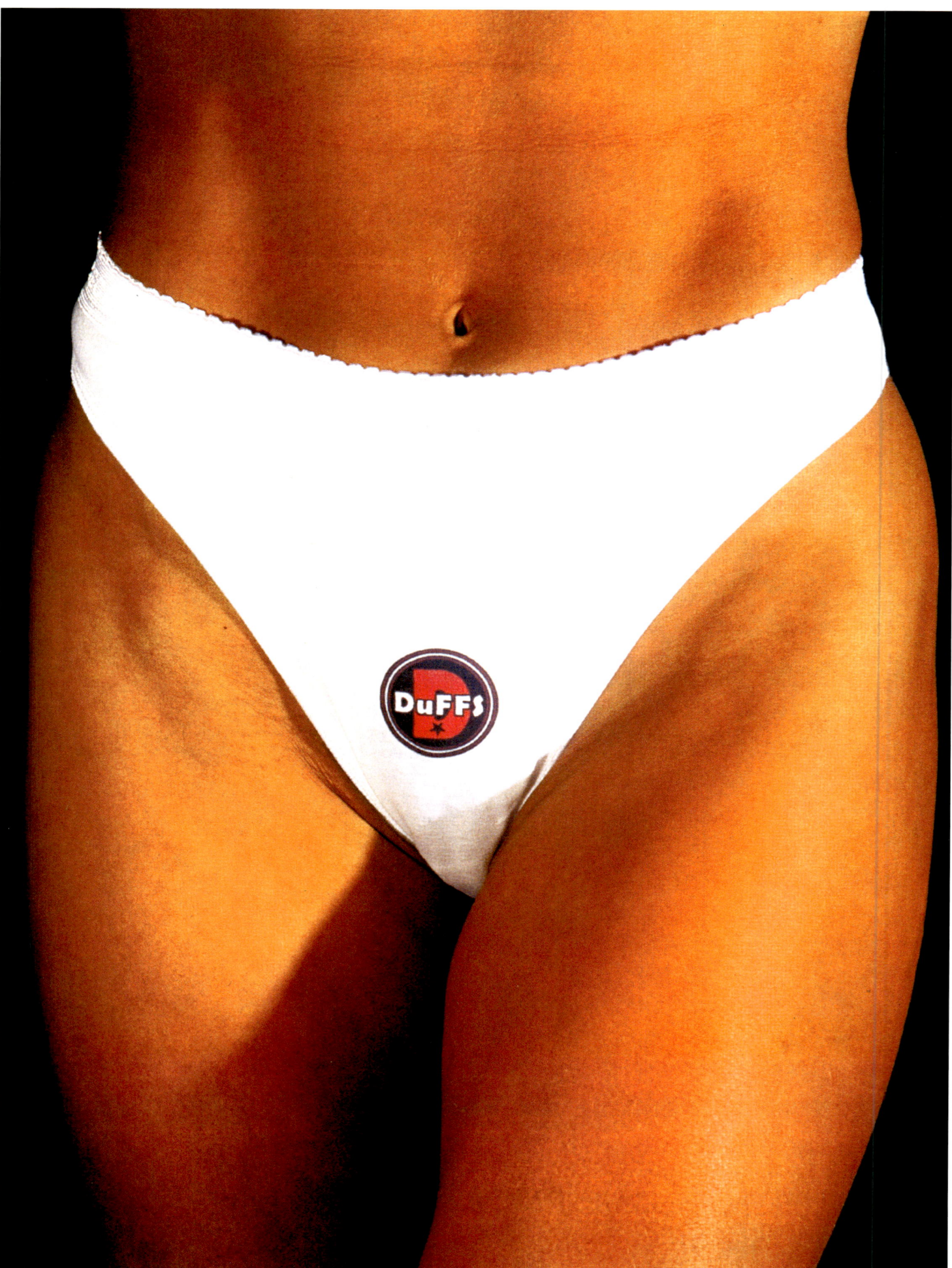

THE 7 INDEX

HARD-COVER

1965 International Surfing Magazine - Sidewalk Flyers

BOOK-JACKETS

Nike - Shogo Kubo at Marina del Ray - Photo by Daniel Josefsohn

Element - Photo by Brian Gaberman

Converse - Anthony Pappalardo - Photo by Jeremy and Claire Weiss

MADE FOR SKATE "Bruiser" Artwork by Todd Bratrud

Page 1	Quote from the Article "Some skate shoe history" by just_bring_it_uk
Page 2	Photo by Wolfgang Burat
Page 13	MADE FOR SKATE - Bright Skateboard Tradeshow 2007 - Photo by FauxAmi
	MADE FOR SKATE - London Nike SB 10 Anniv. Blueprint - Photo by FauxAmi
	MADE FOR SKATE - Vienna at the URBAN LAB - Stil Laden - Photo by FauxAmi

CHAPTER - THE ROOTS

Page 16	SURFER Bi-Monthly Magazine Sept 1964 Article "Skateboard - Kid Stuff or real Sport?"
Page 17	Petersens Surfing Yearbook 1964 Article "How to build a skateboard"
Page 18	"Shoes of August" 1959 - Photo by Tom Corombes
Page 19	1964 Quarterly Skateboarder Article „Surfer - Skier - Skateboarder" Photos by George Schwartz
Page 20	1964 Quarterly Skateboarder Magazine Cover Issue No.1
	1965 Quarterly Skateboarder Magazine Cover Issue No.3
Page 21	1965 Quarterly Skateboarder Issue No.3 Article
	International Skateboard Championships - Photos by Ron Stoner
	1975 SkateBoarder Cover Vol. 2 No. 1
Page 22	1965 May Cover Life Magazine and Article
Page 23	1975 Skateboarder "Who´s Hot" Chris Yandell
	1977 article in German "Skateboard" Magazine

CHAPTER - THE SHOES

Page 37	1976 Dec. Skateboarder Magazine Whos Hot Jay Adams - Photo by Bolster
Page 38	1978 Sep. Skateboarder Magazine „Extra"
Page 40	1979 Oct. Roller Skating Magazine Cover
Page 48	Steve Schneer - Big O Photo and Copyright by Jim Goodrich
Page 50	1979 Curt Kimbel - Del Mar Photo and Copyright by Jim Goodrich
Page 54	1979 Eddie Elguera Boulder - Photo and Copyright by Jim Goodrich
Page 58	1978 Skateboarder Magazine Shogo Kubo Pool Slam Photo sequence by James Cassimus
Page 59	1978 Oct. Skateboarder Magazine - Skate Safe Article by Doug Schneider - Photo by James Cassimus
Page 60	Daniel Josefsohn and Shogo Kubo at Marina del Ray Photo by Daniel Josefsohn
Page 62	1979 May Skateboarder Magazine Subscribe Ad showing Jay Adams - Photo by Wynn Miller
Page 63	1979 The International Skateing Magazine Tony Alva at the "Mad Dog" Bowl in London - Photo by Wynn Miller
Page 64	1978 Steve Alba at Upland skatepark - Photo by Jim Goodrich
Page 67	1978 Dez Skateboard World - Hot Shots Article Jay Smith at the Oxnard Skatepark - Photo by Chuck Saccio
Page 72	1978 German SKATEBOARD Magazin Cover 2/78
Page 74	1977 Sep Skateboarder Magazine Article Photo by Mike Kerley
Page 75	1978 Oct. Skateboard! No.14 Article SKATA DATA
Page 81	1978 Aug. Skateboarder Magazine - Pictrure from the Article "Skatewolves of London" by C. Carrol
Page 82	1986 Monster Magazine - Photo by Florian Böhm

CHAPTER - THE EIGHTIES

Page 86	Thrasher Magazine Cover First Issue 1981
	Back to the Future Part II Poster
Page 87	TRANSWORLD SKATEBOARDING Magazine Cover First Issue 1983
Page 88	TRANSWORLD SKATEBOARDING Magazine Cover Issue Oct. 1990
Page 89	TRANSWORLD SKATEBOARDING Magazine TALK Issue April 1988
	RAD Magazine 1989 NATAS Shoe Competition
Page 95	Skateboarder UK Magazine 1988 Mag Article „Lick My Boots"
Page 98	TRANSWORLD SKATEBOARDING Magazine 1984 Fed. Article "Transaxle"
Page 100	UK Skateboard Magazin 1989 April Article "This is the Stuff"
Page 103	Poweredge Magazine 1989 Article SLASH "Duck Tape"
Page 108	Chin Handplants Photo by Grant Brittain
Page 113	Poweredge Magazine Cover May 1989
Page 139	Thrasher Magazine May 1988 Natas Kaupas Interview Photos by Bryce Kanights
	Thrasher Magazine 1990 April Article "Product Patrol"
Page 148	Ed Templeton Ollie a Hydrant - Photo by O
Page 149	Marc Gonzales 1986 Frontside Rock - Photo by Grant Brittain
	John Kop in Vancouver 1987 - Photo by Swank
Page 153	Thrasher Magazine 1990 Dec. Article "Product Patrol"
Page 159	Rodney Mullen Airwalk 1990 Photo by Claus Grabke
Page 160	RAD Magazine May 1988 "Fun Ramps" Photos by Tim Leighton-Boyce www.whenwewasrad.co.uk
Page 165	RAD Magazine 1988 Aug. "Pacer Hogs Competition"
Page 175	Skatin´ Magazine 1989 oct./nov. Samuca Photo by Dan el Bourqui
Page 176	Mike Vallely Ollie on to Nollie (detail) 1990 Photo by Christian Kline

CHAPTER - THE NINTIES

Page 180	SLAP magazine Vol1 #10 ‚Cover Thrasher Magazine 1993 Oct. Cover
Page 181	Mike Vallely Ollie on to Nollie 1990 Photo by Christian Kline
	Columbia Pictures movie cover, 1994

Page 182   Big Brother Magazine Cover # 7

         Monster Magazin Cover #87

Page 250   Rick Howard k-grind Photo by Lance Mountain

Page 308   Brad Staba 1999 - Photo by Tobin Yelland

CHAPTER - THE NEW MELENIUM

Page 312   Skateboarder Magazine Cover 2003 May
         The Skateboard Mag Cover ONE Premiere Issue 2004 April

Page 318   TRANSWORLD Magazine 2003 March Article „Most Wanted"

Page 329   Skat n´ Magazine 1989 oct./nov. Praca Roosevelt
         Photo by Candido Neto

Page 332   Thrashin VHS Cover

Page 364   NY 2008 - Photo by Daniel Mandell

Page 367   Artwork by Jeremy Fish - The Nike Classic Fish SB

Page 378   „Mega Drop" Rob Lorifice at the X-Games - Photo by Bryce Kanights

CHAPTER - THE FUTURE

Page 382   Thrasher Magzine Cover 1991 April „Future Skateboards"

Page 383   STI Lab Photos provided by Natalie Miller - SoleTechnology

Page 388   Phil Zwijsen - Frontside Feeble - Photo by Bertrand Trichet

CHAPTER - EPILOGUE

Page 390   Big Brother Magazine 1997 Issue 30 Dave Carnie 1997
         Article Sig. Shoe Test

Page 400   MADE FOR SKATE London „AJ1" Artwork by Todd Bratrud

Page 402   Shoe mountain by Cap10

"ENJOY LIFE, RIDE A SKATEBOARD!"